TELL ES-SAʿIDIYEH
Excavations on the Tell, 1964–1966

خلاصه
―――

اجريت الحفريات في تل السعيديه في وادى الاردن المركزى خلال شهور فصل الشتاء عام ١٩٦٤ و ١٩٦٥ على نفقه متحف الجامعه التابع لجامعه بنسلفانيا ويتعاون المعاهد الامريكيه لبحوث المستشرقين وكل ذلك تحت اداره واشراف جيمس بى بريجرد .

قد وجدنا سبع مراتب وطبقات في منطقتين اساسيتين . الطبقه الاولى والثانيه والثالثه منها كانت قد وجدت في الجزء الأعلى من التل . وفي أرض اوسع من أرض الطبقات الثلاث الأولى وشمال غرب الأكمه حفرت أربع طبقات سمينـاها الطبقه الرابعه والخامسه والسادسه والسابعه على الترتيب . أما الطبقه السابعه (٧٩٠ – ٨٢٥ ق م) والطبقه السادسه (٧٥٠ – ٧٩٠ ق م) فكانتا منطقتين سكنيتين والطبقه الخامسه (٧٣٠ – ٧٥٠ ق م) كانت ايضا منطقه سكنيه ولكن لها مميزات أخرى غير مميزات الطبقتين السادسه والسابعه حيث أن أثنى عشر من بيوتها كانت مماثله في التخطيط والحجم وكأنها بنيت كعماره واحده بين الشارعين الشمالي والجنوبي . وخلال زمن الطبقه الرابعه (٦٠٠ – ٧٣٠ ق م) يبدو ان المنطقه كلها كانت تستخدم لتخزين الحبوب في ثماني وتسعين حفره وصومعتين كانتـا بشكل مستطيل مسطـح . أما الجزء الأعلى من الأكمه فكانت تقوم عليه عماره مربعه في العصر الفارسي وكانت مساحتها ٢١,٩٥ × ٢٢,٥ متر ومن المحتمل انها كانت تستخدم كقلعه حينما لم يكن يحيط بالمدينه جدار . أما في العصر الاغريقي فكانت هناك عماره أخرى كانت مساحتها ١٣,٣٠×٢١,٢٠ م تر وربما كانت تستعمل لنفس الغرض . أما الطبقه الأولى التي كانت في العصر الرومانى فكانت تشتمل على بركتين للماء مطليتين بالجبس ، وأساس لعماره مستطيله . الآثار المتبقيه من الجدران الثلاثه للمدينه تدل على نظام الدفاع عن المدينه . الجدار الأول يعـود تاريخه الى وقت قبل عصر الطبقه التي حفرت أولا أعنى الطبقه السابعه . والجدار الثاني يتعلق بمدينه كانت على الطبقه السابعه وربما على الطبقه السادسه والجدار الثالث كان لمدينه قائمه على الطبقه الخامسه . ومن الأشياء المرتبطه اكثر بنظام الدفاع عن المدينه أدراج من ٩٥ درجا ، وأرصفه بنيت على الجانب الشمالي المنحدر من التل والمؤدي من المدينه الواقعه على الجزء الأعلى من التل الى مورد الماء في أسفله ولعل ذلك كان وسيله مأمونه وربما سريه ايضا للحصول على الماء وكان ذلك يقع تحت سطح أرض التل . هذا وكان في وسطه جدار مبني من طوب الطين وكان يستند الى ذلك الجدار سقف يغطي الأدراج .

University Museum Monograph 60

TELL ES-SAʿIDIYEH
Excavations on the Tell, 1964–1966

James B. Pritchard

Published by

THE UNIVERSITY MUSEUM
University of Pennsylvania
1985

Design, editing, production
　Publications Division, The University Museum

Typesetting and Printing
　The Sheridan Press
　Hanover, Pennsylvania

Library of Congress Cataloging in Publication Data
Pritchard, James Bennett, 1909–
　Tell es-Saʿidiyeh: excavations on the Tell, 1964–1966.

　(University Museum monograph; 60)
　Bibliography: p.
　1. Saʿidiyah, Tall (Jordan)　I. Title.　II. Series.
DS154.9.S22P75　　1985　　933　　84-28043
ISBN 0-934718-60-1

Copyright © 1985
THE UNIVERSITY MUSEUM
University of Pennsylvania
Philadelphia
All rights reserved
Printed in the United States of America

Figure 118	Covered drain of Room 101 of Stratum III, looking west
Figure 119	Opening to drain of Room 101 of Stratum III, looking east
Figure 120	General view of Room 101 of Stratum III, looking southeast
Figure 121	General view of Rooms 101 and 102 of Stratum III, looking southeast
Figure 122	Pavements of Rooms 102 and 101 of Stratum III, looking northeast
Figure 123	West side of doorway between Rooms 101 and 102 of Stratum III, looking west
Figure 124	Room 102 of Stratum III, looking east
Figure 125	Room 103 of Stratum III, looking north
Figure 126	Paved area to the north of Room 103, looking west
Figure 127	Room 108, looking west
Figure 128	Room 108, looking southwest
Figure 129	General view of building of Stratum III, looking southwest
Figure 130	General view of building of Stratum III, looking west
Figure 131	General view of building of Stratum III, looking southwest
Figure 132	General view of building of Stratum III, looking northwest
Figure 133	General view of stone foundations of the building of Stratum II, looking west
Figure 134	Rooms 202, 205 (right), 207 and 206 (left), foundations of building of Stratum II, looking west
Figure 135	Foundations of Rooms 203, 204, 205 (right), and 202 (left) of Stratum II
Figure 136	General view of foundations of building of Stratum II, looking northwest
Figure 137	Rooms 203 (center), 204 (upper right), and 202 (upper left) of Stratum II, looking southwest
Figure 138	Rooms 205 (lower), 204 (middle), and 203 and 201 (upper); foundations of building of Stratum II, looking east
Figure 139	Rooms 205 (lower left) and 202 (right of center) of Stratum II, looking east
Figure 140	Rooms 202 (right of center), 205, 204, 203, and 201 (left) of Stratum II, looking east
Figure 141	Rooms 206 (lower), 205 (center), and 204 (right of center) foundations of building of Stratum II, looking north
Figure 142	Room 207 (center) of building of Stratum II, looking northeast
Figure 143	Room 206 (center) at southwest corner of building of Stratum II, looking northeast
Figure 144	East wall of building of Stratum II, looking south
Figure 145	Rooms 203 (lower), 202, 208 (center), and 207 (upper right) of building of Stratum II, looking south
Figure 146	Rooms 204 (lower), 202, 207 (center), and 206 (upper right) of building of Stratum II, looking south
Figure 147	Room 205 (center) foundations of building of Stratum II, looking south
Figure 148	Rooms 203 and 202 (center) and 208 (upper) of building of Stratum II, looking southeast
Figure 149	Top of foundation with reed impressions on south wall of Room 202, opposite Room 207, looking west
Figure 150	Reeds from the roof found on floor in 31-B-6
Figure 151	Charred roof beam in Room 203 of building of Stratum II, looking west
Figure 152	Two clay ovens outside of the building of Stratum II, looking west

Figure 153	Foundations of Stratum I building in 31-C-8, built over the wall of the rectangular building of Stratum II, looking south
Figure 154	Foundations of Stratum I building in 31-B-6, looking east, seen through the doorway between Rooms 205 and 202 of the building of Stratum II
Figure 155	Foundation trench for wall of the building of Stratum I in 31-B-7, looking east
Figure 156	Steps in the north reservoir in 31-E/F-7/8 of Stratum I, looking northwest
Figure 157	South reservoir in 31-F-7, looking northwest
Figure 158	South reservoir in 31-F-7, looking north
Figure 159	City wall on surface of Areas 23 and 13, looking east
Figure 160	City wall on surface of Area 23, looking west
Figure 161	Surface walls in 32-E/F/G-10, looking west
Figure 162	Bin lined with stones on surface of 32-F-9
Figure 163	Shifted strata in 17-H-7/9
Figure 164	Bowls and juglets
Figure 165	Juglets, jugs, and a jar
Figure 166	Jugs, decanters, a chalice, and a pilgrim flask
Figure 167	Storage jars, a krater, and jars
Figure 168	Lamps, cosmetic palette, and a tripod cup
Figure 169	Zoomorphic figurines, human figurines
Figure 170	Loom weights, cloth impression, and stone vessels
Figure 171	Faience cups, gaming pieces, bone tools, bone pendant, bead, and stamped jar handle
Figure 172	Bronze ladle, iron arrowheads, iron point, iron blade, and macehead
Figure 173	Cylinder seals
Figure 174	Incense burner
Figure 175	Inscriptions
Figure 176	Contour map of the tell with excavated areas shown by dotted lines on the grid.
Figure 177	Plan of Stratum VII; later phase, except for the east-west street in 23-F/G-6
Figure 178	Plan of Stratum VI
Figure 179	Plan of Stratum V. *Back cover pocket*
Figure 180	Plan of Stratum IV. *Back cover pocket*
Figure 181	Section of east balk of Areas 23 and 32, Strata VII–IV
Figure 182	Plan of stairway with section
Figure 183	Section of central wall of stairway
Figure 184a	Section of Sounding 4 (14-H/J-9) looking south
Figure 184b	Section of Sounding 1 (14-J-5) looking south
Figure 184c	Section of Sounding 3 (14-J-2/3) looking east
Figure 185	Plan of Stratum III
Figure 186	Plan of Stratum II
Figure 187	Plan of Stratum I
Figure 188	Plan of city wall on surface of tell
Figure 189	Plan of surface structures in Area 32

Abbreviations

AASOR	Annual of the American Schools of Oriental Research.
ADAJ	Annual of the Department of Antiquities of Jordan.
Agora 4	R. H. Howland, Greek Lamps and their Survivals, The Athenian Agora 4, 1958.
APEF	Annual of the Palestine Exploration Fund.
BASOR	Bulletin of the American Schools of Oriental Research.
Beer-Sheba 1	Y. Aharoni, ed., Beer-sheba 1, 1973.
Beth-pelet 1	W. M. F. Petrie, Beth-pelet 1, (Tell Fara), 1930.
Beth Shan	F. W. James, The Iron Age at Beth Shan, 1966.
BMB	Bulletin du Musée de Beyrouth.
Buseirah 2	Crystal-M. Bennett, "Excavations at Buseirah, Southern Jordan, 1972: Preliminary Report," Levant 6: 1–24.
Buseirah 3	Crystal-M. Bennett, "Excavations at Buseirah, Southern Jordan, 1973: Third Preliminary Report," Levant 7: 1–19.
Chapman	S. V. Chapman, "A Catalogue of Iron Age Pottery....," Berytus 21: 55–194.
CIS	Corpus Inscriptionum Semiticarum.
Corinth 7, iii	G. R. Edwards, Corinthian Hellenistic Pottery, Corinth, 7, iii, 1975.
CRAI	Comptes rendus des séances de l'Académie des inscriptions et belles-lettres.
Dhiban 2	A. D. Tushingham, The Excavations at Dibon (Dhībân) in Moab: the Third Campaign 1952–53, AASOR 40.
Gerar	W. M. F. Petrie, Gerar, 1928.
Gezer 3	R. A. S. Macalister, The Excavation of Gezer 3, 1912.
Hazor 1	Y. Yadin, et al., Hazor 1, 1958.
Hazor 2	Y. Yadin, et al., Hazor 2, 1960.
Hazor 3–4	Y. Yadin, et al., Hazor 3–4, Plates, 1961.
Heshbon	E. N. Lugenbeal and James A. Sauer, "Pottery from Heshbon," Andrews University Seminary Studies 10: 21–69.
IEJ	Israel Exploration Journal.
Khaldé	Roger Saidah, "Fouilles de Khaldé," BMB 19: 51–90.
Kheleifeh	Nelson Glueck, "Some Edomite Pottery from Tell el-Kheleifeh," BASOR 188: 8–38.
Lachish 3	Olga Tufnell, Lachish III: The Iron Age, 1953.
Megiddo 1	R. S. Lamon and G. M. Shipton, Megiddo I: Seasons of 1925–34, Strata I–V, 1939.
PEQ	Palestine Exploration Quarterly.
QDAP	Quarterly of the Department of Antiquities in Palestine
RB	Revue biblique.
Sahab	L. Harding, "An Iron-Age Tomb at Sahab," QDAP 13: 92–102.
SS 3	J. W. Crowfoot, G. M. Crowfoot, and Kathleen M. Kenyon, Samaria-Sebaste, III: The Objects from Samaria, 1957.
Sarepta	W. P. Anderson, "A Stratigraphic and Ceramic Analysis of the Late Bronze and Iron Age Strata of Sounding Y at Sarepta (Sarafand, Lebanon)," Ph.D. diss., University of Pennsylvania, 1979.
Tarsus 1	Hetty Goldman, ed., Excavations at Gözlü Kule, Tarsus, I: The Hellenistic and Roman Periods, 1950.
TBM 3	W. F. Albright, The Excavation of Tell Beit Mirsim, III: The Iron Age, AASOR, 21–22.
Tell Keisan	J. Briend and J.-B. Humbert, Tell Keisan (1971–1976): une cité phénicienne en Galilée, 1980.
TN 1	C. C. McCown, Tell en-Naṣbeh I: Archaeological and Historical Results, 1947.
Tyre	P. M. Bikai, The Pottery of Tyre, 1978.
Ugaritica VI	Mission de Ras Shamra, XVII: Ugaritica VI, 1969.
Umm el-'Amed	M. Dunand et R. Duru, Oumm el-'Amed: une ville de l'époque hellénistique aux échelles de Tyr, 1962.
Umm el-Biyara	Crystal-M. Bennett, "Fouilles d'Umm el-Biyara," RB 73: 372–403.
ZDPV	Zeitschrift des Deutschen Palaestina-Vereins.

James B. Pritchard began excavations in Jordan in 1951 at Herodian Jericho, where he was field director for the American Schools of Oriental Research. He dug at el-Jib, the biblical site of Gibeon, for five seasons between 1956 and 1962 under the auspices of the University Museum. Upon the completion of this project he excavated at Tel es-Saʿidiyeh in the Jordan valley for four seasons until the 1967 War terminated what was to have been a long range excavation. Again under the sponsorship of the University Museum he began work at Sarafand, the Phoenician city of Sarepta, in 1969 and continued for four seasons until the disturbances in Lebanon brought the project to a halt. Among his publications are the following books and monographs: *The Excavation at Herodian Jericho, 1951*, New Haven, 1959; *Hebrew Inscriptions and Stamps from Gibeon*, Philadelphia, 1959; *The Water System at Gibeon*, Philadelphia, 1961; *Gibeon, Where the Sun Stood Still*, Philadelphia, 1963; *Winery, Defenses, and Soundings at Gibeon*, Philadelphia, 1964; *Sarepta: A Preliminary Report on the Iron Age*, Philadelphia, 1975; *Recovering Sarepta, A Phoenician City*, Princeton, 1978; *The Cemetery at Tel es-Saʿidiyeh, Jordan*, Philadelphia, 1980. In 1983 he was awarded the Gold Medal for Distinguished Archaeological Achievement by the Archaeological Institute of America.

Introduction

When we began excavations for the University Museum at Tell es-Saʿidiyeh in 1964 we planned that the project would continue for at least ten years, with a campaign of approximately ten weeks each winter. Preliminary reports were to be published at the conclusion of each year's campaign, and a final report was to appear upon the completion of the ten-year project. For each of three seasons, 1964–1966, work went on as planned and the objectives were, in general, achieved. The fourth campaign in 1967, however, was short, for heavy rains during one-third of the six-week season disrupted the planned schedule of work. The enlargement of the area of Stratum VI, the major objective of that season, was not completed sufficiently to allow us to place the newly discovered buildings on the plan with those that had been found during the previous season. Hence, the results of the 1967 season are not included in this report.

Also, the war of June 1967 and the subsequent political and military tensions along the Jordan River made it impossible to continue field work at Tell es-Saʿidiyeh for several years. The director and other members of the staff became involved in the University Museum's excavation at Sarafand, in Lebanon, a project that began in 1969 and continued through 1974, when war in Lebanon brought that effort to a halt. Eventually, in 1977, when conditions in the Jordan Valley seemed to be favorable for the resumption of work at Tell es-Saʿidiyeh, a campaign of excavations was begun under the joint sponsorship of the University Museum of the University of Pennsylvania, the University of Jordan, and the Department of Antiquities of Jordan. After, however, only two days of field work the discovery of evidence of unexploded mortar shells buried within the tell rendered continuation of the project imprudent. The risk to life and limb seemed too great to assume; staff and workmen were removed from the excavation and no further work was carried out.

In this monograph we have presented the evidence which we have for those architectural units that have been recovered sufficiently to provide a fairly complete and intelligible picture of their plans and function. Along with these descriptions of the buildings we have listed and described the associated artifacts.

Yet a full and comparative study of these objects remains to be done. We are aware of the changes that have taken place in the techniques of excavating and recording since we excavated this site. Not only are there new methods in archaeology but today questions are being asked of the data that were not thought of two decades ago. We hope that when excavations are resumed at Tell es-Saʿidiyeh—by far the greater part of the surface of the mound remains untouched—a more comprehensive picture of life in this important city can be discovered to correct and enhance the record of the 1960s.

Surveying the results of our three full seasons of excavations it appears that the most distinctive discoveries were architectural. The pottery, particularly that found within Strata VII-IV, has long been known from other Palestinian sites. The styles of buildings, however, provide some novelty in the record. Of particular interest is the block of rowhouses found in Stratum V, the well-preserved plan of the Assyrian open-court building of Stratum III, and the technique used in building the walls of Stratum II, where a layer of reeds between the stone foundation and the superstructure provided a seal to keep ground water from destroying the mud bricks. Rock-cut tunnels leading from the interior of a walled city to the water source have long been known elsewhere as a measure of civil defense, but the example at Tell es-Saʿidiyeh is unique, in that it was built within a trench cut from the side of a tell of occupation debris. Furthermore, the exclusive use of a large area of approximately 1125 sq. m. for the storage of grain in pits and bins during the period of Stratum IV provides new detail about the organization of city life at the end of the Iron Age. These constructions, covering a period of approximately eight centuries, are the primary concerns of this report.

The records of incomplete soundings, as well as of those made during the short season of excavations in 1967, are deposited in the archives of the University Museum for use when it may be possible to continue work at the site. In Appendix A we have listed some of the important soundings that were begun but not finished.

The provenience for an object found in the course of excavation was recorded according to the 5 by 5 m. plot of the grid in which it was found (fig. 176). When houses or bins were encountered and assigned numbers the locus of an artifact was more specifically defined by entering in the catalogue the number of the house or bin as well as the plot reference.

Well-defined floor surfaces throughout the excavated areas provided the basis for the assignment of artifacts to specific strata (see p. 43 for a description of the way in which the layers of debris had been built up). The artifacts assigned to Stratum I were found lying on the surface of the summit of the mound (Area 31) and in the debris to a depth where the first floor of occupation was encountered; Stratum II consisted of the debris extending from the floor of Stratum I to the surface of the next floor, that of Stratum II; and similarly Stratum III lay below Stratum II in Area 31. Stratum IV, however, designates the first stratum of the adjacent and larger area of the excavation, Area 23-32. Thus, there exists as yet no definite stratigraphic connection between Strata I-III on the one hand and Strata IV-VII on the other (see p. 60).

During the excavation we assigned provisional numbers to the layers of occupation in Area 23-32 as "Levels I–IV." Similarly, we labeled in sequence the layered deposits in Area 31 as "Acropolis Levels I–III." In this final report we have combined the systems into one sequence. The changes from the designations used in the preliminary reports to those employed in the final report are as follows:

Level IV	Stratum VII
Level III	Stratum VI
Level II	Stratum V
Level I	Stratum IV
Acropolis Level III	Stratum III
Acropolis Level II	Stratum II
Acropolis Level I	Stratum I

The excavations were sponsored by the University Museum of the University of Pennsylvania, with the cooperation of the American Schools of Oriental Research. The dates for the field work were: January 1—February 29, 1964; February 12—April 24, 1965; February 7—April 16, 1966. Over each of these periods housing for the staff was made available by the Jordan Cooperative Association at its camp at Wādī el-Yābis. Dr. Awni K. Dajani, Director of the Department of Antiquities of the Hashemite Kingdom of Jordan, extended to the expeditions every courtesy and aided materially in placing at our disposal members of the Department to help in the work of supervision.

The staff consisted of: Terry Ball, draftsman, 1964; Joseph J. DeVault, supervisor, 1965; Joanna Fink (McClellan), supervisor, 1966: Asia G. Halaby, cataloguer and supervisor, 1964, 1965, 1966; Sally Harris (Todd), draftsman, 1966; John E. Huesman, assistant director, 1964, 1965, 1966; Jean-Louis Huot, supervisor, 1966: Moʿawiyah M. Ibrahim, inspector, 1964; Stephan Kroll, supervisor, 1965; Jacques Lagarce, supervisor, 1964; Hassan Mamlouk, supervisor, 1964; Gustav A. Materna, architect, 1964; Ruth Matson, cataloguer, 1965, 1966; Thomas L. McClellan, supervisor, 1964, architect, 1966; Subhi Muhtadi, surveyor, 1964; Magnus Ottosson, supervisor, 1965, 1966; James B. Pritchard, director, 1964, 1965, 1966; Pierre Proulx, supervisor, 1966; Ahmed Shistawi, supervisor, 1964; Robert H. Smith, supervisor, 1964; William H. Stiebing, draftsman, 1965; Fayes Tarawneh, inspector, 1966; Safwan Tell, inspector, 1965; John Van Seters, supervisor, 1965; Oliver M. Unwin, architect 1965; Khair Nimr Yassine, supervisor, 1964. Adrianne Sharples and Polly M. Mackie prepared many of the plates of drawings and a number of the catalogues. Patrick E. McGovern adjusted the older ^{14}C dates for our carbon samples to the ranges of confidence levels of the Radiocarbon International Calibration. William P. Anderson and James A. Sauer made many useful suggestions about both the content and the form of this report when it was in the final stages of preparation.

Preliminary reports written by the director have appeared in the following: *Annual of the Department of Antiquities of Jordan* 8–9: 95–98; *Archaeology* 18: 292–94; and 19: 289–90; *Bible et terre sainte* 75: 6–15; *Biblical Archaeologist* 28: 10–17; and 28: 126–28; *Expedition* 6, no. 4: 3–9; and 7, no. 4: 26–33; and 11, no. 1: 20–22; *Illustrated London News* 28 March, 1964: 487–90; and 2 July, 1966: 25–27; *Revue biblique* 72: 257–62; and 73: 574–76.

In addition the following more specialized or detailed studies, also written by the director of the excavations, have appeared: "An Eighth Century Traveller," *Expedition* 10, no. 2: 26–29; "New Evidence on the Role of the Sea Peoples in Canaan at the Beginning of the Iron Age," *The Role of the Phoenicians in the Interaction of Mediterranean Civilizations*, ed. W. A. Ward, 99–112, 1968; "An Incense Burner from Tell es-Saʿidiyeh, Jordan Valley," *Studies on the Ancient Palestinian World*, ed. J. W. Wevers and D. B. Redford, 3–17, 1972; "On the Use of the Tripod Cup," *Ugaritica VI*: 427–34; "Tell es-Saʿidiyeh," *Encyclopedia of Archaeological Excavations in the Holy Land*, edited by M. Avi-Yonah and E. Stern 4(1978): 1028–32; *The Cemetery at Tell es-Saʿidiyeh, Jordan*, University Museum Monograph, 41.

Additional reports written by members of the staff are: John E. Huesman, *The Catholic Biblical Quarterly* 26: 242–43; T. L. McClellan, "Zarethan," *The Interpreter's Dictionary of the Bible*, Supplementary Volume, edited by K. Crim, 978–79.

I

The Site and its Identification

Tell es-Saʿīdīyeh (hereafter Tell es-Saʿidiyeh, map reference 20461861) is a conspicuous feature of the landscape in the central Jordan Valley (figs. 21–24) and can be seen easily from the road that runs through the village of Kereimeh, 2.5 km. to the east. Situated on the south bank of the Wādī Kufrinjeh, at a distance of 1.8 km. before the wādī reaches the Jordan, the mound rises about 40 m. above the level of a fertile plain and commands a view of long stretches of the winding river to the north and to the south, as well as of the hills and mountains that border the valley on each side. The highest point on the tell is 232.32 m. below sea level; from its summit there is a clear view of Tell el-Mazār and Tell Deirʿ Allā to the southeast, of Qarn Sarṭabeh, across the Jordan to the southwest, and of Tell el-Kereimeh and Tell Abū Dhahab to the east. The fertility of the valley in which Tell es-Saʿidiyeh is situated became dramatically apparent in 1964 with the completion of the East Ghor Canal and its laterals (fig. 21), which irrigated the land so that it produced crops of tomatoes, eggplant, squash, grains, bananas, and citrus fruits. For centuries before the construction of the canal the land had remained a desert wasteland inhabited chiefly by bedouin (*Expedition* 6, no. 2: 3–9), who buried their dead on the top of Tell es-Saʿidiyeh.

The higher and more conspicuous part of Tell es-Saʿidiyeh, to which Nelson Glueck gave the name of esh-Sherqī (*AASOR* 25–28: 292), has a relatively flat top, which measures (along the −244 m. contour line) 180 m. from east to west and 110 m. from north to south (fig. 176). The perimeter of this oval-shaped summit had been contained by encircling city walls, the stone foundations of the uppermost of which remain exposed, particularly on the north side of the tell (figs. 159 and 160). Traces of a city wall also appear at the northeast corner, where an eroded notch in the circumvallation of the tell suggests a gateway, and on the west side of the tell, where another depression in the perimeter probably marks the site of a gateway to the west.

The north side of the tell drops precipitously and the south side is only slightly less steep. The slopes of the east and west sides are considerably more gradual; the leveling at these edges of the mound may have been due to the erosion of the summit by the wash through the principal entranceways into the walled city.

In addition to the evidences for the stone foundation walls that defended the city that were found exposed on the surface, there were numerous stone foundations for houses, particularly in the northeast sector of the tell. Of the surface remains of architecture only the large building in 23-H/J-1/2 (for the grid see fig. 176) has been planned and only the foundation for a fortress tower of Stratum I of the summit in 31-B/D-6/8 (fig. 187) and the scattered walls in 32-C/G-8/10 have been excavated (figs. 161, 189). Surface burials, particularly on the higher part of the tell, made during the last few centuries, were frequently encountered and removed to other locations.

To the west of Tell es-Saʿidiyeh esh-Sherqī (described above), is a lower mound of occupation debris, which has been called el-Gharbī (fig. 23, center). The surface of this lower mound extends in a rectangular to oval shape for a distance of 150 m. from north to south and of about 90 m. from east to west (measured mostly from the −264 m. contour). The surface of the lower mound is about 20 m. below that of the higher. The only building remains visible when we began excavations were the foundations of a large, rectangular building situated toward the north end of the mound. (This is clearly visible in Glueck's photo, ibid., fig. 95.)

The water source for the settlements on the tell consists of a cluster of perennial springs that flow into the Wādī Kufrinjeh opposite the north side of the higher tell (fig. 22). During the rainy season water rushes down the wādī from the hills to the east—at times the water was too deep and swift to allow an automobile to cross—to augment the water that gushes up from the springs. At other times during our stay at Tell es-Saʿidiyeh the wādī to the east of the springs became completely dry, but the springs were always productive.

Former Explorations and Soundings

The first thorough archaeological survey of the tell was made by Nelson Glueck during his explorations of Eastern Palestine from 1939 to 1947 (ibid., 290–95). He reported finding sherds on the top of the higher mound that belonged to the Iron I and Iron II Ages, with those from Iron II predominating; small numbers of sherds from EB I–II and MB I, with several others that he assigned to the MB II and LB II periods; and some Roman and Byzantine sherds (ibid., 292). His discoveries of sherds on the surface of Tell es-Saʿidiyeh el-Gharbī, the bench to the west, he described as belonging mainly to the EB I–III and MB I periods, but there were some MB II and LB II and numerous Iron I–II Age sherds as well as some Roman and Byzantine examples. He reported that on a still lower bench, to the west of the el-Gharbī site, there were, in addition to the EB sherds, several clear examples of forms from the Early Chalcolithic period decorated with bands of chevron or herringbone incisions between alternating bands of reddish-brown paint. He suggested that this westernmost site may have been a Chalcolithic and EB necropolis (ibid., 293, and 483–87 for the publication of the sherds found).

In 1953 Henri de Contenson made several soundings at what he called Tell es-Saʿidiyeh el-Taḥta, a small knoll a few hundred meters west of el-Gharbī (*ADAJ* 4–5: 49–57, figs. 32–36). In a sounding, 3 by 2 m., called Trench 1, he found pottery and flints that he assigned to a late date in Middle Chalcolithic B (ibid., 56), or to Late Chalcolithic with Ghassulian affinities (*ADAJ* 8–9: 37). A human skull found in a pit within the sounding suggested to de Contenson that these slopes leading down to the Jordan River were used as cemeteries for the inhabitants of Tell es-Saʿidiyeh.

Yet another site, named Tell es-Saʿidiyeh esh-Shimālī, was discovered in the survey of 1953 on the north bank of the Wādī Kufrinjeh, opposite Tell es-Saʿidiyeh esh-Sherqī. Its pottery was assigned to the Late Chalcolithic period and described as follows: "jars with everted neck and a raised band at the junction of the neck and the body, hole-mouth jars, flat bases, vertical loop-handles and ear-handles with elongated attachments" (ibid., 37). On the surface of Tell es-Saʿidiyeh el-Gharbī de Contenson recorded EB I material ("indented ledge-handles, bowls with inverted rim, pattern burnished sherds, hole-mouth jars, jars with an everted neck") as well as lamps with several spouts of the Middle Bronze I period (ibid., 37).

In the 1975 survey conducted by Ibrahim, Sauer, and Yassine, sherds were noted on the tell itself from the following periods: EB I–III, MB II, LB, Iron I, Iron II, Early Roman (1), and Byzantine (few). From the cemetery site there were sherds from EB II–III (dominant), Iron Age (few), and Byzantine (few) (Moʿawiyah Ibrahim, J. Sauer, and K. Yassine, "The East Jordan Valley Survey, 1975," *BASOR* 222:41–66, site no. 92).

Identification of the Site

Various attempts at attaching an ancient name to the modern site of Tell es-Saʿidiyeh have been made, on the assumption that such a prominent landmark on the horizon could hardly have escaped mention in the biblical narratives about events that took place in this part of the eastern Jordan Valley. The modern name does not evoke any ancient associations; in fact, it may be that it was brought by bedouin from Arabia, where there are at least six places bearing the name. The position of the tell, standing alone as it does on the plain, and its size, both in area and in height, make it a landmark that can be seen for miles around as the principal man-made feature from Wādī el-Yābis in the north to Tell ed-Dāmieh in the south. Only Tell el-Mazār and Tell Deir ʿAllā stand out with comparable prominence, but both are considerably smaller in size.

There are three cities in the biblical narratives that appear to belong to the general region of the eastern bank of the central Jordan Valley: Zaphon (Josh. 13:27; Judg. 12:1), Zarethan (Josh. 3:16; 1 Kings 4:12; 1 Kings 7:46; and possibly in Judg. 7:22; 1 Kings 11:26; and 2 Chron. 4:17), and Succoth (Gen. 33:17; Josh. 13:27; Judg. 8:5–16; 1 Kings 7:46; Ps. 60:8, 108:8; 2 Chron. 4:17). Since Succoth has often been identified with the modern Tell Deir ʿAllā (however, Magnus Ottosson has tentatively proposed that Succoth is Tell es-Saʿidiyeh, *Gilead: Tradition and History*, 1969, 225; and H. J. Franken, the excavator of Deir ʿAllā, prefers to place Succoth at Tell el-Ekhṣāṣ, *Encyclopedia of Archaeological Excavations in the Holy Land*, ed. M. Avi-Yonah, 1, 1975, 321.) the two principal contestants for the ancient name of Tell es-Saʿidiyeh are Zaphon and Zarethan.

In 1926, W. F. Albright proposed the tentative identification of Tell es-Saʿidiyeh with Zaphon (identical with Asophon, mentioned by Josephus in *Antiquities*, 13.12. 5, as the scene of Ptolemy Lathyrus'

Figure 81	Partition wall between front and back rooms of House 12, looking east
Figure 82	Portion of pavement of House 12, and brick foundation for column, looking north
Figure 83	House 13, looking east, cut by Bin A of Stratum IV
Figure 84	Pavement of House 14, looking west
Figure 85	House 16, looking east
Figure 86	House 16, east part with stairs and bin, looking east
Figure 87	Back room of House 16, with bin, looking north
Figure 88	Loom weights on floor of back room of House 16, looking west
Figure 89	Loom weights found beside column wall of House 16, looking northwest
Figure 90	Street running north-south in 32-F-8/9, looking south
Figure 91	Paved section of the front room of House 14 and the north-south street, looking southeast
Figure 92	Houses 19 (foreground) and 17 (upper), looking south
Figure 93	Paving of House 25, looking north
Figure 94	House 27 (right) and courtyard between Houses 27 and 29, looking east
Figure 95	Beam and roof material on floor of House 27, looking northeast
Figure 96	West north-south street of Stratum V, looking north
Figure 97	West north-south street of Stratum V, looking south
Figure 98	Upper course of west north-south street in Stratum V, looking south
Figure 99	Pit 14 with posthole, in Stratum IV, looking southwest
Figure 100	Rectangular Bin A of Stratum IV, looking northeast
Figure 101	Rectangular Bin A, looking southwest
Figure 102	Rectangular Bin B of Stratum IV, looking northwest
Figure 103	Rectangular Bin B (foreground) and Bin A (upper), looking east
Figure 104	Rectangular Bin B of Stratum IV, looking southwest
Figure 105	General view of west end of the north side of the tell
Figure 106	North side of the tell at the beginning of the excavation of the stairway
Figure 107	Segment of stairs in 14-H/J-5/6, looking south
Figure 108	Stairway in 14-H/J-8/9, looking south
Figure 109	Stairway seen from upper steps, looking toward the springs and the Wādī Kufrinjeh (upper)
Figure 110	Treads of six steps between the landing at the bottom of the main north-south section and the first broad platform; to the right is the wall separating the tunnel from the street outside; looking west
Figure 111	Steps of the east-west segment of the stairway and the landing, looking west
Figure 112	Street to the north of the east-west wall of the tunnel, looking south
Figure 113	Plaster on a stone from the west wall of the stairway
Figure 114	Stairway, looking south
Figure 115	Lower part of stairway, with the north wall in the foreground
Figure 116	Sounding 3, at the head of the preserved portion of the stairway, looking east
Figure 117	Pavements of Rooms 101 and 102 of Stratum III, looking south

Figure 38	Platform of House 64, looking northeast
Figure 39	Tripod cup *in situ* on platform in House 64
Figure 40	Shells and stone ring on floor of House 64
Figure 41	House 66, looking north
Figure 42	East-west street in 23-F/G-6, with House 35 at the right and House 37 at the left, looking west
Figure 43	General view of the north-south street and Houses 41, 37–39, 35, 33, and 31, looking north
Figure 44	Clay oven in House 35 constructed of broken cooking pots and jars
Figure 45	Millstone and rider found in House 35
Figure 46	Stone pavement in House 41, looking west
Figure 47	House 37, looking west
Figure 48	House 37–39 and kitchen area to the east beside main north-south street, looking southeast
Figure 49	Crushed pottery vessels in House 39, looking southeast
Figure 50	Faience cosmetic cup (S1084/M274) and juglet beside south wall of House 37
Figure 51	Chalice (S1078/P625), jug (S1094/P635), and decanter (S1057/P619) found beside north wall of Room 37, looking west
Figure 52	Loom weights and juglets along north wall of Room 39
Figure 53	House 43, looking west
Figure 54	Remains of pavement in House 1 (right center), looking east
Figure 55	House 3, looking east
Figure 56	House 3, looking west
Figure 57	House 5, looking west
Figure 58	House 5, looking east
Figure 59	House 7, looking west
Figure 60	Balk between 23-G-4 and 23-G-5, looking north
Figure 61	House 7, looking east
Figure 62	House 7, looking south
Figure 63	House 9, looking east
Figure 64	House 9, looking northwest
Figure 65	Charred beam in House 9, looking north
Figure 66	House 11, looking east
Figure 67	Pavement of House 2, running beside foundation for city wall, looking west
Figure 68	Original pavement in the northwest corner of House 4, looking north
Figure 69	Second pavement imposed on original in the northwest corner of House 4, looking west
Figure 70	Pit in the unpaved room of House 6 north of columns, looking west
Figure 71	Plastered bin with hole, in House 6, looking south
Figure 72	Skeleton of infant buried in the floor of House 6
Figure 73	Lower layer of loom weights found in House 6, looking west
Figure 74	Upper layer of loom weights found in House 6, looking west
Figure 75	House 6, with its four columns, looking northwest
Figure 76	House 6, looking southeast
Figure 77	Bin between two columns of House 6, looking northwest
Figure 78	House 8, looking east
Figure 79	House 8, looking west
Figure 80	House 25 (foreground, left), House 23 (foreground, right), and House 12 (upper), looking east

defeat of Alexander Jannaeus near the Jordan), largely on the basis of the reference in Judg. 12:1 to the passing of the Ephraimites over the Jordan to Zaphon in order to attack Jephthah (*AASOR* 6:46–47). F.-M. Abel followed this identification (*Géographie* 2:448), as did F. V. Filson in his note on the reference to Asophon in Josephus (*BASOR* 91:27–28). More recently Y. Aharoni has suggested Zaphon as his choice for the identification (*The Land of the Bible: A Historical Geography*, 2nd ed., 1979, 126, 207). Albright noted that the name Zaphon was old, since Baʿal-Zaphon was a popular Canaanite deity, and "we may safely look for it in a Bronze Age tell" (*AASOR* 6:45–46). Thus the requirements of a tell for this identification would be the presence of remains of the Bronze Age, Iron I, and Hellenistic periods. But unfortunately Albright was never able to visit this area of the Jordan Valley in his exploration for potsherds owing to the hostility of local tribesmen, especially the Suḫûr (ibid., 14).

Nelson Glueck, in reporting on his explorations of the central Jordan Valley in 1942, proposed an identification of Tell es-Saʿidiyeh with the biblical Zarethan, principally on the basis of an emendation of the text of Josh 3:16, which had been suggested by Albright in 1925 (*BASOR* 90: 6ff). The latter had reconstructed the Hebrew text of the passage that describes the damming up of the Jordan so as to allow the Israelites to pass over dry land as follows: "And the water coming down from above stood still, (and) rose up into a single mass as far from ʾAdamah as beside Saretan (Zarethan)" (*Journal of the Palestine Oriental Society* 5: 33, n. 37). Glueck proposed a further change in the reading (and Albright concurred) to "as far from ʾAdamah as the fortress of Zarethan" (*BASOR* 90: 6). On the basis of this emended and revised reading of the Hebrew text, Glueck made the following arguments: "It is obvious (a) from Josh. 3:16 that Zarethan is north of Adamah,—and, it would seem, a fair distance north of it. The text means to be taken literally, that this wall of water damming up the Jordan extended north as far as Zarethan . . . . It is furthermore obvious (b) that Zarethan must have been a very well-known landmark, (c) that it must have been also an important site, (d) that it must have been occupied in the Late Bronze Age as well as in the Early Iron, and that (e) like Adamah (Tell ed-Dâmieh) it must have been in or very near the Zôr of the Jordan" (ibid., 6).

Since Tell es-Saʿidiyeh seemed to meet all of these requirements, Glueck was convinced that its proper identification was Zarethan and that there was no other site that met all of the conditions. As further confirmation of his identification Glueck cited a talmudic reference by a third-century scholar, Rabbi Johanan, which speaks of Adamah and Zarethan as being 12 miles apart. This is the distance between Tell ed-Dāmieh and Tell es-Saʿidiyeh (ibid., 8).

As corroborative evidence for his identification Glueck makes use of 1 Kings 7:46, which locates the casting of the copper vessels for use in the Jerusalem temple "in the earthen foundries (or in the thickened earthen moulds) between Succoth and Zarethan" (Glueck's translation, ibid., 14). In his explorations in the region between Deirʿ Allā, the site often identified with Succoth, and Tell es-Saʿidiyeh Glueck found seven Early Iron Age sites and ventured the opinion that "at any or at all of these places, smiths may have been at work, manufacturing the copper vessels required for the new temple" (ibid., 13). In the final publication of his explorations in Eastern Palestine Glueck reaffirmed this view (*AASOR* 25–28: 345–46).

The arguments that have been adduced for the identification of Tell es-Saʿidiyeh with places mentioned in the Bible rest too much upon uncertain and emended texts to provide us with any high degree of confidence. At the present stage of archaeological work in the area, and at Tell es-Saʿidiyeh in particular, any conclusions about the ancient names of the sites must of necessity remain hypothetical.

II

Stratum VII

The earliest buildings recovered on the tell were those of Stratum VII, found in 23-F/G-2/9 (fig. 30 for a general view; fig. 177 for the plan). Within this area of slightly less than 400 sq. m. there appeared nine identifiable housing units, a system of streets, a drain, and a segment of the city wall. The plan of this part of the city remained virtually unchanged throughout the occupation of Stratum VII, except for slight alterations that were made in the principal east-west street (in 23-F/G-6) and to the buildings and paved area lying to the north of it.

Two substrata, VIIA and VIIB, were recognized in the group of buildings and the streets of this particular area of Stratum VII. No evidence for these two phases could be found in the streets and buildings that lay to the south of the east-west street (with the possible exception of House 60-62). A possible explanation for the anomaly of two phases of occupation to the north of the east-west street is that, since this lower and sloping section of the city was flooded at times during heavy rains, modification of the floors of streets and of houses was made more frequently than in the more stable area of the higher ground to the south of the east-west street. Even though the evidence for two separate phases of occupation is for the most part a localized and explainable phenomenon, we have used the designations of Stratum VIIA for the second and later use of the streets and buildings and Stratum VIIB for the earlier substratum of occupation. The artifacts, however, from these two substrata have been listed together.

When a small sounding was made in the floor of House 51 of Stratum VII it was discovered that this stratum had been built on the debris of an earlier occupation that had been destroyed by fire (see below). The evidence for the end of the city of Stratum VII, however, suggests that it was abandoned and not burned. Nearly everywhere there were evidences of a reddish silt deposit, averaging about 10 cm. in thickness, between Stratum VII and the succeeding Stratum VI (see the section in fig. 181). Nowhere was there evidence for a general burning of Stratum VII.

One general feature should be noted about the houses of Stratum VII: the mud-brick walls were almost always built upon a foundation of stone. These foundations ranged in depth from that of a single row of stones to a wall about 1 m. deep (fig. 27 for the north wall of Houses 51, 53, and 55, which served also as a retaining wall above the paved area). Stone was also generously used for the paving of streets, the lining of gutters (figs. 31 and 32), as well as for the floors of houses, especially in Stratum VIIA.

The City Wall

At the north of the excavated area a portion of the city wall was encountered in 23-F/G-9. The orientation of the more than 9 m. segment of the mud-brick structure is almost exactly east-west. The northern part of the wall had been lost through the erosion that had taken place at the north side of the tell but the south and inner line of the wall remained and could be seen in the mud bricks of the wall itself or in the line of its stone foundation. The greatest preserved width of the brick wall is 2.85 m., but soft, mud-brick material above foundation stones at about the center of the excavated segment indicated that the width of the city wall had been at least 3.50 m. Very little of the superstructure remained. At the remaining west balk a thin section of bricks, belonging to the inner face of the wall, stood 1.10 m. above the level of the adjoining pavement (fig. 25, right). In the west balk there could be seen the erosion line of the tell, on which lay about 8 cm. of black earth that had accumulated after the erosion of the upper part of the city wall. The bricks of the wall were reddish yellow in color. The upper surface measured 36 by 46 cm.; the bricks that were measured from the houses of Stratum V ranged from 32 by 48 cm. to 38 by 56 cm. (see p. 35) The thickness of the bricks could not be determined accurately from the few available samples.

Since the stone pavements of Stratum VII in 23-F/

G-8 ran up to the foundation stones of the city wall, it would appear that the wall had been built to fortify the city of Stratum VII. At the close of the 1966 season Magnus Ottosson, who had supervised the area of the city wall, made a sounding in 23-G-7 through the floor of House 51 of Stratum VII. After removing about 1 m. of debris containing roof fall, burned brick, and a charred roof beam he reached the stone floor of a house which belonged to a stratum on which Stratum VII had been constructed (fig. 28). When a trench was cut from the pavement of the floor of the house of what would have been Stratum VIII northward through the paved area to the line of the city wall, it was apparent that the floor of Stratum VIII was well below the level of the foundation of the city wall and its accompanying stone pavements. It seems clear, therefore, that Stratum VII was build upon the burned remains of an earlier city and surrounded by the city wall described above.

The erosion of the edge of the tell has made it impossible to determine how long the city wall of Stratum VII remained in use, since all connections between any part of it and the remains of Strata VI and V have disappeared. It is quite possible that the city wall of Stratum VII was maintained as a fortification for the city of Stratum VI, since the general orientation of its houses in the north is similar to those of the plan in Stratum VII. But the orientation of the plan of houses in Stratum V and the line of the foundation for its city wall are different from those of Strata VII and VI.

Paved Area between Houses 51-53-55 and the City Wall

The open area between the city wall and the north wall of Houses 51-53-55 was solidly paved in each of the two phases, Stratum VIIB (lower) and Stratum VIIA (upper). The lower pavement first became apparent at the west end, where a segment of it, measuring .65 m. at the south and 3 m. at the north, lay 20 cm. below the upper pavement (fig. 26). The north edge of the pavement of Stratum VIIB abuts the city wall; how far it reaches to the south could not be determined without the demolition of the pavement which overlays it. It is thus probable that the earlier pavement of Stratum VIIB is contemporary with the building of the city wall to the north.

Later, in Stratum VIIB, but sometime before the building of the north wall to Houses 51 and 53, a new pavement, 3 m. wide at the west balk and 3.50 m. wide at the east balk, was laid over the first (fig. 25). It was upon this pavement that the north wall of Houses 51 and 53 was built. The missing section at the west end of this later pavement is difficult to explain. The stones may have been robbed for use in a later period of construction.

It can readily be seen that the pavement of the upper layer of this street or plaza is by far the best masonry to be found in Stratum VII (figs. 25 and 27). It consists of stones of uniform size set with pebbles laid between them. The pavement could have served as a street running parallel to the city wall; if this was its use, it was considerably wider and better paved than any other street encountered in this stratum. It must be observed that there were no doorways leading from it to the houses that adjoined it. The street to the east of House 51 was found to have had an accumulation of about 30 cm. of pebbles; in the opinion of the supervisor it may well have been in use through both phases of Stratum VII.

The area of the houses to the north of the east-west street is known as two phases of Stratum VII. The plan shown in fig. 177 is that of their later phase, Stratum VIIA, when all three houses, 51, 53, and 55, had the same general plan. Each had a small front room on the street and a larger back room. The south wall of the houses ran parallel to the street, but most of the brickwork had disappeared, except for a short segment to the east, where the bricks were preserved to a height of about 50 cm. It was observed during the excavation that the principal north-south walls were leaning toward the east. Each had been cut by a pit dug from a higher level.

House 51 (fig. 29, upper)

The doorway to the front room of this two-room house was on the principal east-west street and was provided with a sill that served to divert the water which ran down the sloping street from the house. The floor of the front room sloped toward its north wall, in which there was an entranceway into a larger back room.

Within the house there were found two floors. That of Stratum VIIB, the earlier, was of beaten earth throughout. Within the back room, 95 cm. from its southwest corner and 55 cm. from its south wall, was a pit, measuring 80 cm. in diameter and 35–40 cm. deep. Its walls were plastered with a grayish green clay (*qaṭṭārah*), as was the stone-lined bottom.

Two oblong grinding stones were found in the northeast corner of the room. A clay oven, 50–54 cm. in diameter, had been constructed in the southeast corner of the front room.

The floor of Stratum VIIA lay from 25 to 30 cm. above that of Stratum VIIB. As can be seen from fig. 177 the front room had a stone pavement sloping to the north and there were remnants of a similar paved surface in the northeast corner of the back room. There were no changes made in the walls of the house in Stratum VIIA.

OBJECT:
Frit Bead,
 S1253/J70 (fig. 5:24).

House 53 (fig. 29, center)

The general plan of House 53 is the same as that of House 51, although the doorway between its two rooms could not be traced. The first floor of the house, in Stratum VIIB, was of beaten earth and had been cut by a stone-lined storage bin that had been dug from a higher level. Although the level of the floor of the back room was about 35 cm. lower than that of the front room, no evidence could be found for steps that must have led from one to the other. It is possible that they had been removed in the cutting of the bin.

About 20 cm. above the first floor was the floor of Stratum VIIA. In the center of the front room a millstone was found, as well as a puzzling single line of mud bricks, about 50 cm. high, that ran along the west wall of the front room (not shown in the plan of fig. 177), giving the impression of a bench. The back room in this phase was paved with stones in some places, especially in the northwest and northeast corners. Since the level of the floor of the front room was considerably lower than that of the street there must have been steps inside the room at the entrance. Stones which might have been from this structure were reported by the supervisor.

House 55 (fig. 29, lower)

In the early phase of Stratum VII in the area which later became House 55 of Stratum VIIA, there was a street paved with stones leading from the main east-west street in 23-F/G-6 to the stone pavement in 23-F/G-8. At the south of this passageway three or four steps led downward to the north.

In Stratum VIIA the street was closed off and a house of two rooms, patterned after Houses 51 and 53, was built (see fig. 177). The stairway of the former street seems to have been incorporated into the paved front room in which a millstone had been set. The north wall of the back room, unlike the wall that separates Houses 51 and 53 from the paved area to the north, was poorly built without a deep stone foundation.

OBJECTS:
Juglet,
 S1155/P649 (fig. 5:7). Possibly from House 53.
Tripod Bowl,
 S1180/St81, basalt fragment, D.13 cm. Possibly from House 53.

The East-West Paved Street in 23-F/G-6 (figs. 31 and 32)

In contrast to the pebbly north-south street in 23-F-2/5 this street was built with large foundation stones and easily identifiable curbs to channel the water that flowed from west to east in the rainy season. Two phases of construction were noted and designated in the order of their construction as Stratum VIIB and VIIA.

The earlier Stratum VIIB street had a well-built water channel, 80 to 85 cm. wide, built of small stones set in a grayish green plaster made from the local marl (*qaṭṭārah*). The south wall of this channel can be traced as it encircles the north and the east walls of House 57 (see black line in 23-F/G-6 in fig. 177). As it curves from west to south the wall was found to be 1 m. deep. The purpose, obviously, of this plastered channel was to protect the foundations of the houses on each side of the street from being undermined or weakened by the water that flowed down the streets from the west and the south.

At the west end of the east-west street there is a

paved platform of stones extending about 1.25 m. from the west balk (top of fig. 31). In the center of this platform the water channel is only about 30 cm. wide and leads into a small basin (fig. 32, lower; and fig. 31, upper). The function of this pit, or basin, can only be conjectured. It could have been a settling basin for collecting water for use by the owners of the houses beside it.

During the later phase of Stratum VII, called Stratum VIIA, the water channel was filled in with large stones to provide a new pavement for the street, thus enlarging it to almost the maximum distance that separates the walls of the houses on each side. During this phase of occupation large curb stones were placed as fenders against the house to protect the vulnerable brick walls (see fig. 177 and fig. 31, where a line of large stones is visible at the left).

It was probably during the phase represented by Stratum VIIA that a pit was dug at the east end of the street (fig. 32, top; and fig. 33, top left). It was found to be lined with a poor quality of plaster, described as "mud-brick" material by the supervisor, on the sides and on the stones that formed the bottom. The purpose of this pit, like that of the basin at the west end of the street, is not clear. Possibly it was a secondary arrangement for the control of the considerable amount of water that must have come from the streets that converged in what appears to have been an open square. The eastern limit of the square is not yet apparent since the boundary is beyond the limits of the excavation.

The alterations of the east-west street and its water system probably took place in a comparatively short time. Water from the heavy winter rains must have constituted a constant threat to the foundations of the buildings along the street. The absence of discernible levels of deposit on a street that was also a water channel made it impossible to correlate its rebuildings with those within the adjoining houses.

The last phase of the east-west street of Stratum VII is attested by a heavy deposit of reddish silt, upon which the foundation stones for the walls of the southeast corner of House 35 of Stratum VI were laid. The evidence of silt here, as elsewhere between Strata VII and VI, suggests a gap in occupation.

House 57-59 (fig. 33)

To the south of the main paved east-west street, in 23-F/G-6, are two well-defined rooms, 57 and 59, which probably constituted a single house. The doorway from the street into Room 57 was at its northwest corner, and its floor was paved with large stones and pebbles. The west wall of the room was reported by Fayez Tarawneh, the supervisor of the area, to have had in all probability an opening leading into Room 59, which adjoins it on the west. This room, of which the west wall should be beyond the limits of the excavation, was only partly paved. It may once have been the western part of one long room, which was subsequently divided into two. The complex is bordered on the north, east, and south sides entirely by streets. On each of these sides there was evidence for a stone curbing which had served to protect the mud-brick walls from the water of the streets.

OBJECTS:
Iron Arrowhead,
 S1153/F62 (fig. 5:18).
Pestle,
 S1195/St84, basalt, unbroken. H.9.1 cm., D.6 cm.
Base,
 TS (fig. 3:15). (For TS, Type Series, see p. 43).
Storage Jar,
 TS (fig. 4:6).
 TS (fig. 4:13).

The North-South Street (fig. 34)

A slightly sloping street, 1.40 to 1.70 m. wide and surfaced with small pebbles, runs for ca. 17 m. from south to north in 23-F-2/5 and then turns eastward. The west side of the street is slightly higher than its east side. Since the walls along the east side of the street were more vulnerable to the water that ran in the gutter, deeper foundations of stone were constructed for the west walls of the houses on this side of the street. The level of the street was higher than that of the floors of the houses that adjoin it, especially those houses on the east side of the street.

House 60-62 (fig. 35)

House 60-62 lies to the north of House 64 and shares a common wall with it. In their first phase, Stratum VIIB, Rooms 60 and 62 were divided by the stub of a mud-brick wall running east-west (fig. 35). Associated with this wall of Stratum VIIB were two small clay ovens in the southwest corner of Room 62 (fig. 35) and a pit, probably dug to contain the ashes from the ovens. Later, in Stratum VIIA, the partition between the two rooms was removed in order to make one large room (fig. 177). Sections of stone pavements lay in the southwest and the southeast; six loom weights were found in the segment of paving at the southeast, measuring 1.25 by 1.25 m. Imbedded in the stone floor to the southwest was a mortar; a clay oven, 40 cm. in diameter, was found beside the west wall of the room surrounded by ash. Immediately to the north of the clay oven there was a plastered rectangular pit, 85 cm. deep, filled with ashes. The opening to the pit, 1 by 1.20 m. was circled with stones.

OBJECTS:

Spouted Jug,
  S1198/P674 (fig. 5:9).
Jug,
  S1191/P670 (fig. 5:1).
Pilgrim Flask,
  S1237/P692 (fig. 5:17).
Ring,
  S1264/M293, white frit, D.3.5 cm., H.1.3 cm.
Jug,
  S1219/677 (fig. 5:5).

House 63

The long room of House 63 was well protected by curb stones along the outside of its east wall. It may well have been divided into two rooms by an east-west partition wall, although no evidence for it or its foundation was preserved. The floor of the north half of House 63 was lower than the floor of the southern half. No doorways could be observed in the existing walls. The open area to the north of House 63 was possibly a wide street or plaza.

House 64 (figs. 36, lower, and 37)

The large room of House 64 (fig. 37) belonged to a complex of at least three rooms; the back rooms continued eastward beyond the limits of the excavation. The west wall of House 64 could be recognized only by its foundation stones and those of the curb of the street (fig. 37, left). There seem to have been two doors from the street, each ca. .90 m. wide, separated by a stone column. Evidence for the doorways consisted principally of two steps by which one entered the room, the floor of which was considerably lower than the level of the street. On the plan (fig. 177) these steps can be seen protruding beyond the line of the house wall into the room. The north wall of the room had a stone foundation supporting the mud bricks. The south wall (fig. 36) divided Room 64 from Room 66, the floor level of which is ca. 60 cm. above that of Room 64.

Against the east wall of Room 64 there appeared a mud-brick table or platform, measuring 1.20 m. long, .55 m. wide, and .48 m. high (fig. 38). The entire structure had been plastered with lime plaster, as had the stub of house wall that extends from the table to the doorway to the north. The original platform was later enlarged. An extension of about the same size as the original construction, but with a more rounded corner, appears to the south. On the top of each of the two parts of the platform there is a basin. The depression on the south part of the table is elliptical, measuring 30 by 13 cm.; in this basin was found the incense burner (fig. 5:11), surrounded by charcoal and ashes (fig. 39). The floor of the room immediately before the platform was plastered; paving stones were found in the northeast corner of the room. In the southwest corner of the room there was a clay oven, which belonged to a period of use later than that represented by the plastered and paved floor. To the south of the platform the north-south wall was badly damaged (not shown on the plan) and it is quite possible that at this point there was a doorway leading into the room to the east.

OBJECTS:

Jug,
  S1222/P680 (fig. 5:2).

S1223/P681 (fig. 5:4).
S1260/P697 (fig. 5:6).
Juglet,
S1257/P695 (fig. 5:10).
S1220/P678 (fig. 5:8).
Lamp,
S1182/P661 (fig. 5:15).
S1183/P662 (fig. 5:13).
S1185/P664 (fig. 5:14).
S1124/P682, brown ware, small black grits, H.6.1 cm., D.14.2 cm. P.
Tripod Cup,
S1187/P660 (fig. 5:21).
S1199/P675 (fig. 5:12).
S1221/P679 (fig. 5:11).
Rubbing Stone,
S1196/St85, black pumice, H.2.5 cm., L.8.5 cm., W.4.3 cm.
Bead,
S1245/J68 (fig. 5:25).
S1246/J69AB (fig. 5:23).
Iron Needle,
S1247/F73, L.10.2 cm., found beside plastered platform. P.
Iron Arrowhead,
S1265/F79 (fig. 5:19). On platform.

The large assemblage of artifacts from House 64—almost half the catalogued items found in Stratum VII—includes a number of objects that may indicate a specialized rather than a more general or domestic use of the house. Distinctive among the items of the inventory is the tripod cup, of which there are three examples. One of these was found on the top of the plastered table or platform (fig. 39), and the two others were found lying on the floor of the room not far away. A collection of nine shells was found on the floor beside the south wall, 2.25 m. east of the west wall (fig. 40). The four lamps recorded from this house are the only lamps found within the entire Stratum VII; also worthy of note are the three beads from the house. But in addition to these relatively rare artifacts found in House 64 there are utilitarian objects which are common in areas of domestic occupation, such as juglets, jugs, a rubbing stone, and a needle. While these objects of everyday life would suggest that the house served as a living area, as did other houses of this stratum, the discovery of the tripod cup in situ lying in charcoal and ashes on top of the plastered platform can hardly be explained as an utilitarian arrangement, since the bowl of the tripod cup is too small to have been effective as a brazier for heating a room as large as Room 64. We may conclude from the position of the cup in ashes and from the burning on the rims of other examples of this type of tripod cup that the vessel served as a kind of censer for burning incense or some type of aromatic compound (see James B. Pritchard, "On the Use of the Tripod Cup," *Ugaritica VI:* 427–34). When the presence of three tripod cups within this room is considered along with that of the plastered table or platform, on which one of the cups was found in situ, it seems likely, at times at least, that the house served a specialized purpose.

House 65

Only the northeast corner of House 65, in 23-F-2, was excavated (fig. 177). A doorway, measuring ca. 1 m. in width, from the north-south street at the south end of the wall may be postulated from the presence of large stones that could have provided a foundation for a threshold. To judge by a path of paving, 1.10 by .90 m., which remained near the west balk, the room once had a stone pavement. A clay oven was situated at the northeast corner of the room.

OBJECTS:
Alabaster Cup,
S1144/St79 (fig. 5:26).
Bronze Ring,
S1255/Br83, D.2.9 cm. P. From street to the east of House 65.

House 66 *(figs. 36, upper, and 41)*

House 66 (fig. 41), in 23-G-2, lies to the south of House 64, with which it shares a common wall. The doorway to House 66 from the street seems to have been at the south-west corner, where a step in the street leads to the stone threshold. Another step appears within the room. The conjectured entranceway measured ca. .95 m. wide. Scattered stones that had once constituted the pavement of the room were found along the east wall. Three clay ovens were located in the northwest corner of the room. Since the oven at the north wall of the room lay partly under the foundation of the wall, it evidently belonged to an earlier use of the area. The east wall of the room lay beyond the line of the east balk.

OBJECTS:
Iron Fibula,
  S1207/F65 (fig. 5:22). Possibly from House 64.

OBJECTS FROM STRATUM VII FOUND OUTSIDE THE HOUSES:
Stopper,
  S1151/M284, 23-F-5 (fig. 5:16).
Silver Ring,
  S1216/J66, 23-G-3. Possibly Stratum VI.
Iron Arrowhead,
  S1152/F61, 23-G-8 (fig. 5:20).
Basalt Stopper,
  S1206/St88, 23-G-8, hole pierced in shank, H.5.4 cm., L.7 cm. A.
Bronze Fibula,
  S1214/Br 77, 23-G-8, L.5.2 cm., H.3.5 cm. P. Possibly from House 51.

Summary

The architectural remains that were uncovered in Stratum VII consist of nine identifiable building units (Houses 51, 53, 55, 57-59, 60-62, 63, 64, 65, 66). Four of these are sufficiently complete in plan for determining the inside measurements:

House 51: 2.5 by 6 m. (= 15 sq. m.)
House 53: 2.75 by 6 m. (= 16.5 sq. m.)
House 60-62: 4 by 6.25 m. (= 25 sq. m.)
House 57-59: ca. 3 by 5.5 m. (= ca. 16.5 sq. m.)

Houses 51 and 53 are two-room units, as is probably House 60-62. The area of these houses is small when compared to that of the houses of Stratum V, which average 40.42 sq. m. Some dwellings are arranged in clusters, like Houses 51, 53, 55, and 60-62, 64, 66, but House 57-59 is more isolated from its neighbors by streets. The same isolation is exhibited by what has been recovered of House 63. The most common plan is that of a rectangular building divided into two rooms. The one exception is the three-room structure of House 64, which seems to have had a specialized use. Circular clay ovens are commonly found. Houses 51, 63, and 65 each had one oven. Houses 60-62 and 66 each had three ovens, and House 64 had two. Another form of household equipment was the stone mortar or grinding stone. In House 51 there were found two oblong grinding stones. The base or lower element of a circular stone mill was found in situ in three of the houses of this stratum: 53, 55, and 60-62 (see fig. 177). In addition to these indications of the domestic activities of baking and milling, there is evidence that weaving had been done in House 60-62. Six loom weights were discovered on the floor that was in use during the later phase of occupation.

Among the objects catalogued from the rooms of Stratum VII are the following: 3 juglets, 2 storage jars, 1 jar, 1 base, 6 jugs, 1 pilgrim flask, 4 lamps, 3 tripod cups, 2 stoppers, 1 tripod bowl, 4 beads, 3 arrowheads, 1 pestle, 3 rings, 1 rubbing stone, 1 needle, 1 alabaster cup, 2 fibulae.

The relative dearth of well-preserved personal possessions of value, when considered along with the stratigraphic evidence for a gap in occupation between Stratum VII and Stratum VI, supports the theory that the city was abandoned rather than destroyed in a sudden catastrophe. The inhabitants had been able to take most of their household possessions as they abandoned their dwellings to take up residence elsewhere. Stratum VII seems to have come to a peaceful end, only to be rebuilt subsequently by the founders of the city of Stratum VI.

III

Stratum VI

The remains of Stratum VI (fig. 178 for the plan) consist of six houses (31, 33, 35, 37-39, 41, and 43), a north-south street, and two east-west streets that meet it at right angles. These were all built upon the remains of the abandoned city of Stratum VII (the lines of silt or reddish brown soil in the section of 23-G-2/3 shown in fig. 181 run over the walls of Houses 64 and 66 of Stratum VII and under the street of Stratum VI). The plan of the settlement is new and the house units, where their size can be determined, are generally larger than those in the earlier stratum. Houses 33 and 35 have areas of 24.44 sq. m. and 23.38 sq. m. respectively. The houses consist of one room, except for House 37-39, which had two, and House 43, which was originally a one-room structure but was divided into two rooms in its second phase of use.

House 31 (fig. 178)

The evidence for House 31 consists of the stub of a wall that is the northern continuation of the east wall of House 33, and fragments of stone pavement to the north of the north wall of House 33. The erosion at the north edge of the tell seems to have destroyed any further information about it. Against the hypothesis that there was a house in this area is the observation that the south face of the city wall of Stratum VII appears just 2.50 m. to the north of House 33. If the Stratum VII city wall was indeed in use during the time of Stratum VI—the orientation of the houses of Stratum VI is similar to that of the houses of Stratum VII, when the wall is known to have been in use—the space left to the north of House 33 is not adequate for a house of anything like the usual dimensions. Yet, if the fragments of pavement in House 31 belonged to a paved area like that found to the south of the city wall in Stratum VII, it is difficult to explain the stub of wall that projects northward from the northeast corner of House 33. We consider the evidence, scant though it is, to favor the hypothesis that there had been a building in this area.

OBJECTS:

Jug,
    S1161/P651 (fig. 7:17).
Iron arrowhead,
    S1145/F60 (fig. 8:17). Possibly House 33.

House 33

The entrance into this well-defined house is from the north-south street to the east of it (fig. 178). The threshold had been built up with stones to keep out the water from the street. Remnants of paving stones were found in the southwest corner and along the north wall. Just west of the center of the house was a well-laid platform that could have served as the foundation for a pillar or column to support the roof. A clay oven was found in the southwest corner (not shown on the plan), and it was noted that the bricks in the wall to the south of the oven had been colored by the heat of the fire in the oven. This house had two levels of occupation; to the later belonged the clay oven and the pavement at the southwest corner. The north half of the west wall had been destroyed, as had most of the north wall.

OBJECTS:

Juglet,
    S1095/P636 (fig. 7:2).

S1163/P653, black ware, burnished, H. 7.2 cm., D. 5.5 cm., form like fig. 7:2. P.
S1164/P654, black ware, burnished, H. 8.3 cm., D. 5.6 cm., form like fig. 7:1. P.
TS (fig. 7:13).
Storage jar,
S1102/P643 (fig. 9:13).
Lamp,
S1098/P639 (fig. 7:32).
S1100/P641 (fig. 7:33).
Mortar,
S1106/St76 (fig. 8:26).

Krater,
TS (fig. 8:7).
TS (fig. 8:14).

OBJECTS FROM STREET EAST OF HOUSE 33:
Iron plow point,
S1131/F58, L. 7.9 cm. P.
Pottery mold,
S1133/M282 (fig. 8:21).
Tripod,
S1134/St78 (fig. 8:27).

House 35

The walls of House 35 could be traced easily (fig. 43, upper). The entrance was in the east wall, and the door sill had been built up with stones to divert the water of the street from the house. The pavement at the south side of the house (fig. 42, right) was well preserved. An oven, 77 cm. in diameter (fig. 44), in the northeast corner belonged to the later phase of occupation and had been crudely repaired with large fragments of jars and cooking pots. A stone mill with its rider was found in situ on the floor of House 35 (fig. 45).

OBJECTS:
Lamp,
S1097/P638 (fig. 7:34).
S1099/P640 (fig. 7:31).
Bead,
S1132/J62, white, D. 1.2 cm.
Spindle whorl,
S1148/M276, tan stone, H. 2.4 cm., D. 3.9 cm. P.

House 37-39

This house consisted of a large oblong room, 37 (fig. 47), and a long narrow room, 39. The absence of mud bricks for about 1 m. of the west end of the east-west wall that separates Rooms 37 and 39 suggests the possibility that there might have been a doorway between them at that point. The main entrance into Room 37 was possibly by a door from the east-west street, since the mud bricks of the north wall could not be traced with certainty for a short section beginning 1.5 m. east of the west balk (not shown on the plan, but suggested by the supervisor). Two patches of pavement appeared in Room 37, one in the northeast corner and another to the west of it along the north wall (fig. 47).

To the east of this house there appeared an area that was walled off from the main north-south street by a row of stones set upon the floor of the street. Within this enclosed area there was an oven, 72 cm. in diameter, surrounded by ash and other evidence of burning (fig. 48). About 50 cm. northeast of the oven there was a large stone that may have served as a table or shelf. The enclosed area was not surfaced with pebbles as was the surface of the north-south street outside. If this enclosure was a cooking area belonging to House 37-39 one would expect to find an entrance to it from one of the rooms of the adjacent house; yet no indication of such a doorway was apparent. Since the stones that lined the east side of the "kitchen" were not wide enough to have served as the foundation for a mud-brick wall, one can best interpret the construction as a temporary structure built upon the street to keep the water that flowed down the street from south to north from the enclosed cooking area.

Rooms 37 and 39 were unusually productive of artifacts. Along the north wall of Room 39 there were found a number of jugs, juglets, and cooking pots (not reconstructed), lying on the floor where they had been crushed when the building collapsed (fig. 49). Beside the same wall farther to the east there were complete juglets and a number of loom weights (fig. 52). For other objects in situ in Room 37 see figs. 50 and 51.

OBJECTS FROM ROOM 37:
Jug,
S1094/P635 (fig. 7:25).

Juglet,
　S1058/P620 (fig. 7:11).
　S1059/P621 (fig. 7:7).
　S1060/P622 (fig. 7:10).
　S1079/P626 (fig. 7:9).
　S1080/P627 (fig. 7:5).
　S1081/P628 (fig. 7:4).
　S1090/P631 (fig. 7:3).
　S1092/P633 (fig. 7:8).
Storage jar,
　S1101/P642 (fig. 9:12).
　TS (fig. 9:5).
　TS (fig. 9:6).
　TS (fig. 9:7).
Chalice,
　S1078/P625 (fig. 7:30).
Lamp,
　S1082/P629 (fig. 7:35).
Decanter,
　S1093/P634 (fig. 7:29).
　S1057/P619 (fig. 7:26).
Bead, carnelian,
　S1138/J64, H. 1.3 cm., D. 1.5 cm.

Bronze ring,
　S1077/Br59 (fig. 8:16).
Krater,
　TS (fig. 8:5).
　TS (fig. 8:15).
Spindle whorl,
　S1083/M273, buff stone, D. 3.8 cm., H. 2.2 cm. P.
Faience cup with lid,
　S1084/M274 (fig. 8:22).
Iron chisel,
　S1085/F48 (fig. 8:23).
Iron spear,
　S1086/F49 (fig. 8:24).

OBJECTS FROM ROOM 39:

Jug,
　S1056/P618 (fig. 7:21).
Juglet,
　S1021/P612 (fig. 7:12).
Decanter,
　S1055/P617 (fig. 7:28).
Bone spatula,
　S1074/B33 (fig. 8:20).

House 41

House 41 was built upon the debris of what had been parts of Houses 60-62, 64, the north-south street, and House 63, of Stratum VII. The west wall of the house evidently lies beyond the west balk. At the south there are curb stones along the east-west street and fragments of the wall that fix the southern boundary. It was conjectured that the main entrance from the east-west street was somewhere in this wall, but no clear evidence for it could be obtained. The line of the east wall was established by the location of foundation stones. The north wall is preserved only in a short segment, 30 cm. in width, that runs westward at the offset in the line of the north-south walls of Houses 41 and 37-39. Beyond this short stub there are no traces of the wall to the west. It is possible that the mud bricks of the north wall of the house were dissolved during the period when they were exposed after the abandonment of Stratum VI. The segment of pavement shown in fig. 46, made of large stones, remains from the floor of the room. Another feature of House 41 is a clay oven, 77 cm. in diameter, found in its northeast corner. Black ash covered the floor around the oven.

OBJECTS:

Bowl,
　S1019/P610 (fig. 6:2).
Jug,
　S1162/P652 (fig. 7:22).
Juglet,
　S1053/P615 (fig. 7:6).
Decanter,
　S1023/P614 (fig. 7:27).
Iron spear point,
　S1034/F44, L. 9.9 cm., W. 2.7 cm.
　S1037/F47, with tang, L. 7.2 cm., W. 1.9 cm. P.
Shell,
　S1068/M268, cream, pierced, D. 4.3 cm. P.

House 43 (fig. 53)

This house has a well-defined east wall running parallel to the principal north-south street. The main entrance from the street was probably where there appears a 70 cm. gap in the stones that had bordered the mud-brick wall. The south wall is clearly defined in 23-F-2 and the supervisor of the area reported traces of mud-brick material which followed its line of continuation to the east over the stone pavement in the southeast corner. A few bricks at the southwest corner of the house suggest a back wall on the west side. The north wall is almost completely eroded or otherwise destroyed; only the section at the east end remains. Obviously, this wall of the house bordered the east-west street to the north of it.

There were two principal phases of occupation. In the earlier phase, that of Stratum VIB, the house consisted of only one room. At the center of the east wall there was a clay oven, 77 cm. in diameter, and a second oven (not shown in the plan) beside the line of the north east-west wall. The pavement in the southeast corner belonged to this phase of occupation. In the second phase of use, Stratum VIA, a north-south wall was built through the middle of 23-F-2, dividing the house into two rooms. The stone pavement and the clay oven in the northwest corner of the house were built, and the mill surrounded by stones was installed slightly to the north of the center of the house.

OBJECTS:

Juglet,
  S1096/P637 (fig. 7:1).
Decanter,
  S1136/P647 (fig. 7:24).
Iron tube,
  S1121/F56, L. 8.2 cm., D. 0.8 cm. P.
Iron spear point,
  S1087/F50, tang curled, L. 11.6 cm., W. 3.4 cm. P.
Iron knife,
  S1109/F52, curved (fig. 8:18).

OBJECT FROM STREET E OF HOUSE 43:

Iron knife,
  S1141/F59, L. 12.1 cm, W. 2 cm.

Summary

The furnishings and artifacts found within the houses and on the streets of Stratum VI are more numerous than those found in Stratum VII below it. Ovens were situated in four of the six houses (Houses 33, 35, 41, and 43, which had three ovens) and in the north-south street before House 37-39. Evidence for milling was found in House 35, where both a mill and its rider were recorded; House 43 had a circular mortar imbedded in the floor and surrounded by stones; a stone mortar was catalogued from House 33 (fig. 8:26), and another mortar came from the street to the east of House 33 (fig. 8:27). A row of 11 loom weights was found on the floor of Room 39 of House 37-39 (fig. 52). In addition to the ovens, mills, and loom weights the following 58 artifacts were recorded from Stratum VI: 15 juglets, 5 storage jars, 5 lamps, 4 jugs, 4 kraters, 5 decanters, 1 chalice, 1 bowl, 3 spear points, 2 knives, 2 beads, 2 spindle whorls, 1 arrowhead, 1 plow point, 1 pottery mold (?), 1 ring, 1 faience cup, 1 chisel, 1 bone spatula, 1 shell, and 1 iron tube.

These artifacts can be classified under the rubrics of vessels, tools, weapons, and articles of personal adornment and thus considered to be the usual complement of household objects from a domestic quarter of an Iron Age city. Although there is no evidence for a general destruction of the houses of Stratum VI by fire—ash was frequently found in the vicinity of ovens—the evidence for the collapse of the north wall of Room 39 upon a number of utensils in House 37-39 (29 of the catalogued objects from Stratum VI came from this house) suggests that a catastrophe may have occurred at least in this house, and a considerable cache of objects were broken and buried in the debris.

IV

Stratum V

The houses of Stratum V were built upon the fill that had accumulated over the floors and stubs of walls of Stratum VI. Where the later city plan can be compared with that of its predecessor the houses are larger, more uniform in plan, and set at a slightly different orientation. The streets run both north-south and east-west, as they do in the two earlier strata.

The most obvious feature noted in the uncovering of the remains of Stratum V was the evidence for the destruction of its houses and their contents by fire. A layer of ash was found on the floors of most houses; sun-dried bricks had turned reddish brown under the influence of an intense heat; and roof material, in the form of charred beams of wood and clay from the roof with impressions of reeds still visible, was frequently found lying on the floor. A jar of grain, found in House 9, had been carbonized by the heat from the burning of the house. That a considerable number of household goods have survived in fair condition is due to the destruction of the city by fire before personal possessions could be removed. Evidently the burning was as sudden as it was complete.

House 1 (fig. 179)

Although most of House 1 had been removed by the erosion that had taken place at the north edge of the tell, its plan can be recovered with a fair degree of certainty. The actual remains of the house consist of most of its south wall, appearing in 23-E/F/G-7 and shared by House 3 as a common wall, a line of curb stones along the west side of the street in 23-G-7/8, a segment of the east wall covered by paving stones in 23-G-8, and a patch of pavement (fig. 54, center right) belonging to the larger of the two rooms (assuming that the plan is that common to the houses found in Stratum V in Area 23) found in 23-F-7. The north wall of the house was probably built against a city wall, the foundation of which can be seen in fig. 188. Allowing for a width of 50 cm. for the north wall, the width of House 1 would have been approximately 4.50 m. The doorway into the house may well have been in the east wall, where a segment of paving stones (fig. 54, top) is preserved beside the larger stones that served as one side of a gutter in the street. Similar thresholds are found in other houses of this complex. It has been assumed in the reconstruction of the plan (fig. 179) that the house had a partition wall dividing it into two rooms, with a door in between, and that it shared a common back wall with House 2 to the west. Evidence for these elements had been destroyed by erosion and the reconstruction is based entirely upon the assumption that House 1 was similar in plan to the others of this block.

House 2 (figs. 54 and 179)

House 2 lay in 23-D/E-7/8 and has been restored from a fragment of its south wall, 1.10 m. of its west wall, and a considerable portion of stone pavement at the north. On the plan (fig. 179) a back room has been reconstructed from the measurements of others in the block. The stone foundation of the city wall shown in fig. 188 appears to the north of the north edge of the pavement, separated from the pavement's edge by only a half meter (fig. 67) and running parallel to it. It seems reasonably certain, therefore, that this house was built against the wall of the city. The evidence for the door indicated in the reconstruction is merely the finished ending of the south end of the stone-faced segment of the west wall.

House 3 (fig. 179)

A rectangular house divided into two rooms lies in 23-E/F/G-6/7 and is clearly defined on all sides either by complete walls or fragments. The outside of the east wall was faced with a line of stones set in mud (fig. 56) for its entire length along the street, with the exception of the threshold located 75 cm. north of the south wall of the house. A large stone, possibly serving as a doorjamb at the north of the door, stands 45 cm. above the threshold. The opening for the door is 85 cm. wide. The paved threshold is higher than the floor level of the house; obviously one had to step down when entering the room from the street. It is probable that the street had built up faster than had the level of the room, since the street served also as a gutter for water that coursed down it during the rainy season.

The larger of the two rooms had portions of pavements on both the north and the south sides. However, the paving of the north side could have been a later modification, since it averages 22 cm. higher than that at the south. In the center of the room along its east-west axis were two large stones, one 40 cm. and the other 45 cm. high, which served as supports for the roof (fig. 55). They were found in positions which suggest that there were originally four columns in a line through the long axis of the room. A doorway, 85 cm. wide, led into a smaller room at the back. The threshold was not paved; nor was there evidence for paving on the floor of the room. Nine loom weights were reported to have been found on the floor at the southwest corner of the room; another was found about 1 m. east of the doorway leading into the second room of the house (text fig. 1). The context of these artifacts was reported as soil of decomposed yellow brick mixed with very thin pieces of organic matter.

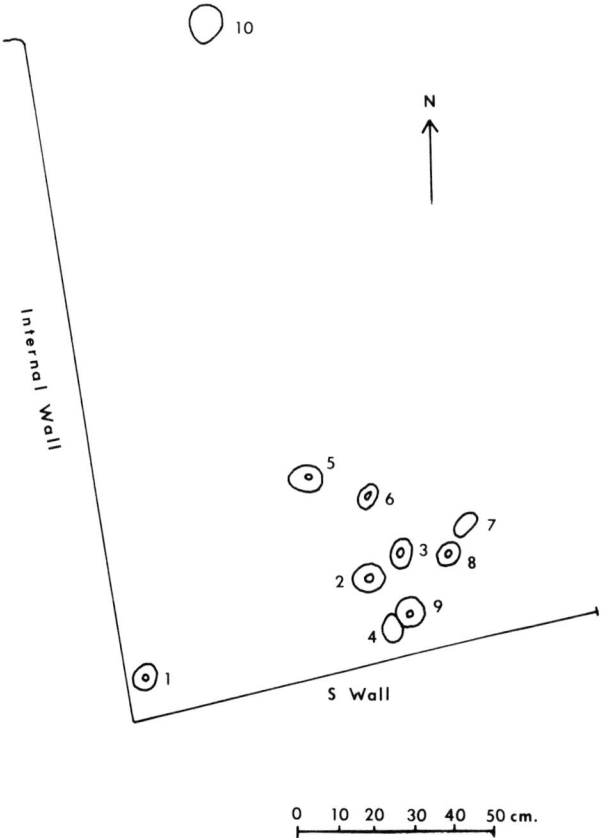

Text Fig. 1. Loom Weights in House 3.

OBJECTS:

Krater,
  S845/P483 (fig. 12:16).
7 Game pieces,
  S70/M62 (fig. 14:22). Possibly House 4.
Bead,
  S205/J3, carnelian, barrel shaped, perforated lengthwise, L. 1.4 cm. Possibly House 4. P.
Bone,
  S206/M95, hole drilled at one end, L. 6 cm., D. 1.3 cm. and 1.8 cm. at ends, D. of hole, .6 cm. P.

House 4 (fig. 179)

South of House 2 and west of House 3 is a well-defined structure with a doorway in the west wall leading into a north-south street. The south wall is completely preserved for the entire length of the house; the back wall, shared with House 3, is indicated by a stub at the south; and the line of the north wall is mostly preserved. The partition wall that should separate the larger front room from the back room is missing entirely. The paving in the northwest corner and along the north wall (fig. 68) was fairly well preserved over a large area and found to be covered with a thin layer of black ash; many of the stones were blackened by fire. This original, uneven pavement had been repaired by spreading a layer of 10 cm. of loose, brown soil over the area and laying a new pavement on top of it (fig. 69). There was noted a thin layer of gray-white plaster on one section of the upper pavement. Projecting from the west wall of the room is a short brick wall set on a stone foundation. At its east end was a circular pit, filled with loose, brown soil and surrounded by a row of stones (fig. 68, center). There as no evidence of burning or ash in the pit; possibly it was the socket for a wooden post that had supported the roof.

OBJECTS:

Juglet,
   S334/P171 (fig. 11:5).
Alabaster bowl,
   S316/St25, globelike body, disk base, H. 4.5 cm., D. of base, 3.5 cm.
Bead,
   S200/J2, spreader (fig. 14:36).
Spindle whorl,
   S1300/M300 (fig. 14:23).

House 5 (fig. 179)

The entrance into House 5 from the street was an opening in the east wall, 1.10 m. wide, at its south end. The threshold was paved with stones, from which there was a step of about 26 cm. down into the house. The east side of the east wall was lined with stones. A portion of the west side of the east wall of the room had been eroded by water that had once collected in the northeast corner of the room (see fig. 58). A part of the stone pavement of the larger room of House 5 remained along the north wall (fig. 57). Beside this pavement, about 1.25 m. from the north wall and at about the same distance from the west wall, Jacques Lagarce, a supervisor of this area, reported the remains of a brick column supported by a brick foundation wall that ran to the east. The alignment of this wall and the position of the one column suggest that the room had had four brick columns as supports for the roof. A pavement of smaller stones was found along the south wall of the room. To the east of this pavement and in the southeast corner of the room the floor was covered with burnt organic material, possibly reeds, but this residue probably belonged to a secondary use of the house. A clay oven was in the northeast corner of the room, and a small bin was found to have been built beside the south wall (fig. 179). Four loom weights were reported from the stone pavement in the north.

The smaller room to the back of House 5 had a temporary partition wall (not shown on the plan in fig. 179) running roughly east-west that divided it into two parts. A thin layer of gray organic material, possibly grass or straw, was observed on the floor of the south portion of this room. The south portion of the room had evidently been used as a storage area; on the clay floor of the north part of the room there was no evidence of burning.

OBJECTS:

Cooking pot,
   S530/P288 (fig. 13:20). Possibly House 6.
Cup,
   S513/M149A (fig. 14:21).
Fibula,
   S400/Br7, bronze and iron, (fig. 14:32). Possibly House 3.
Arrowhead,
   S1007/Br50, bronze (fig. 14:29). Possibly House 3.
   S401/F8, iron, L. 7.5 cm., W. 1.5 cm. Possibly House 3. P.

House 6 (fig. 179)

From the points of view of its architecture and of its contents, House 6 is the most distinctive of the houses of Stratum V. It was everywhere apparent that the house had been destroyed completely by a fire that had burned with enough intensity to turn the sun-dried bricks of the walls and columns to a red color. Evidence for the catastrophic destruction of the walls and roof of this house is to be seen in the frequent references in the supervisors' notebooks to ash, burned bricks, pieces of roof material, and plaster. The roof and much of the upper walls had collapsed as some highly combustable materials within the house had fed the fire.

The entrance from the street is at the north end of the west wall, which was protected on the outside by pebbles set in plaster over its surface. The doorway leads into an unpaved portion of the room, situated to the north of a row of columns. In the center a large pit had been dug (fig. 70), with sides sloping downward at an angle of about 45°. The north side of the pit was lined by a row of four large stones; at the bottom there was a millstone, or mortar, in which there was a depression about 20 cm. in diameter and from 10 to 15 cm. deep. To the north of the opening between the first and second columns from the east there was a rectangular basin with plastered walls and bottom (fig. 71). In its center there was a round hole, 18 cm. in diameter and about 14 cm. deep, which was also plastered. The bottom of the basin was reported to have been covered with gray ash. Immediately to the north of this basin were found the fragmentary remains of the skeleton of an infant (fig. 72). The body was lying in a crouching position on the right side, with the head to the east and the face to the north; the skull was crushed. Since there was no evidence of burning among the bones it was concluded by the supervisor that the body had been buried beneath the floor of the room before the house had burned. A line of the pit in which the child had been buried could be traced along the north of the grave but not on the other sides. The bones were in general disorder; a tooth was found within the area of the chest.

South of the row of columns there was a pavement overlaid with 10 cm. of tan clay of putty-like consistency, which in turn was covered over with a layer of fine black ash. In the east, unpaved end of House 6, directly before the opening between the projecting east wall and the first column, two layers of clay loom weights were found embedded in the soft, dark soil and ash that covered the floor of the room. The lower layer of loom weights appears to lie in two rows, as though they had fallen along a straight line (fig. 73, and sketch in text fig. 3). In the balk immediately above the area in which they were found there was evidence of lines of charred beams, which could possibly have been parts of the frame of the loom to which the weights had belonged. The destruction of the room by fire had, however, been so violent and complete (it was the heaviest burning within the excavation) that it was impossible to reconstruct the positions of the wooden part of the loom. It is, of course, possible that the beams had belonged to the roof and had had no connection at all with the loom weights found nearby. The upper layer of loom weights is probably to be associated in use with the lower, since there was no occupation layer between the two (fig. 74 and sketch and text fig. 2). One can only say that

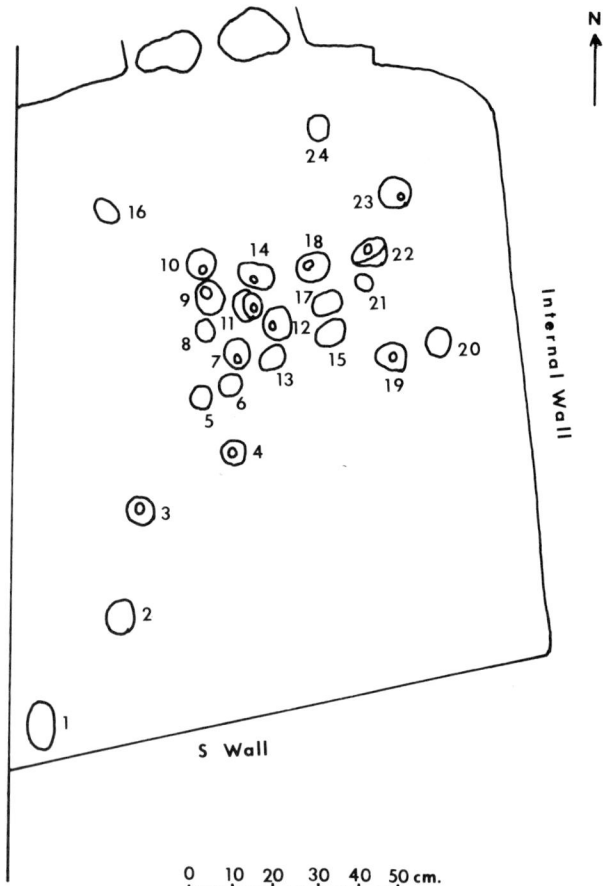

Text Fig. 2. Loom Weights in House 6, Upper Layer.

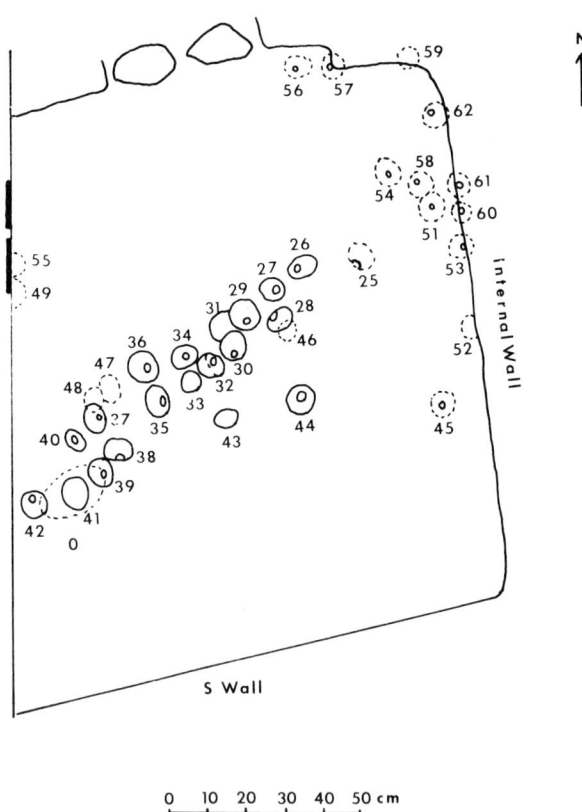

Text Fig. 3. Loom Weights in House 6. Lower Layers (Layer 3, dotted).

the upper layer seems to have fallen later than the lower layer.

A line of four brick columns, numbered from east to west, and two pilasters or antas (figs. 75 and 76) divide the paved from the unpaved portion of the front room of House 6. In the opening between the pilaster at the east and the first column, a bin or cell was built with bricks set on edge at the north and south of the opening, although the brick at the north side was difficult to distinguish clearly. The bin in the second opening, between columns 1 and 2, is much more clearly defined, and the thin brick walls are preserved on both the north and the south sides (fig. 77). Between columns 2 and 3 the north wall of a bin was preserved; and between columns 3 and 4 a line of stones on the north side may well have served as a foundation for the brick wall of the bin in this place. The passageway from the unpaved to the paved part of the room must have been between column 4 and the pilaster attached to the west wall. (Similar receptacles were found between the columns of the pillared building of Stratum VIII of Area A at Hazor [*Hazor* 1: 12, pl. 9:4–6; *Hazor* 2: 6, pls. 4, 5, 200]. They were built of two rows of rubble stones and measured .40 m. deep. Inside there were found fragments of storage jars and kraters.)

The back room of House 6 was entered by a doorway at the north end of the partition wall; it was found to be filled with a heavy deposit of burned brick. The south part of the floor of the back room was reported to have been covered with a layer of ash, 5 cm. thick. The room had been divided into two parts by a thin partition, the stub of which was found extending for almost 1 m. from the east wall.

OBJECTS:

Bowl,
  S127/P46 (fig. 10:13).
  S217/P85 (fig. 10:5).
  S111/P34 (fig. 10:11).
  S123/P42, tan ware, mixed black and white grits, burnished on rim and inside, rim fragment. Form like fig. 10:12, 15. P.
  S224/P92, tan ware, mixed black and white grits, rim fragment. P.
  S229/P97, red-brown ware, gray core, mixed black and white grits, burnished on rim, rim fragment. Form like fig. 2:20. P.
  S241/P108, red-brown ware, mixed black and white grits, burnished on rim and inside, rim and body fragment. P.
  S227/P95, buff ware, small black and some white grits, rim fragment. P.
  S172/P69, tan ware, red slip on rim and inside, rim fragment. Form like fig. 2:1. P.

Jug,
  S118/P40 (fig. 11:21).
  S182/P78 (fig. 11:20).

Juglet,
  S207/P79, tan ware, gray core, small black and white grits, narrow and wide horizontal lines on exterior in shades of brown, red, and white, vertically burnished. P.
  S222/P90, strainer spout (fig. 11:23).

Krater,
  S267/134 (fig. 12:9).
  S270/P137 (fig. 12:4).
  S268/P135 (fig. 12:2).
  S340/P177, red ware, thick tan core, mixed black and white grits, three rim and body fragments. Form like fig. 12:11. P.
  S171/P68, tan ware, mixed black and white grits, two rim and body fragments, D. of rim, 30 cm. Form like fig. 12:13. P.
  S173/P70, buff ware, burnished on rim. Form like fig. 12:5. P.
  S237A/P104, red-brown ware, gray core, mixed black and white grits, rim and body fragment. Form like fig. 12:11 (for neck) and fig. 12:9 (for rim).
  S333/P170 (fig. 12:14).

Cooking pot,
  S125/P44 (fig. 13:11).
  S124/P43 (fig. 13:4).
  S225/P93 (fig. 13:9).
  S266/P133 (fig. 13:14).
  S112/P35 (fig. 13:10).
  S341/P178, red-brown ware, mixed white and crystalline grits, rim and handle fragment. Form like fig. 13:19. P.
  S336/P173, brown ware, mixed white and crystalline grits, small black grits, carbon traces on exterior, rim fragment. Form like fig. 13:18. P.
  S269/P136 (fig. 13:3).
  S237/P103, brown ware, mixed black, white, and crystalline grits, carbon on exterior, rim and handle fragment. Form like fig. 13:18. P.
  S239/P106, tan ware, mixed black, white, and crystalline grits, rim fragment. Form like fig. 13:9. P.
  S236/P102, brown ware, mixed black, white, and crystalline grits, rim and handle fragment. Form like Fig. 13:18. P.
  S238/P105, red-brown ware, mixed black, white, and crystalline grits, rim fragment. Form like fig. 13:15. P.
  S240/P107, tan ware, mixed black, white, and crystalline grits, rim fragment. Form like fig. 13:9. P.

Storage jar,
  S122/P41 (fig. 14:10).
  S126/P45 (fig. 14:1).
  S331/P168 (fig. 14:11).
  S113/P36 (fig. 14:16).

S226/P94, buff ware, gray core, small black and white grits, rim fragment, D. of rim, 9 cm. Form like fig. 9:3. P.
D174/P71, tan ware, gray core, mixed black grits, rim and shoulder fragments, straight neck with shoulder going out at right angle. P.
S219/P87, buff ware, mixed white grits, rim and neck fragment, slightly thickened rim with ridged neck. P.

Sherd,
S223/P91, buff ware, very well-levigated, gray core, white slip inside and out, highly burnished inside and out, body fragment. P.
S218/P86, brown ware, buff wash on exterior with three horizontal brown bands, body fragment. P.
S220/P88, buff ware, mixed black and white grits, two vertical red-brown bands on exterior, body fragment. P.
S221/P89, tan ware, gray core, four red-brown horizontal bands on exterior, wheel burnished outside, body fragment. P.
S339/P176 (fig. 10:35).

Pilgrim flask,
S157/P67 (fig. 11:17).
Decanter,
S265/P132 (fig. 11:12). Possibly House 4.
Animal figurine,
S700/Pfig10 (fig. 10:30).
Cup of kernos ring(?),
S228/P96, buff ware, white grits, cream slip with horizontal pink band, carinated profile. P.
Disk,
S365/P203 (fig. 14:24).
S366/P204 (fig. 14:25).
Mortar,
S69/St4, basalt (fig. 10:34).
Bone point,
S368/B8 (fig. 14:37).
Bone spatula,
S596/B11, polished, L. 6.5 cm. A. (fig. 171:8)
Pestle,
S117/St9, black, two circular depressions on opposing sides, L. 12 cm., W. 7.3 cm., Th. 4.5 cm.

House 7 (figs. 59, 61, 62, 179)

Most of the east wall of House 7 had been destroyed by the digging of Pit 22 from Stratum IV. The line of the east wall, however, is clear from a stub preserved to the south of the doorway and from stones that line the north door jamb at the level of the threshold. Paving stones on the street side of the threshold seem to indicate the position of the entrance into the house. A well-preserved pavement, 1.68 m. wide, extends over the length of the north half of the front room from the west wall to the east. A column of mud brick appears along the east-west axis of the room, 2.49 m. east of the partition wall between the larger and the smaller room of the house. A mass of fallen burnt bricks was found to the north of it, in a position that indicated the column had collapsed when the house burned. In line with the mud-brick column are two large flat stones, both of which probably served as bases for other columns. Standing on the base to the east was a large pillar (fig. 60), which had supported the roof. The bricks of the south wall had turned red from the heat produced in the burning of the house. Heavy burning was reported to be evidenced on the floor of the stone pavement in the west half and along the south wall of the room. A fireplace, bordered on the north by a mud-brick wall, appeared along the east wall at about the center of the room, and a clay oven, 30 cm. in diameter, sitting on a mud-brick platform, appeared beside the south wall slightly east of center. The charred remains of a beam were found on the floor extending east-west for a distance of 1.50 m. (fig. 65), just to the south of the row of columns. Its position was such that it was impossible to determine with any degree of certainty from which side of the row of columns it had fallen. The floor of the back room of House 7 was found to be covered with a thin layer of organic material, possibly decomposed straw. There was no evidence of burning on this floor.

OBJECTS:

Cooking pot,
S525/P281 (fig. 13:17).
S752/P424, red-brown ware, black, white, and crystalline grits. Form like fig. 13:9. P. Possibly House 9.
Bowl,
S523/P281 (fig. 10:6).
S768/St57, Basalt, H. 5.9 cm., W. 16 cm., L. 18.7 cm. A.
Jug,
S479/P257 (fig. 11:24).
Juglet,
S758/P428, black ware, vertical burnishing, D. 5.2 cm. Form like fig. 11:9. P.
S494/P254, black ware, vertical burnishing, D. 5 cm. Form like fig. 11:9. P.
Spindle whorl,
S1018/M252, tan stone, H. 2 cm., D. 3.6 cm. Form like fig. 14:23. P.

Ring,
S772/F21, iron (fig. 14:31). Possibly House 9.

Sickle,
S1009/F40, iron (fig. 14:26).

House 8 (figs. 78, 79, 179)

The west wall of House 8, unlike that of the neighboring House 6, had not been faced with stone pebbles at its base to protect the mud bricks from erosion and consequently was not so well preserved. There was an entranceway from the street into the larger of the two rooms. The threshold was paved with stones and stood 12 cm. higher than the level of the dirt floor of the room. Along the east-west axis of the front room there were two columns and a low brick wall that joined the east column with the east wall of the room. This short wall stood at a height of 49 cm. above the level of the dirt floor to the south and may well have been at its original height, serving only as a barrier between the two sections of the room at the east side. Just 10 cm. to the west of the southwest corner of the column to the west there was found a segment, 35 cm. long and 9.5 cm. in diameter, of a wooden roof beam. Its position suggests that the section of the room with a dirt floor was roofed. The north sector of the room was completely paved with stones that extended even to the area between the columns. A narrow, and possibly secondary, wall extended east from the west wall of the room to the north of the doorway. This may well have served to contain the ramp that led downward from the street into the front room. It was preserved for a course of only 75 cm. The entire east part of the paved floor was covered with wood ash, which bore witness to the burning of the house. Entrance was had into the back room by means of a doorway slightly to the south of center.

OBJECTS:
Bowl,
S103/P26 (fig. 10:9).
S105/P28 (fig. 10:10).
S106/P29 (fig. 10:20).
S107/P30 (fig. 10:19).
S230/P98 (fig. 10:17).
Jug (?),
S104/P27 (fig. 11:16).
Juglet,
S312/P165 (fig. 11:8).
S378/P210, tan ware, brown core, white grits.
S1003/P602 (fig. 11:2).
S1310/P700 (fig. 11:6).
Storage jar,
S108/P31 (fig. 14:2).
Sherd,
S109/P32, Gray ware, buff slip, mixed white grits, horizontal groove on exterior. P.
S110/P33, buff exterior, pink and gray core, painted line.
Arrowhead,
S306/F3, iron (fig. 14:27). Possibly House 10.
Cosmetic palette,
S311/St24 (fig. 14:20). Possibly House 10.
Funerary jar,
S343/P181 (fig. 10:33).
Decanter,
S342/P179 (fig. 11:25).

House 9 (fig. 179)

The entrance to the house from the street was at the south end of its east wall. The doorway, 80 cm. wide, was filled with fallen stones, which may have belonged to the doorposts of the house. A row of four brick columns along the east-west axis of the front room of the house divided it into two equal parts. The area to the north was paved with stones, which were in place over most of the area (fig. 63). The two columns to the west were connected at their north sides by a narrow brick wall, about 15 cm. wide, which continued westward to join the west wall of the room. The paved area to the north of this narrow partition wall was covered with burned material, and on the floor between the two middle columns there was found a jar of carbonized grain (two-row barley hulled). A bin for storage was identified in a rectangular area, extending 1.02 m. from the east wall, bounded on the north by the north wall of the room, and on the south by the column. The paving of the remaining north part of the room stopped at the edge of this enclosed area, and bricks were noted at various places in the borders to this area. A segment of a charred wooden beam (apparently from the roof) was found within the area of the bin. At the southwest corner of the room there was a clay oven, the bottom of which was 27 cm. lower than its rim. The back room of the house had a dirt floor, on which there was observed no trace of burning (fig. 64).

OBJECTS:

Jug,
S1004/P603 (fig. 11:22).

Juglet,
S719/P409, brown ware, many mixed white grits, vertically burnished, fired black in places, H. 8.4 cm., D. 4.2 cm. A.
S720/P410, tan ware, many mixed black and white grits, traces of red-brown slip, H. 12 cm., D. 6.8 cm. P.

Cooking pot,
S545/P303 (fig. 13:19). Possibly House 11.

Jar,
S715/P407, tan ware, brown core, many mixed black and white grits, red-brown paint on neck and shoulder, vertical red-brown bands on body intersected by one or two horizontal bands, H. 12.5 cm., D. 11.8 cm. A. (fig. 165:9)

Lamp,
S730/P405 (fig. 14:19).

Tripod cup,
S744/P419 (fig. 10:29). Possibly House 11.

Tripod bowl,
S717/St53, basalt, H. 12 cm., D. 26.5 cm. A.

Disk,
S789/Br33, bronze, (fig. 14:30).

Alabaster flask,
S721/P411, surface eroded and burnt, H. 10.5 cm., D. 8.5-6.8 cm. P.

Stones,
S733/St54, (A) red whetstone, well polished, L. 5.5 cm., W. 3.5 cm., H. 1.8 cm.
(B) gray whetstone, well polished, L. 6.4 cm., W. 6.3 cm., H. 1.6 cm.
(C) gray stone, H. 3.3 cm., D. 3.6 cm.

House 10 (fig. 179)

This house was damaged by pits cut from Stratum IV, especially Pit 3, which removed about half of the partition wall between the two rooms of the house, and Pits 5 and 7, which damaged the center and the southwest corner of the front room. The entrance into the house from the street, like that to House 8, was in the southwest corner, and the floor of the room was considerably lower than the threshold. The north sector of the front room was paved, except for a clay platform at the northwest corner. The platform seems to have been bounded on the south by a wall, 30 cm. in width, which was represented only by a stub extending to the east. The south border of the paved area consisted of a narrow line of bricks that divided the room into two parts. It was observed by the supervisor, Moʿawiyah M. Ibrahim, that such a thin wall could not have served as a support for the roof. To the south of the center of this line of bricks was a posthole, 25 cm. in diameter and 25 cm. deep, which was obviously in the position where there should be a roof support. The corresponding posthole to the west would have been destroyed when Pit 5 was cut from Stratum IV.

In the unpaved area of the front room a mill, with an indentation 15 cm. deep, was found in place beside a stone foundation that ran along the south wall of the building. The only possible explanation offered for a foundation in this position was that it may have been set for the repair of the south wall of the building. It could hardly have belonged to a building of an earlier stratum. Evidence for repairs in this area of the building can be seen in the rather wide buttress on the street side of the north-south wall of the room at the southwest corner. The back room of the house is practically identical to that of House 8, except for the segment of wall foundation that extends from the south wall in line with the stone foundation along the south wall of the front room. This element also could have served to repair the south wall.

OBJECTS:

Bowl,
S538/P296 (fig. 10:16).

Juglet,
S495/P255, black, traces of burnishing, H. 7 cm., D. 5 cm. Form like fig. 11:10. P.
S367/P205, buff ware, some black and white grits, D. 6.4 cm. P.

Fibula,
S310/Br3, bronze (fig. 14:33).

Spindle whorl,
S556/St40, light gray stone with black on surface, H. 2 cm., Base D. 3 cm., D. of hole, 1 cm.

Lamp,
S536/P294, tan ware, mixed black and white grits, carbon deposit on nozzle, L. 11.5 cm., H. 3.4 cm. P.

House 11 (fig. 179)

Only a fragment of the east wall of this house could be reached because of the limit of the excavation on the east (fig. 66). However, the abrupt and well-finished ending of the south wall at its east end, short of where it would have met the north-south wall, suggests that the entrance may have been from the south rather than from the east street, as was customary in the houses of this block. Four mud-brick columns situated in a row slightly to the north of center, along the east-west axis, were obviously designed to support the roof. It was noted that there was more than one brick in each course of the columns; whole and half bricks were probably used in each of these fairly uniform pillars. A stone blocked the space between the first and second columns (counting from the west) and probably served to form one side of a storage bin. The entire north section of the room was paved with stones to a width of 1.58 m. The unpaved section of the room was covered with white, sometimes reddish soil, which appeared to be the sediment from wood and reed ash washed down through the debris of destruction by water that deposited it in a layer on the smooth floor of the room. The clay oven near the east wall of the room contained some pieces of iron slag and other pieces of iron slag were reported from the floor of Stratum V, slightly to the north of the clay oven. The back room of the house is deeper than that of the adjoining room of House 9; in fact, it is the largest back room of the entire complex. The floor is entirely of clay. The south wall of the room at the rear had been cut by Pit 29, which had been excavated from Stratum IV.

OBJECTS:

Juglet,
   S706/P403, tan ware, many mixed white grits, H. 11.2 cm., D. 7.2 cm. P.
   S775/P437, black ware, vertical burnishing, D. 5.8 cm., H. 8.5 cm. Form like fig. 11:10. P.
   S718/P408, dipper, tan ware, tan core, mixed black and white grits, H. 13.6 cm., D. 7.6 cm. Form like fig. 11:3. S.

Cooking pot,
   S731/P406 (fig. 13:21).

Knife,
   S708/F20, iron, corroded, L. 10 cm., W. 2.3 cm., Th., 1 cm. P.

Spatula,
   S716/B20, bone, (fig. 14:35).

Adze,
   S785/F23, iron, tang missing, L. 21.7 cm. A.

Nail,
   S786/F24, iron (fig. 14:34).

Plow points (2),
   S787/F25, L. 19 cm. P.

Spindle whorl,
   S707/M200, gray stone, H. 2.1 cm., D. of base, 3.6 cm., D. of hole, .9–1.2 cm. P.

House 12 (figs. 80–82, 179)

This house had the standard plan of a large partly paved front room and a smaller back room. Four pits cut from Stratum IV had done considerable damage to the walls and floors of the house: Pit 7 had cut away the walls at the northwest corner of the house; Pit 23 had been cut through the floor of the center of the front room; and Pits 24 and 25 had been responsible for the disappearance of most of the wall of separation between the two rooms. The line of the west wall of the house was clear, and a wide buttress-like facing on the street side could be assumed from the absence of the usual pebbles for about 50 cm. to the west of the house wall. One stone of the facing remained in place opposite the south doorjamb: Opposite the entrance to the front room was a quernstone, 52 cm. in diameter; in the southwest corner there was a clay oven, 74 cm. in diameter. The north sector of the front room was paved. A fragment of brick work, about 1 m. west of the partition wall and south of the south line of the paved section, was thought to be the base for a column that had supported the roof (fig. 81). John Huesman, supervisor of the area, reported that pieces of mud plaster, 14 cm. thick, and marked with the impressions of reeds, were found directly on the paved area of the front room. The position of this roof material is an indication that the paved area was covered.

House 13 (figs. 83 and 179)

Only the general outline and some of the pavement of House 13 were preserved, since four pits and a bin cut from Stratum IV had severely damaged the remains of the house. The east wall was apparently outside the present area of excavation. Pit 47 cut the south end of the row of columns in 23-G-1/2; the cutting of Pit 41 was responsible for the removal of a portion of the pavement to the west of the north-south wall; and the construction of a large rectangular bin, Bin A, of Stratum IV accounts for the absence of the entire southwest corner of the house. The north wall of the house had been cut by Pits 29 and 87. Since it is fairly certain that a major east-west street of the city ran to the south of this house it is not surprising that its south wall should have had a well-built stone foundation to protect the mud-brick wall from the erosion, to which it would have been subjected from the water that ran down the street sloping as it did from east to west. The west wall of the house is preserved in 23-F-1 and is in line with the shared back wall of the block of houses to the north. It is possible to reconstruct a house of approximately the same dimensions as those of the standard house of the block of 12 houses to the north, although the internal arrangements are not the same. There are remnants of columns, between which there appear to have been bins like those in House 6. Evidence for the destruction by fire was apparent from a layer of ash covered by a deeper layer of fallen bricks lying over the stones of the pavement in the north part of 23-F-1.

OBJECTS:
Bowl,
  S1020/P611 (fig. 10:3).
Juglet,
  S732/P418, buff ware, burnished vertically, H. 14 cm., D. 7.2 cm. Form like fig. 11:1. P.
Cooking pot,
  S751/P423 (fig. 13:16).
  S750/P422, brown ware, brown core, black and white grits, D. 16 cm. Form like fig. 13:16. P.
  S749/P421, brown ware, many mixed black and white grits, D. 18.5 cm. Form like fig. 13:16. P.
Two sickles,
  S784/F22, iron, L. 20 cm., L. 24 cm. P.
Lamp, seven spouted,
  S790/P443, tan ware, mixed white grits, D. 7.4 cm.

House 14 (figs. 84, 91, and 179)

Despite the damage done to the remains of House 14 by Pits 80, 81, 83, 84, 56, 57, and the large Bin B, enough of its plan was recovered to indicate that it was similar in plan to those of the block of houses. Yet it was bounded by streets on three sides, rather than on one, as Houses 1–12.

The entrance was probably on the east street. Although most of the east wall was missing it is possible that the stones to the north of the preserved stub of wall were the threshold of an entranceway. The large front room was evidently divided into a paved and an unpaved section. The west portion of the foundation for the row of dividing columns may be seen extending eastward from the partition wall in 32-D-9, and its course eastward is marked clearly by the fairly straight line of the north side of the paving stones. The north wall of the front room has been almost completely destroyed by the cutting of Pits 56, 57, and a rectangular bin; this work from Stratum IV also removed most of the northwest corner of the house. The house was bounded on three sides by streets.

OBJECTS:
Decanter,
  S893/P511 (fig. 11:15).
  S1006/P605 (fig. 11:13).

House 15 (fig. 179)

Enough remains of House 15 to show that it could well have been of the same plan and proportions as those of the other houses of the block. However, pits dug from Stratum IV, and possibly erosion that took place following the destruction of Stratum V, were responsible for the loss of some important details. The entire west wall of the house was preserved along the north-south street in 32-F-8/9, but there is no evidence for a doorway in its entire length. The north wall of the house exists only in a small section to the east in 32-G-9, and the east wall is obviously beyond the area of excavation. The north face of the south wall is apparent partly within the balk at the south of the excavation. A small projection of bricks from it to the north, in 32-F-8, may have belonged to the partition wall that divided the front room, with its paved and unpaved sections, from the smaller unpaved room at the back. If this hypothetical arrangement is correct then the entrance to the house must have been in the east wall, beyond the limit of the excavated area. In the removing of the balk 32-G-8/9, Magnus Ottosson noted bricks that he considered could have come from fallen columns that separated the paved from the unpaved portions of the larger room. In this same balk he found, amid heavy burned material, a collection of 42 loom weights lying on the floor of an area that covered approximately 50 by 30 cm.

OBJECTS:

Jug,
S982/P567, trefoil mouth, tan ware, mixed black and white grits, H. 16.2 cm., D. 12.3 cm. A. (fig. 165:6)

Stamped jar handle,
S1014/S11, tan ware, gray core, many mixed white grits, scarab impressions upside down. A.

Whetstone,
S1038/St71, white, well cut and polished, L. 2.3 cm., W. 1.9 cm., H. 1 cm. J.

Shell,
S1041/M253, cowrie, punctured at top P.

House 16 (figs. 85–89, 179)

House 16 conforms in plan and measurements to the standard house of Stratum V. From an entrance in the east wall along the north-south street in 32-F-8/9 one descends by several steps to the larger portion of the front room, the floor of which was 88 cm. below the level of the street outside. Although the foundation wall that separated the front room into two parts was continuous, it was observed during the excavation that several columns had once stood on this foundation, but it was impossible to fix their original positions. The wall that separates the front room from the back is continuous, but there must have been a doorway at a level above the remaining foundation layer of mud bricks. The north wall of the house had been cut by Pit 84 from Stratum IV, and a portion of the south wall at the west end had been disturbed by the digging of Pit 77. The entire south sector of the front room had experienced some of the heaviest burning within Stratum V. At about its midpoint the south wall of the house had cracked and toppled, and the surface of the brick had been turned red by the heat. In the northeast corner of that area charred beams were found lying on the floor, along with pieces of roofing material bearing the impressions of reeds. At about the midpoint of the foundation wall for the columns there was found a collection of 31 loom weights, lying approximately in line, and in association with burned material of a fine consistency, which Magnus Ottosson, the supervisor of the area, suggested could have been the ash from wool. Five additional loom weights were found on the floor near the southwest corner of the room. It was on the floor of this room, near the southeast corner, that the cylinder seal, S978/S5 (fig. 173:1) was found. Two bins, constructed of mud brick and stone, were found in the southeast corner of the room. The north sector of the front room appears to have been paved. Two ovens were reported from the area adjacent to the foundation wall that divides the front room. The back room had a packed earth floor and was covered by a thin layer of ash. A storage bin appeared near the northwest corner. Fourteen loom weights were found on the floor beside the bin (fig. 88). An impression of woven cloth in clay was found within this house (fig. 170:2).

OBJECTS:

Bowl,
S941/P549, buff ware, pinkish-red slip on inside wall and rim, many mixed black and white grits, H. 6 cm., D. 17.3 cm. Form like fig. 10:6. P.

Juglet,
S981/P566 (fig. 11:10).
S1012/P608, brown ware, mixed white grits, H. 12.3 cm., D. 6.7 cm. P.

Cylinder seal,
S978/S5, Stone, brown, L. 3.5 cm., D. 1.3 cm. A. (fig. 173:1)

Human figurine,
S979/Pfig18 (fig. 10:31).

Spindle whorl,
S983/M231, buff stone, D. 3.6 cm., D. of hole, .8 cm. P.

House 17 (figs. 92, upper; 179)

Only the northeast corner of this house has been excavated; the remainder lies beyond the limits of the excavation. Pit 72 had cut away part of the north wall of the house. The doorway is apparent from a threshold of stones in the line of the east wall. It was observed that there was plaster on the inside of the east wall to the south of the door. Mud-brick debris and burning were evidenced on the floor throughout.

House 19 (figs. 92, foreground; 179)

The part of House 19 lying within the excavation limits consists of a room divided by two large stones, which may have served as foundations for columns. The area to the south of the stones is paved. The entire floor was covered over with fallen brick and burnt material. Unfortunately each of the three walls had been cut by pits dug from Stratum IV. There is no indication of a doorway, although one would expect it to have been from the street to the east.

OBJECTS:

Decanter,
S892/P510 (fig. 11:11).
Spindle whorl,
S899/M225, gray stone, D. 3.7 cm., D. of hole, .8 cm. at top and 1 cm. at bottom. P.

House 21 (fig. 179)

Only the southeast corner of this house remains; both of the walls have been cut by pits from Stratum IV. It was noted that there was no burning on the floor of this house.

House 25 (fig. 179)

House 25 consists of parts of two rooms. Part of the room to the north is paved, the remainder was cut by Pit 28, dug from Stratum IV. In the northeast corner of the south room there is an oven, 60 cm. in diameter; another was found to the west of it along the north wall of the room. Even farther to the west is a stone mill, 44 cm. in diameter. The entrance to the house was not found.

OBJECTS:

Juglet,
S842/P480 (fig. 11:4).
Point,
S1026/B31, bone with very sharp point, L. 7.5 cm., W. 2.4 cm., Th. .2 cm. P.

House 27 (figs. 94, 95, 179)

House 27 could only be partly excavated since the west part of the building extends beyond the west limits of the excavation. The east wall of the house had been destroyed by Pit 9, cut from Stratum IV, and much of the brick work had been eroded. It was impossible to get any evidence for a doorway. Resting on a stone pavement in the northeast corner of the building was a clay oven, 62 cm. in diameter, standing to a height of 55 cm. On the outside there was a layer of broken sherds. The bottom of the oven was formed by stones set in mud plaster. A thin partition wall that separated the paved area to the east from the dirt floor to the west extended from the south of the north wall. Heavy burning was noted on both sides of this partition wall; to the west of the partition there appeared pieces of clay from the roof bearing impressions of reeds. The clay had been applied to the reeds in two layers; the first consisted of lime and clay mixed; the second was only clay. A piece of charred beam from the roof was found lying on the floor about 1 m. directly north of the north end of the mud-brick wall that extended northward from the middle of the south wall of the house (fig. 95). The beam had a length of 1.26 m. and a maximum diameter of 11.5 cm. There were three cross beams attached to it. Near them were numerous reed impressions in the clay that had once covered the roof (see fig. 95). At the north end of the dividing wall, projecting from the south wall, there is a fireplace between two lines of stones. Immediately to the north there were found bones of a sheep or goat.

OBJECTS:

Storage jar,
  S611/P327, tan ware, small white grits, D. 11 cm. Form like fig. 14:10. P.

Lamp,
  S362/P200, tan ware, gray core, many mixed black grits, carbon on spout, H. 5 cm., D. 12 cm. P. (fig. 168:5)

House 29 (fig. 179)

This partially recovered house has the plan of the block houses to the east, but it is turned at an angle of 90°. The east wall, running parallel to the street, seemed to have had no doorway. It was buttressed by stones which had been placed against it to preserve the mud bricks of the wall. The partition wall between the larger and the smaller rooms appears running east-west in 23-C-6, and there is the possibility that a pilaster or pillar is to be found in the stub of a wall that projects from the south wall in 23-C-5. Throughout the entire house there was evidence of heavy burning and the collapse of house walls in a conflagration. Three charred beams are reported to have been found on the floor. In the smaller room, in 23-C-6, there is a clay oven, a feature which does not appear elsewhere in the back rooms of the block houses of this stratum.

OBJECT:

Tripod bowl,
  S496/P256 (fig. 10:32).

East North-South Street in Area 23 (fig. 179)

The street to the east of the block of houses in Area 23 appeared in 23-G-5/6/7. Over a course of 15 m., the grade from south to north had a fall of 9.5 cm. in each meter. The south end of the recovered portion of the street was covered with small pebbles, while the north end was paved with larger stones carefully set. The width was difficult to determine, but in 23-G-6 it seemed to have been about 1 m., and was constricted by buttressing walls in 23-G-7 to something like 50 cm. Originally the street had been wider, but the building of buttresses along the outside of house walls had narrowed it considerably.

West North-South Street (figs. 96–98, 179)

The longest straight stretch of street in Stratum V is that which can be traced from 23-D-1 to 23-C-7. The width, measured between the brick walls of the houses on each side, averages about 1.50 m. However, as stone-faced buttressing walls were built to protect the mud-brick walls, the paved area of the street was narrowed, so that in 23-D-3, for example, the passageway between Houses 10 and 27 is only about 75 cm. wide. The surface of the street consists of small pebbles, pieces of broken pottery, and soil between the occasional larger stones. A representative sample of street surface can be seen in Fig. 96. Undoubtedly the surface of the street had built up as rain washed away the soil and carried down more pebbles. Three distinct layers were seen in the street in 23-C-6. This considerable deposit was near the bottom of the long street; it probably was the accumulation deposited by three heavy rains, or three rainy seasons; it indicates very little of the periods of occupation or use. A check of the elevation points taken in the street shows that there is a gradual slope to the north, a drop of 7 cm. to the meter over the 28 m. of distance from the recorded level of −241.14 in 23-D-2 to the point −243.10 in 23-C-7. The extension of the street to the south in 23-D-1, however, is lower than the highest part of the preserved street in 23-G-2; and the slope is toward the south, rather than to the north as in the remainder of the street. One possible explanation of this apparent reversal in the direction of the drainage is that in this section the north-south street was intersected by another running east-west with a slight slope to the west.

Courtyard between Houses 27 and 29 (figs. 94, 179)

To the west of the north-south street, directly opposite the front of House 8, is a courtyard in which there were four clay ovens. The wall that had separated this area from the street had been cut at the north end by Pit 10. The floor of this area consisted of ash mixed with mud, which was 25 cm. thick in some places. Over the floor lay a heavy layer of white, wood ash that seemed to have come from the ovens. Above the ash was a second burned layer, in which several animal bones were found. The oven in the southeast corner had an average inside diameter of 60 cm. The rim was missing but the walls stood to a height of 65 cm. The floor of the oven was 30 cm. below the level of the floor of the courtyard, and the outside of the oven was plastered with a layer of mud plaster, 15 cm. thick. A small oven, with an inside diameter of 30 cm., was found to the west of the larger oven. It was standing to a height of 25 cm.; the outside was plastered with mud and the bottom was made of lime plaster.

The larger of the two clay ovens in the north part of the courtyard had an average inside diameter of 55 cm., and its base lay 20 cm. below the latest floor of the court. The smaller of the ovens (to the west) is badly damaged. Its floor was 15 cm. below the floor level of the courtyard and was plastered with lime plaster. The absence of a north wall to this area and the lack of fallen roof material suggest that the ovens were located in an open court.

OBJECTS:
Millstone,
  S183/St17, basalt, one-half of the rider of a mill, L. .15 m.
Shell,
  S193/M90, cockle, dark gray, P.

North-South Street in the Southwest (fig. 179)

A 15-meter section of a north-south street in the southwest of the excavated area is to be seen running through 32-C-8/10. It is about 1.50 m. wide, but was somewhat wider before the buttresses had been placed against the exposed walls of the houses. The surface consists of pebbles, with an occasional use of larger stones, particularly in two preserved patches at the north end of the section. The course of the street is lost in 23-C-1, where it must have connected with the longer part of the north-south street, which is to be seen in the few pebbles in 23-D-1. Either there was a jog to the east of about 1.50 m., or there was an open square at the junction of the east-west with the north-south streets. Unfortunately all the evidence for this detail has been removed by erosion after the destruction of Stratum V.

The East-West Street (fig. 179)

For this rather large area of the Stratum V city there was only one east-west street for which traces can be seen in 32-E/G-10. The evidence for this cross street is scant, consisting of a patch of pebbles in 32-G-10 beside a stretch of east-west wall which could well have been the north wall of a house east of House 14 and north of House 15, and some paving in 32-E-10, which is also beside the north wall of House 14. The street slopes gently, 4.4 cm. to the meter, to the west. It is possible that there was an open court in 23-C/E-1 and 32-C/E-10. The position of this east-west street is roughly parallel to the east-west street of Stratum VI below, but it runs about 3 m. to the north of it.

North-South Street in the Southeast (figs. 90, 179)

In 32-F-8/9 there is a short segment of less than 10 m. of street that separates Houses 15 and 16. Its width, measured between the mud-brick walls on each side, averages about 1.50 m., although the actual passageway is lessened in places by the addition of buttressing walls added to protect the brick facing of the sides of the houses. The street drains to the north, with an average fall of 11 cm. to the meter.

CATALOGUED OBJECTS FROM STRATUM V, NOT IDENTIFIED WITH HOUSES:

Bowl,
    23-C-4 (fig. 10:7).
    32-C-10, S818/P459 (fig. 10:21).
    32-C-10, S817/P458 (fig. 10:2).
    32-C-10, S820/P461 (fig. 10:18).
Basalt bowl,
    32-C-10, S849/St60, black, D. 30 cm. A.
Juglet,
    23-E-1, S759/P429, Black ware, black core, vertical burnishing, D. 4.9 cm. P.
Krater,
    32-C-10, S846/P484 (fig. 12:15).
Pierced horn,
    23-G-5, S582/B10.
Spindle whorl,
    32-C-10, S812/M222, D. 3.7 cm., H. 2.2 cm. S.
    32-E-10, S898/M224, gray stone, black surface, D. of base, 3.4 cm. P.
Bracelet,
    32-G-10, S1028/Br53, Bronze, D. 5.3 cm., Th. .3 cm. P.
Juglet,
    23-E-1, S757/P427 (fig. 11:9).
Pilgrim flask,
    23-D-6, S421/P232 (fig. 11:18).
Cooking pot,
    23-C-4, S181/P77 (fig. 13:8).

INSIDE MEASUREMENTS OF THE HOUSES OF STRATUM V

House Number	Average Width	Average Length	Area sq. m.
3	4.60	8.55	39.33
5	4.88	8.40	40.99
7	4.73	8.20	38.79
9	4.88	8.08	39.43
11	5.05	8.15	41.16
4	4.90	8.15	39.94
6	5.05	8.55	43.18
8	4.80	8.30	39.84
10	4.70	8.55	40.19
12	4.70	8.80	41.36
Average	(4.83)	(8.37)	(40.42)
16	5.25	8.78	46.10
14	5.20(?)	8.90	46.28
15	5.00(?)	—	—
13	4.55(?)	—	—
27	5.60(?)	—	—
29	—	8.30	—

The Block of 12 Pillared Houses

From the general plan (fig. 179) and the Table of Inside Measurements of the Houses of Stratum V it is obvious that at least 10 of the houses of Stratum V are almost identical in plan and size (Houses 3–12). In addition, two more (Houses 1 and 2) have walls and pavements sufficiently preserved to suggest the same plan; and six more houses (Houses 13–16, 27, 29), while only partly preserved, have features and measurements that are comparable to those of the standard house of Stratum V.

Each of the standard block of Houses 3–12 has a single doorway opening from the street into a large front room, one half to one third of which was usually paved with stones. A row of columns, or roof supports, separated the paved from the unpaved portion of the room. With the possible exception of House 3, the entrance from the street was into the unpaved portion of the room. At the back of the room a second doorway led from the unpaved portion into a smaller room, which had a floor of packed earth. The block was built solidly, with the houses on one street sharing a common back wall with those that opened into the other street. Each house also shared a common side wall with its neighbor. Further evidence that these houses had been built as a unit is the observation that in a number of places the bricks at the corner of a house overlapped and were bonded with those of the adjoining house. From the table of inside measurements for the houses within the block it will be seen that there is but slight variation from the following averages for Houses 3–12:

Width: 4.83 m.
Length: 8.37 m.
Area: 40.42 sq. m.

Mention has been made in the descriptions of the individual houses of roofing materials found on the floors. This consisted of charred beams and mud impressions of the reeds that had been laid across the beams (figs. 65 and 95). In House 8 the roof material is reported to have been found lying on the unpaved area of the floor, but in Houses 9 and 12 beams and clay roofing material were found lying on the paved area. In House 7 a charred beam was found just south of the row of columns, but it was impossible to determine exactly from which side of the columns it had fallen.

There are three models to be considered for determining the method of roofing the houses. First, the entire block of 10 houses (probably 12) was completely covered with a roof that drained into one or both streets that bordered the block. This arrangement, however, would have excluded all light from the houses, except that which came in through the doors to the street. Another difficulty to this method of covering would have been that smoke from the ovens (found in Houses 5, 7, 9, 11, and 12) would have had no means of escape except through the doorways.

Both of these difficulties could have been eliminated, however, by the building of a system of clerestory openings in the upper walls. Such an arrangement, however, would have involved a sophistication in building technique that is thus far unattested for the Iron Age in this area.

A second possibility is that the paved area of the front room and the back room were roofed over to provide shelter from the rain in the winter season and from the sun in the summer. The difficulty with this hypothesis is that the larger portion of the front room, with its dirt floor, would have been rendered unusable by the water that drained into it from the adjacent roofs during the rainy season.

The third possibility is that the unpaved portion of the front room and the back room were covered with a roof. The paved area would have functioned as an open courtyard that had its drainage through the loosely set stones on the floor. The seemingly negative evidence for this arrangement, the presence of roofing material on the paved portions of Houses 9 and 12, might be removed by the supposition that the roof had slipped from an adjoining house. One difficulty, however, with this arrangement is that in Houses 1 and 3 and Houses 6 and 8 the paved portions of their respective front rooms adjoin each other and the common house wall is between the two courtyards. If the roofing plan was as we have suggested then the top of the partition walls between Houses 1 and 3 and between Houses 6 and 8 would have been exposed to the weather and subject to erosion. But this difficulty could have been overcome by plastering the tops of the walls with roofing material and renewing it periodically, as indeed the roofs themselves were renewed. Of the three hypothetical models the third seems the most likely.

The construction of 12 houses according to such a uniform plan and at the same time might suggest that they had been built for public or industrial purposes. Yet every indication is that these were private dwellings, with the furniture and artifacts appropriate to residences. There were clay ovens for baking (Houses 5, 7, 9, 11, 12), mills for grinding grain (Houses 6, 10, 12), and bins for storage (Houses 5 and 9). The only suggestion of industrial activity is the discovery of large collections of loom weights in Houses 3, 5, and 6, as well as a few scattered examples in other houses. It seems more plausible to suppose that these weights belonged to family rather than to industrial looms (see pp. 35–36).

Although the houses were built according to a standard plan there were secondary features that suggested individual ownership. The number of posts designed to support the roof varies from house to house. Some are built of brick, others of stone, and in House 10 there is evidence that wooden posts were used as roof supports. Such temporary features as bins for storage and clay ovens for baking seem to have been placed according to need and family convenience. On the west street the owner of House 6 had apparently faced the outside of his wall on the street side with stones to protect it from erosion. His neighbor to the south, in House 8, seems to have left his wall completely exposed to this hazard. Noticeably absent from the houses of this level are deep storage bins or pits dug into the floor. Bins in the corner of rooms and in the back storage room seem to have taken their place.

The Pillared House in Palestine

The plan of the Tell es-Saʻidiyeh standard house is well known from the Palestinian sites of Tell Beit Mirsim, Khirbet el-Mshāsh, Beer-Sheba, Tell en-Naṣbeh, and Hazor (see Y. Shiloh, "The Four-Room House–the Israelite Type-House?" (in Hebrew), *Eretz-Israel* 11: 277–85, especially fig. 1 for the plans of the three-room sub-type; "The Four-Room House: Its Situation and Function in the Israelite City," *IEJ* 20: 180–90; Volkmar Fritz, "Bestimmung und Herkunft des Pfeilerhauses in Israel," *ZDPV* 93: 30–45. A recent study of this type of house lists 12 Palestinian sites where the plan is to be found (Frank Braemer, *L'architecture domestique du Levant à l'âge du Fer*, 60–65). Below are listed some examples of this style of architecture, with the inside measurements and the approximate areas of the buildings. These figures may be compared with the average width of 4.83 m., the average length of 8.37 m., and an area

MEASUREMENTS OF PILLARED HOUSES

	Length	Width	Area		Length	Width	Area
Tell Beit Mirsim, NW 11:4, 5 (*TBM* 3: pl. 7)	8.80 m.	5 m.	44 sq. m.	Khirbet el-Mshāsh, House 74, A, Str. IIIA (*ZDPV* 96: 124, fig. 2; *Tel Aviv* 4: 142, fig. 3)	12.60 m.	8.50 m.	107.10 sq. m.
Tell Beit Mirsim, NW 13:8, 9 (*TBM* 3: pl. 7, p. 53)	8.60 m.	4.80 m.	41.28 sq. m.	Beer-Sheba, House 76, Str. III–II (*Beer-Sheba* 1: pl. 94)	ca. 8 m.	ca. 5 m.	ca. 40 sq. m.
Tell Beit Mirsim, NW 31:10, 11 (*TBM* 3: pl. 6)	10 m.	5.80 m.	58 sq. m.	Beer-Sheba, House 75, Str. III–II (*Beer-Sheba* 1: pl. 94)	ca. 7.8 m.	ca. 3.5 m.	ca. 27.3 sq. m.
Tell Beit Mirsim, NW 31:7, 8, 9 (*TBM* 3: pl. 6)	9.60 m.	4.60 m.	44.16 sq. m.	Tell en-Naṣbeh, House 580 (*TN* 1: plan, AC/AD-17/18)	7.80 m.	4 m.	31.2 sq. m.
Tell Beit Mirsim, NW 32:10,11 (*TBM* 3: pl. 6)	8.80 m.	5.40 m.	47.52 sq. m.	Hazor, Area A, loc. 48, Str. VI (*Hazor* 1: pl. 173)	8.50 m.	6 m.	51 sq. m.

of 40.42 sq. m. for the ten best-preserved examples from Tell es-Saʿidiyeh. The number of pillars running the long axis of the front room is four, with the exception of the house in Tell Beit Mirsim, Area NW 31:10, 11, which has three pillars and a short wall in the position usually occupied by the fourth.

These examples of the three-room pillared house, with the exception of that at Khirbet el-Mshāsh, generally fall within the range of the sizes of our houses in Stratum V; only House 75 at Beer-Sheba and House 580 at Tell en-Naṣbeh are appreciatively smaller. The plan appears throughout Palestine, extending from Beer-Sheba in the south to Hazor in the north. The tradition for the plan of our houses in Stratum V must be connected with the well-documented architectural tradition of sites to the west of the Jordan in the latter part of the Iron Age.

Uses and Function of the Houses of Stratum V

Although the individual houses found in Stratum V have been described in detail and their contents inventoried in the lists of catalogued objects, we shall now consider the furniture and artifacts found throughout the stratum for the purpose of determining, if possible, the kinds of activities that took place in this area. The most prevalent type of artifact, apart from pottery sherds, in Stratum V is the clay loom weight, of which 215 examples were found. These have been recorded and discussed in a separate section of this report (pp. 35–38).

Among the larger and more fixed household equipment are 15 ovens for baking. Eleven had been built within houses (Houses 5, 7, 9, 11, 12, 16 (2), 25 (2), 27, and 29); four were found outside, in the courtyard situated between Houses 27 and 29. Wherever ovens were found within a house of the standard plan (Houses 3–12) they were always in the front room, and with one exception, House 5, always in the unpaved portion of the front room. An oven in House 29 appears to be within the back room. A stone mill, or mortar, was found as a feature of Houses 6, 10, 12, and 25. Clay bins or receptacles had been constructed between the columns of Houses 6 and 13; and other storage bins were found in Houses 5, 9, and 16.

Of the smaller artifacts that came from the floors and the streets of Stratum V, 174 were catalogued. Of these 90 are shown on the plates of drawings (figs. 10–14), others are shown in the photographs of objects in figs. 164–175. In addition to the catalogued objects from Stratum V there are drawings of sherds, which are included within the Type Series and appear in figs. 10–14. In the following classification of the 174 catalogued objects within the total assemblage of Stratum V an effort has been made to place objects within categories that define function and use. Needless to say such a classification cannot be absolute, but it may serve to make possible some valid generalizations as to what were the activities in which the inhabitants of the houses of Stratum V engaged. Following is a listing of the objects in a suggested classification.

VESSELS AND CONTAINERS:

  21 bowls
   6 jugs
  22 juglets
  10 kraters
  22 cooking pots
   9 storage jars
   2 pilgrim flasks
   5 decanters
   1 jar
   1 faience cup
   1 alabaster flask

LAMPS:

  4 lamps

TOOLS AND WEAPONS:

  6 bone tools
  3 arrowheads
  3 sickles
  4 whetstones
  1 knife
  1 adze
  2 plow points
  8 spindle whorls

ARTICLES OF PERSONAL ADORNMENT:

  2 fibulae
  2 beads
  1 ring
  1 bracelet
  1 cosmetic palette
  2 shells

EQUIPMENT FOR THE PREPARATION OF FOOD:

  1 mortar
  2 stone bowls
  3 pestles (two in loom weight catalogue)
  2 tripod bowls

NON-UTILITARIAN OBJECTS:

  1 zoomorphic figurine
  1 human figurine
  1 cylinder seal
  1 tripod cup
  7 gaming pieces
  1 fragment of kernos ring

MISCELLANEOUS:

  1 alabaster bowl
  7 decorated sherds
  2 clay disks
  1 bronze disk
  1 nail
  1 stamped jar handle

From this classification of artifacts it is apparent that there is a predominence of vessels and containers for food and drink. Among the remaining items there seems to be no substantial evidence for either a specialized industrial or a ceremonial use for the building. We can only conclude that this area of the city was a residential section in which the normal household activities were carried on at the time of its destruction.

Summary

The domestic quarters of the city of Stratum V are significantly different from those found in the preceding period of occupation. The pillared house is an innovation in this period in the life of the city, and the duplication of the same plan and the arrangement of houses back to back in two rows opening on to parallel streets is unique for the Iron Age in Palestine and Transjordan. The plan of this sector of the city testifies to effective city planning. Even though the houses were built according to the same plan and at the same time, there is evidence for a diversity of furnishings. Variations in partition walls within the back room, bins for storage, shelves between the pillars, and ovens evidence the freedom of the individual occupant or family to make arrangements to suit individual family needs. One could bake in an oven within the house or make use of ovens in a courtyard, like those between House 27 and House

29. Although the furnishings and arrangements differ from house to house and there is a variety of artifacts found on the floors throughout the area, there is no evidence to suggest that the houses within this section of the city were used for purposes other than living quarters.

^{14}C Dates of Samples from Stratum V

In the course of the excavation of Stratum V, 12 samples of charcoal were collected from the floors of houses and from the streets of that stratum and submitted to the Radiocarbon Laboratory of the University of Pennsylvania for analysis. The resulting dates were published by Robert Stuckenrath, Jr. and Elizabeth K. Ralph, "University of Pennsylvania Radiocarbon Dates VIII," *Radiocarbon* 7:195, and B. Lawn, "University of Pennsylvania Radiocarbon Dates XIII," *Radiocarbon* 12:581–83. Three of the samples, P-832, P-835, and P-836, have been discarded from the following tabulation because of the discovery of an uncertain or wrong stratigraphic attribution. The remaining nine samples are retained and the radiocarbon ages (5568 half-life) before present (BP—A.D. 1950) for each are listed along with their calibrated date ranges at a 67% (1 sigma) and 95% (2 sigma) confidence levels according to the Radiocarbon International Calibration (see Jeffrey Klein, J. C. Lerman, P. E. Damon, and E. K. Ralph, "Calibration of Radiocarbon Dates: Tables Based on the Consensus Data of the Workshop on Calibrating the Radiocarbon Time Scale," *Radiocarbon* 24:103–50.

^{14}C DATES OF CHARCOAL SAMPLES FROM STRATUM V

Sample No.	Age BP (5568 Half-Life)	RIC Calibrated Date (1 sigma)	RIC Calibrated Date (2 sigma)	Sample No.	Age BP (5568 Half-Life)	RIC Calibrated Date (1 sigma)	RIC Calibrated Date (2 sigma)
P-834 23-D-4 House 8	2730 ± 160	1105–780 B.C.	1250–600 B.C.	P-830 23-G-6 Street opposite Houses 3, 5	2570 ± 60	810–755 B.C.	825–585 B.C.
P-1444 23-G-3 House 9	2630 ± 60	835–775 B.C.	880–620 B.C.	P-831 23-G-6 Street	2540 ± 50	800–600 B.C.	810–430 B.C.
P-1101 23-G-4 Room 7	2610 ± 60	825–770 B.C.	865–610 B.C.	P-833 23-G-5 House 7	2540 ± 50	800–600 B.C.	810–430 B.C.
P-829 23-C-4 Oven area	2600 ± 60	820–765 B.C.	850–605 B.C.	P-1100 23-F-3 House 9	2430 ± 60*	625–415 B.C.	780–400 B.C.
P-1099 23-G-2 House 11	2580 ± 50	810–760 B.C.	830–590 B.C.				

* Originally published as 2420 ± 60
Note: All but P-829, P-830, and P-833 had NaOH pretreatment.

The average age for the entire group of samples from Stratum V is 2580 ± 80 B.P., which corresponds to date ranges of 825–600 B.C. (1 sigma) and 1000–420 B.C. (2 sigma) according to the international calibration. However, since sample P-1100 is without a specific stratigraphic record and its date proves to be statistically inconsistent by the Chi-square test with those of the other eight samples of the group, it should probably be excluded from the average. With this omission the average is 2600 ± 60, giving date ranges of 820–765 B.C. (1 sigma) and 850–605 B.C. (2 sigma).

Measurements of Bricks Used in Houses of Stratum V

Joanna Fink McClellan made a series of measurements of bricks that had been used in the building of some well-preserved walls of Houses 5, 6, 8, and 9 of Stratum V. The following measurements, in centimeters, are those appearing on the face of the wall after it had been scraped with a trowel to produce a smooth, vertical scarp. Since the walls of these houses (the west wall of House 6 is an exception) were built generally with a single row of bricks laid as headers—that is, the width to the face of the wall—the measurements that were obtained from the scraped scarps were those of the width and the thickness of the individual bricks. The measurements for lengths were more difficult to obtain, since the faces of some walls had been plastered and others had been reduced by erosion or by scraping in the process of cleaning. The lengths of bricks given below in parentheses are those of the average width of the wall as it was recorded in the general plan of fig. 179. Thus, this measurement is only an approximation.

HOUSE 5, ONE COURSE OF THE NORTH WALL, FROM EAST TO WEST:

(55) × 36 × 12, (55) × 34 × 12, (55) × 27 × 10, (55) × 34 × 10.

HOUSE 6, THREE COURSES OF THE WEST WALL, FROM SOUTH TO NORTH:

— × 56 × 12, — × 54 × 13,
— × 52 × 12, [missing] — × 56 × 13,
— × 56 × 12, — × 50 × 12.

HOUSE 8, WEST WALL, TOP TO BOTTOM:

(50) × 39 × 12, (50) × 39 × 12,
(50) × 36 × 12, (50) × 38 × 12, (50) × 30 × 10, (50) × 32 × 12,
— × 50 × 12, — × 54 × 12, (50) × 34 × 10, (50) × 34 × 10,
(50) × 38 × 12, (50) × 37 × 12, (50) × 38 × 12 (50) × 38 × 12,
(50) × 38 × 12, (50) × 38 × 12, (50) × 38 × 12, (50) × 38 × 12, (50) × 38 × 12, (50) × 38 × 12, (50) × 38 × 12.

HOUSE 9, THREE COURSES OF THE NORTH WALL, FROM WEST TO EAST:

(50) × 36 × 10, (50) × 40 × 10,
(50) × 38 × 10, (50) × 36 × 10, (50) × 38 × 10, (50) × 25 × 10, (50) × 38 × 10,
(50) × 34 × 10, (50) × 34 × 10, (50) × 34 × 10, (50) × 20 × 10, (50) × 38 × 10.

HOUSE 9, TWO COURSES OF THE SOUTH WALL:

(48) × 34 × 10, (48) × 34 × 10, (48) × 32 × 10, (48) × 32 × 10, (48) × 32 × 10, (48) × 36 × 10.

HOUSE 9, ONE COURSE OF THE NORTH WALL, BACK ROOM:

(52) × 34 × 10, (52) × 34 × 10, (52) × 34 × 10.

MEASUREMENTS OF SINGLE BRICKS

House 3, south wall: — × 37 × 10.
House 5, west wall: — × 36 × 12, — × 36 × 10.
House 5, south wall: 48 × 44 × —.
House 6, west wall: 50 × 36 × —.
House 6, buttress: 50 × 36 × —.
House 6, fallen: 55 × 32 × 15, 50 × 31 × 15.
House 7, column: 56 × 36 × 10.
House 8, west wall: 44 × 40 × —.

LENGTH MEASUREMENTS

If the last of the measurements for single bricks is rejected on the grounds that it was a cut or broken brick, the others have lengths ranging from 48 to 56 cm. This range of measurements corresponds in general to that for the width of the walls found in the houses. Thus, the bricks seem to have been laid in header fashion, with the longest axis of the brick running across the wall. The exception to this generalization is to be seen in eight bricks found in the west walls of Houses 6 and 8, which will be discussed below.

WIDTH MEASUREMENTS

In the list of measurements given above for 62 bricks, the distribution is as follows:

Width in cm.	Number of examples
20	1
25	1
27	1
30	1
31	1

Width in cm.	Number of examples
32	5
34	12
36	10
37	2
38	15
39	2
40	2
44	1
50	2
52	1
54	2
56	3

Forty-four examples, or 71 percent of the total, fall within the range of 32–38 cm., with the greatest number of examples measuring 38 cm. If a mold of standard size was used in the fabrication of bricks, the variation of 6 cm. within this range of measurements could have been due to the shaving of a brick, shrinkage in the process of baking, or the spreading of the mud after its removal from the mold. The smaller width, from 20 to 27 cm., can perhaps best be explained as that of half or trimmed bricks. The eight examples that range from 50 to 56 cm., however, should possibly be considered as lengths of bricks set as stretchers. They were all found in one segment of wall, that of the west wall to Houses 6 and 8. This wall would then have been an exception to the more common type of header construction.

THICKNESS MEASUREMENTS

The thickness of 58 bricks, for which measurements are recorded, is remarkably consistent.

Thickness in cm.	Examples
10	29
12	25
13	2
15	2

The range of thickness for 93 percent of the measured bricks is from 10 to 12 cm. The remaining four examples were probably made by heaping up the mud on the form or by the use of mud of a consistency that did not settle upon the removal of the form. It is of interest to note that the two bricks with measurements of 15 cm. for thickness had widths of 32 and 31 cm., measurements that are below the average.

The material used in the fabrication of the bricks for this section of houses was of two types. Most of the bricks were made of reddish brown to brown clay, which could hardly be distinguished during the excavation from the fill that surrounded the walls. The regularity of the edges of the bricks and the lines of mortar between them frequently provided the only means for distinguishing a wall from the filling packed against it. Less frequent was the use of a gray-green clay (*qaṭṭārah*) for the bricks. The material is still available on the low-lying hills between the tell and the Jordan River. There seemed to have been no pattern in the choice of bricks of gray-green clay or of those of the brown material. The former were noticed in House 5 set in a course of brown bricks. Obviously the bricks had been supplied from more than one brick field.

SUMMARY

Although the sizes of bricks used in building the standard houses in Area 23 of Stratum V varied slightly they fell predominately within the range of 48–56 × 32–38 × 10–12 cm. They were laid in single rows, generally in header fashion, with the divisions between bricks of a course staggered with those of the courses above and below. The mortar was a mud that was hardly distinguishable from the material used in the manufacture of the brown bricks.

Catalogue of Loom Weights

Next to pottery the most common artifact found on the floors of Stratum V was the clay loom weight. The dominant form among the 215 examples noted is that of a globular ball of clay pierced through its shorter axis and usually slightly flattened at the points of perforation (fig. 170:1). The average measurement for the height (axis of the hole) is 5.7 cm.; the larger diameter averages 7.9 cm. while the average diameter of the hole is 2.1 cm. In addition to the usual type there are a few examples of a bag-shaped or tear-drop weight, perforated horizontally toward the top of the neck of the bag (see especially extreme left of rows 3–5 from the top, fig. 170:1). All examples of loom weights exhibit some degree of firing, although the hardness varies considerably. Many were found in burned areas and it is possible that these had received an additional degree of hardness in the burning of the house. Others were so brittle that they broke apart in the process of removing them from the debris that covered them. It is probable that the firing of weights at a high temperature, such as that used in kilns, would have cracked or even exploded them; however, they could have been burned in an open fire after having been molded by hand around a reed or stick. The colors range from shades of tan to grayish brown.

Loom weights were generally found in groups. Ninety percent of the examples were found in five houses:

House 6: 79
House 16:51
House 15:42
House 3: 13
House 5: 9.

The largest single collection of loom weights appeared in a mass of ash over the pavement to the south of the bin between the east pilaster and the adjoining column of House 6 (figs. 73, 74, and text figs. 2, 3). In the excavation of these weights three levels were recorded, but it is unlikely that these layers represent anything but the accident of their deposit during the conflagration that destroyed the house. The layers are separated only by ash and other burned material with no trace of floors or occupation levels between. It is apparent from the plan of the second and third layers that the weights were deposited, or fell, in a fairly straight line. Although some examples had rolled or fallen out from this line, it is likely that the arrangement in which the weights were found had been due to their dropping from a horizontal beam to which they had been attached by threads. Additional support for this assumption is to be seen in the line of charred beams remaining in the balk beside the weights on the floor (fig. 74). At Lachish a charred beam was found near loom weights in Room H.15:1003 (*Lachish* 3:107–108 and pl. 20:5). In House 3, where 13 weights were found in the southwest corner of the front room, they were scattered over a considerable area; 42 loom weights in House 15 were reported to have been spread over an area of 30 by 50 cm. of the floor.

In House 16 loom weights were found in three areas. Thirty-one weights were found arranged in a fairly straight line to the south of the wall that served as a foundation for the columns that separated the front room into two parts (fig. 89). Five more loom weights appeared in the southwest corner of the room. In the back room of the House 14 more examples appeared in a fairly straight line beside a storage bin (fig. 88).

It is interesting to note that the heaviest burning to be noted within the entire complex of buildings was within the houses that had the largest collections of loom weights. If Houses 6 and 16 had contained large quantities of combustable material for weaving, as well as wooden beams for looms, they would have provided fuel for the fire which burned there so hotly.

While most of the loom weights were found within the debris of Stratum V, some were also found in the other strata. In the houses of Stratum VII only six examples were recorded; 11 weights were found in Room 37-39 of Stratum VI (fig. 52); and eight weights were found in Stratum IV, three of which were conical. But the continued use of the spherical variety in Stratum IV is attested.

CATALOGUE OF CLAY LOOM WEIGHTS*

House	No. on Plan	Catalogue No.	Height	Diam.	Diam. of Hole
STRATUM V					
3	2	S480/M137	6.	8.	2.
3	4	S476/M134	6.	8.	2.
3	5	S478/M135	—	—	—
3	6	S479/M136	6.	8.	1.9
3	9	S475/M133	7.	7.	2.
3		S403/M118	4.4	6.8	2.
3	10	S431/M124	7.5	7.5	2.5
3		S433/M125	7.5	8.3	2.3
3		S434/M126	7.	7.2	2.4
3		S435/M127	7.5	8.	2.3
3		S481/M138	6.	8.	1.5
3		S482/M139	5.	7.	2.
3		S755/M213	5.7	6.5	2.
4		S234/M97	5.	7.	—
5		S485/M142	5.	7.	2.
5		S486/M143	5.	5.5	1.9

House	No. on Plan	Catalogue No.	Height	Diam.	Diam. of Hole
STRATUM V					
5		S487/M143A	5.	7.2	1.8
5		S488/M144	4.5	7.	2.
5		S489/M145	6.	10.	2.
5		S490/M146	5.5	7.	1.8
5		S491/M147	5.	9.	2.5
5		S492/M148	5.	6.5	—
5		S550/M150	7.	9.	2.
(First layer of House 6)					
6	3(?)	S43/M39	5.2	7.8	—
6	4	S50/M46	4.4	6.7	—
6	5	S26/M21	5.	7.6	—
6	6	S45/M41	5.5	8.1	—
6	7	S48/M44	5.9	7.2	—
6	8	S19/M14	6.	8.	—
6	9(?)	S60/M56	5.6	8.3	—
6	10	S46/M42	5.1	9.7	—

* NOTE: Measurements are in centimeters; height is the measurement along the axis of the hole. House 6, first layer, nos. 1, 2, 16, 20 of the plan are stones; second layer, no. 41 is a loom weight not catalogued; third layer, nos. 46 and 50 are stones, and no. 49 is a loom weight not catalogued.

CATALOGUE OF CLAY LOOM WEIGHTS—(Continued)*

House	No. on Plan	Catalogue No.	Height	Diam.	Diam. of Hole
STRATUM V					
6	11	S58/M54	6.6	8.6	—
6	12	S27/M22	6.6	8.3	—
6	13	S11/M6	5.6	8.6	—
6	14	S44/M40	9.3	8.6	—
6	15	S49/M45	5.2	7.8	—
6	17(?)	S61/M57	5.6	8.3	—
6	18	S59/M55	8.6	8.1	—
6	19	S56/M52	5.	8.3	—
6	21	S42/M38	5.7	7.3	—
6	22(?)	S53/M49	9.6	7.8	—
6	23	S47/M43	5.7	7.8	—
6	24(?)	S51/M47	8.4	7.	—
(Second layer of House 6)					
6	25	S18/M13	6.3	7.7	—
6	26	S25/M20	5.5	8.7	—
6	27	S14/M9	5.	8.3	—
6	28	S23/M18	5.4	5.8	—
6	29	S22/M17	6.2	8.4	—
6	30	S54/M50	5.6	8.2	—
6	31	S16/M11	5.4	7.1	—
6	32	S29/M24	4.4	8.4	—
6	33	S57/M53	4.4	7.8	—
6	34	S15/M10	5.8	8.3	—
6	35(?)	S17/M12	5.5	7.8	—
6	36	S20/M15	5.6	7.8	—
6	37	S55/M51	5.7	7.7	—
6	38	S12/M7	5.4	7.8	—
6	39	S28/M23	5.5	8.3	—
6	40	S52/M48	5.	5.8	—
6	42	S32/M27	5.5	7.4	—
6	43	S24/M19	5.	7.8	—
6	44	S21/M16	5.5	8.4	—
(Third layer of House 6)					
6	45	S31/M26	6.2	8.3	—
6	47	S32a/M28	5.8	8.1	—
6	48	S39/M35	5.3	7.9	—
6	51	S36/M32	6.3	8.4	—
6	52	S37/M33	5.8	8.	—
6	53	S38/M34	4.5	8.3	—
6	54	S34/M30	5.8	7.5	—
6	55	S35/M31	4.2	6.3	—
6	56	S33/M29	5.1	9.	—
6	57	S40/M36	5.7	8.	—
6	58	S30/M25	5.5	8.5	—
6	59		(broken)		
6	60	S13/M8	6.3	8.5	—
6	61		(broken)		
6	62	S41/M37	5.4	8.1	—
6		S155/M75	—	—	—
(House 6, scattered)					
6		S65/M61	9.4	10.	(bag-shaped)
6		S119/M67	5.	8.3	2.3
STRATUM V					
6		S120/M68	6.	8.2	2.3
6		S121/M69	5.	9.	2.5
6		S149/M71	4.	7.	1.8
6		S153/M73	—	—	(bag-shaped)
6		S164/M77	5.	7.	1.5
6		S165/M78	6.	9.5	—
6		S167/M80	5.	6.	2.
6		S168/M81	7.	10.5	2.2
6		S169/M82	4.5	7.5	2.
6		S235/M98	5.	8.	2.
6		S314/M100	4.	7.	2.
6		S315/M101	4.	7.	—
6		S322/M106	4.5	7.5	—
6		S323/M107	5.	7.5	2.4
6		S326/M110	5.5	8.	2.
6		S319/M103	4.	6.5	2.
6		S320/M104	6.	8.	2.2
6		S321/M105	5.	10.	2.8
6		S324/M108	6.	8.	2.2
6		S328/M112	6.7	10.	3.7
6		S329/M113	5.5	7.7	2.5
6(?)		S430/M123	5.5	6.	2.
7		S493/M149	8.	9.	2.
7		S440/M128	5.5	7.5	3.
7		S483/M140	5.6	7.5	2.
7		S1045/M257	—	6.8	—
8		S64/M60	4.6	7.6	—
8		S148/M170	5.	9.	2.5
8		S309/M99	5.	7.5	3.
8		S138/M102	8.	8.	1.4
8		S330/M114	4.5	6.7	2.5
9(?)		S770/M215	—	8.	—
9		S736/M204	5.1	8.3	1.5
9		S769/M214	—	14.	—
11		S734/M203	4.5	7.1	1.7
13		S747/M211	4.3	7.8	1.9
14		S1051/M263	—	7.	—
15		42 examples not catalogued			
16		S1048/M260	—	9.5	—
16		31 examples not catalogued (see fig. 89)			
16		14 examples not catalogued (see fig. 88)			
16		5 examples not catalogued			
23-C-1		S738/M206	4.9	7.5	—
23-C-1		S748/M212	5.7	8.7	—
23-E-1		S771/M216	—	8.	—
23-G-6		S746/M210	7.7	11.3	2.6
23-E/F-10		S1049/M261	7.7	8.7	—
STRATUM IV					
23-E-5		S5/M1	5.3	7.	—
23-E-5		S6/M2	5.	8.3	—

*NOTE: Measurements are in centimeters; height is the measurement along the axis of the hole. House 6, first layer, nos. 1, 2, 16, 20 of the plan are stones; second layer, no. 41 is a loom weight not catalogued; third layer, nos. 46 and 50 are stones, and no. 49 is a loom weight not catalogued.

CATALOGUE OF CLAY LOOM WEIGHTS—(Continued)*

House	No. on Plan	Catalogue No.	Height	Diam.	Diam. of Hole	House	No. on Plan	Catalogue No.	Height	Diam.	Diam. of Hole
STRATUM IV						STRATUM IV					
23-E-5		S7/M3	5.8	8.3	—	23-E-4		S163/M76	—	—	—
23-E-5		S8/M4	8.5	8.6		23-D/C-4		S166/M79	5.	6.5	—
					(conical)	23-F-7		S327/M111	6.	10.	2.5
23-E-5		S9/M5	9.	7.8		23-E-1		S737/M205	6.8	8.2	—
					(conical)	STRATUM UNDETERMINED					
23-E-4		S100/M66	(damaged)			23-D-7		S62/M58	5.6	7.1	—
23-D-3		S150/M72	6.5	5.7	—	32-E-9/10		S1050/M262	—	8.2	—
					(conical)	32-E-9/10		S1050/M262	—	8.2	—
23-E-5		S170/M83	4.5	6.5	—	32-E-9/10		S1050/M262	—	8.2	—
SURFACE						32-E-9/10		S1050/M262	—	8.2	—
23-E-4		S63/M59	2.5	6.5	—	23-F-6		S484/M141	4.5	6.	2.

* NOTE: Measurements are in centimeters; height is the measurement along the axis of the hole. House 6, first layer, nos. 1, 2, 16, 20 of the plan are stones; second layer, no. 41 is a loom weight not catalogued; third layer, nos. 46 and 50 are stones, and no. 49 is a loom weight not catalogued.

V
Stratum IV

Of the excavated area of the tell Stratum IV is unique in that it was devoid of buildings. It consists of an area of 1125 sq. m. (23-C/G-1/6 and 32-C/G-8/10) on which there was a clearly identifiable floor, from which 98 circular pits and two rectangular bins had been cut (fig. 180). This large occupational surface overlay the remains of the houses of Stratum V; when this stratum had been destroyed by fire its walls and other debris were leveled to make a flat surface. Not only were there no house walls that belonged to Stratum IV, but there were no well-defined streets or paths through the area. At the time of Stratum IV this area of the tell was given over to activities that involved the use of pits and bins. When these characteristic features of the stratum ceased to be used most of the area does not appear to have been built upon or used for any other purpose; only in 32-D/G-8/10 are there building remains which belonged to a later occupation (fig. 189).

The floor of Stratum IV consisted of an irregular surface that differed noticeably from the usual house floors of Stratum V. It appeared generally to have been beaten down by use, but it lacked the inclusions of small bits of charcoal and lime which characterize the floors of houses. There were some areas of burning, as for example 23-F-3, where burned material was noted on the floor to a depth of 20 cm., and there was a ḥawārah floor in both 23-G-2 and 23-E-1. But generally, with the exception of small spots of light burning that had resulted from a cooking or camp fire, the floor was distinguishable from the soil above and below it only by its hard surface, which evidenced traffic and use. Artifacts were relatively scarce, when compared with the wealth of pottery and other objects found in the houses of Stratum V. Some objects came from the filling within the pits and undoubtedly had belonged to those who used the storage area; other artifacts, particularly the smaller sherds, could easily have been washed down the slope from the later buildings to the south. In general the pottery from the stratum was sparse and the provenience of some of it was not as definite as that which had been sealed into the earlier strata.

Evidence that the area of Stratum IV had, on occasion, been used for baking is supplied by the presence of three clay ovens built on its floor (32-C-10; 32-C-9, where the oven had been partly destroyed in the cutting of Pit 69; and 23-G-4). The only indication that any of the area had been covered is to be seen in the presence of several holes that may have provided a seat for the posts of temporary sheds or a roof. In 23-E-4 a posthole, 13 cm. in diameter and 25 cm. deep, was found beside Pit 14 (fig. 99). Another posthole, 18 cm. in diameter and 25 cm. deep, was found to the southeast of Pit 11, in 23-D-4, and yet another hole was found in the southeast corner of 23-C-4. Undoubtedly there were other postholes, the outlines of which have been obscured or lost.

Most of the pits are circular in plan (fig. 180) and have vertical walls. The elliptical Pit 19, and the two larger, irregular pits, Pits 21 and 22, are exceptions. The diameters of the more normal, circular pits vary greatly, from the small Pit 2C, with a diameter of only 80 cm., to Pit 23, which has a diameter of 2.74 m. The average diameter is 1.73 m. There is also considerable variation in the depths to which the pits had been cut, as can be seen from the Table of Measurements (pp. 41–42). The range is from a depth of 1.77 m. for Pit 75 to only 30 cm. for Pit 2C. The average is 93 cm. In no example of these cuttings was there found evidence that the sides or the bottoms had been plastered. Occasionally a few stones were found embedded in the bottom, but these may well have belonged to a house floor of Stratum V, into which the pit had been dug.

It was obvious that not all the pits had been dug at the same time. When Pit 64 had been filled in, Pit 55 was cut through a segment of it. It was similarly observed that Pit 61 was later than Pit 60; Pit 63, later than Pit 62; Pit 57, later than Pit 56; Pit 80, later than Pit 79; Pit 31B, later than Pit 31A; Pit 34, later than Pit 25; and Pit 40, later than Pit 39. In one instance it was clear that there had been three periods in the digging of pits. In 32-D-8, Pit 77 had been dug and then filled in; later, Pit 76 was cut through a segment of the fill of Pit 77; later, Pit 76 was filled in, and in a third stage of the use of the area for storage, a part of its rim was removed when Pit 75 was cut. Yet despite such evidence for the filling and cutting of these circular bins, the floor level of the area seems to have remained fairly constant. The soil from a new excavation was utilized to fill in an older pit, and thus did not serve to raise the floor level. While it is obvious that not all of the 98 pits were in use at any one time, it is impossible to correlate the evidence for the fillings and the recuttings and to determine how many pits were used simultaneously. Probably the use of the area was fairly continuous over the period of time represented by Stratum IV.

Most of the bins were filled with soil, though several provided samples of other materials. The entire bottom of Pit 10 was covered with a layer, 3 mm. thick, of a soft gray powder containing easily powdered lumps and a considerable amount of short, needle-like crystals. An analysis of this material by A. E. Parkinson in 1968 revealed that this was a mixture of silicates of calcium, magnesium, iron, and aluminum. In Pit 59 there was found a small sample of grain, which proved to be 75 percent two-row barley hulled, and 25 percent wheat; in Pit 3 there were burnt grains of two-row barley hulled; and in 23-E-3, to the east side of Pit 3, there was a collection of kernels of two-row barley hulled.

Because of the evidence of grain in and about the pits there can be little doubt that the pits were used for storage. The prevailing wind from the northwest would have made the area at the northwest of the tell a suitable and advantageous location for threshing of grain. Some of the larger pits, and possibly the two brick-lined bins (see below), could have been used for the storage of straw. The storage space provided by the pits and bins would have been serviceable only in the dry summer season; before the coming of the fall rains the grain would have had to have been removed. What evidence there is for temporary occupation of this area of Stratum IV, such as ovens and pottery, would have been left by the farmers who remained to look after their grain until it could be moved for storage elsewhere.

Rectangular Bin B (figs. 102–104, 180)

A rectangular bin had been cut, almost exactly within the lines of our grid 32-D-10, to a depth of about 1 m. below the surface of Stratum IV. The bin measured 4.80 m., from east to west, and 4.50 m., from north to south. It was lined on all of its sides with a single row of gray mud bricks, each measuring 36 by 35 (?) by 12 cm., set in a plaster that was of a powderlike consistency. The brick lining of the bin was preserved to its original height only at the southeast corner, where the elevation was −239.79 m., a level that corresponds roughly to the recorded floor level of −239.75 m. for the floor of Stratum IV in the adjacent plot 32-E-10. The walls of the bin had been cut by Pits 53, 59, 55, 68, and 56A; other portions of the brick lining had been damaged in the upper courses of erosion. From an examination of the inner and outer surfaces of the brick lining it was clear that the bin had been exposed to the weather. The outer surface of the lining, protected as it had been by the soil filled against it, was not eroded; the inside surface (the wall of the open bin), however, was badly worn away, especially in the upper courses of bricks. Obviously, an area slightly larger than the bin had been excavated and the free standing walls built up in the form of a rectangular structure. A filling was then placed against the outside of the mud-brick walls until the floor level around the bin stood at the level of the highest course of mud bricks. There was no evidence for any openings in the walls of the lining; nor were there steps or a stairs leading from the surface to the bottom of the bin.

Rectangular Bin A (figs. 100, 101, 180)

About 5 m. to the east of Bin B, in 32-F-10 and 23-F-1, there appeared another bin of approximately the same size and having a similar brick lining. Its inside measurements are 4.95 m., east-west, and 3.77 m., north-south; and the walls consist of a single row of gray mud bricks, which measured 36 by 35 (?) by 12 cm. The original height of the brick lining seems to have been preserved at the southwest corner (fig. 100), which has an elevation of −239.68 m., a level that is only 14 cm. lower than that of the floor in 32-F-10. The floor of the bin seems to have been like that of the bin to the west of it and approximately 1 m. deep. From fig. 100 it is apparent that the outer surface of the lining of this bin shows no wear from exposure to the weather, while the inner surface of the lined pit appears to have been partially dissolved by the action of rain. As in the case of Bin B, there was no evidence for steps. Two earlier pits had been cut through by the builders of Bin A. The excavators had cut through the north edge of Pit 66, as well as the south rim or Pit 52. No later pits had been cut into Bin A.

CATALOGUED OBJECTS FROM STRATUM IV:
Bowl,
    S2/P2 (fig. 15:6).
    S141/P60 (fig. 15:13).
    S115/P38 (fig. 15:23).
    S1/P1 (fig. 16:14).
Jug,
    S85/P10 (fig. 16:2).
    S116/P39 (fig. 16:4).
    S91/P15 (fig. 16:5).
Krater,
    S89/P13 (fig. 15:15).
    S98/P22 (fig. 15:18).
    S90/P14 (fig. 15:19).
    S139/P58 (fig. 15:20).
Cooking pot,
    S137/P56 (fig. 15:25).
    S92/P16 (fig. 15:27).
    S138/P57 (fig. 15:28).
    S114/P37 (fig. 15:29).
Storage jar,
    S88/P12 (fig. 16:3).
    S87/P11 (fig. 16:7).
    S83/P8 (fig. 16:8).
    S338/P175 (fig. 16:13).
    S393/P221 (fig. 167:2).
Tripod bowl,
    S140/P59 (fig. 16:11).
Lamp,
    S66/P4 (fig. 16:17).
    S441/P245 (fig. 16:18).
Iron point,
    S552/F9, 23-F-4, two pieces, L. 15 cm., W. 2 cm., Th. 1 cm.
Iron knife,
    S1015/F41, 32-D-10, L. 13.8 cm., W. 2 cm.
Needle,
    S966/Br46, Bronze, three pieces, L. 7.1 cm., D. 0.2 cm.
Cosmetic palette,
    S703/St51, stone, cream, fragment, D. 7.5 cm., H. 2.6 cm.
Shell,
    S195/M92, 23-D-4, saucer shape, hole through border, off-white and very light yellow, L. 2 cm., W. 1.2 cm.
    S190/M87, 23-C-4, fanlike, hole at edge.
    S192/M89, 23-D/E-5, fanlike, pierced at tapering end, off-white.
Mortar,
    S160/St13, 23-D-7, stone, circular, black/dark gray. A.
    S701/St50, 23-F-2, stone, black, central depression polished, H. 7.5 cm., D. 10 cm.
Pestle,
    S443/St37, 23-E-3, stone, black, H. 6.7 cm., max. D. 5.7 cm.
Rubbing stone,
    S86/St8, 23-D-4, spongelike texture, black, shoe-shaped, upper part pierced, L. 9 cm., W. 7 cm.
Human figurine,
    S142/Pfig2 (fig. 16:12).
    S944/Pfig16 (fig. 169:3).
Zoomorphic figurine,
    S971/Pfig17, 32-G-8, bull's head, tan ware, reddish brown slip, black and white paint, L. 5.5 cm., H. 8 cm.
Incised sherd,
    S84/P9 (fig. 16:15).

The total of 38 catalogued objects from Stratum IV is small in comparison with the assemblage of 174 items from Stratum V. Although the two strata are equal in area there is less than one-fourth the number of artifacts from Stratum IV than from Stratum V. When the objects are classified according to function (cf. p. 32) there are only minor differences in proportions between the two groups:

	Stratum V		*Stratum IV*	
	No.	%	No.	%
Vessels and containers	100	57	20	52
Lamps	4	2	2	5
Tools and weapons	28	16	3	8
Articles of personal adornment	9	5	4	11
Equipment for preparation of food	8	5	3	8
Nonutilitarian objects	12	7	3	8
Miscellaneous	13	8	3	8
Total	174		38	

Stratum V has a higher percentage of vessels and containers and double the percent of tools and weapons; in other categories Stratum IV has equal or higher percentages.

MEASUREMENTS OF PITS IN STRATUM IV

Pit No.	Location	Depth	Diameter	Pit No.	Location	Depth	Diameter
1	23-E-3	.52	1.25	44	23-C-1	1.28	1.46
2	23-E-3	.49	1.87	45	23-C-1	1.09	1.82
2A	23-F-3	.60	1.75	46	23-C-1	.67	.98
2B	23-F-3	.50	1.30	47	23-G-1	1.48	1.92
2C	23-F-3	.30	.80	48	23-E-1	.94	2.04
3	23-E-3	1.26	2.50	49	23-E-1	.85	1.42
4	23-E-3	.35	1.35	50	23-E-1	.85	1.94
5	23-D-3	.56	2.05	51	23-E-1	1.06	1.52
6	23-D-3	.22	1.00	52	23-F-1	1.03	1.64
7	23-D-3	.77	1.90	53	23-D-1	.63	1.70
8	23-D-3		1.70	54	32-C-10	1.48	1.46
9	23-C-3		1.85	55	32-D-10	1.48	1.68
10	23-C-4	.87	1.30	56	32-E-10	.86	1.56
11	23-D-4	1.13	1.20	56A	32-E-10		1.37
12	23-D-4	.46	1.15	57	32-E-10	1.17	2.28
13	23-E-4	1.05	1.75	58	32-D-10	1.08	1.92
14	23-E-4	.43	1.37	59	23-D-1	.66	1.52
15	23-E-4	.59	1.90	60	32-D-9	.42	2.15
16	23-D-4		1.05	61	32-D-9	.77	1.90
17	23-D-4		1.50	62	32-D-9	.61	1.78
18	23-C-4		1.60	63	32-D-9	.86	2.14
19	23-C-5		1.20	64	32-C-9	1.28	1.76
19A	23-C-5		1.50	65	32-C-9	1.56	1.88
20	23-F-5	.67	1.75	66	32-G-10	1.34	1.72
21	23-F-5	.66	3.25	67	32-G-9	.69	1.48
21A	23-F-6		1.20	68	32-D-9	1.21	1.95
22	23-G-5	.78	ca.5.00	69	32-C-9	1.57	2.52
23	23-E-2	.49	2.74	70	32-G-9	1.17	2.18
24	23-E-2	.81	1.92	71	32-C-8	.66	1.62
25	23-E-2	.83	1.50	72	32-C-8	1.31	2.10
26	23-E-2	.71	1.46	73	32-C-8	.88	1.86
27	23-D-2	.80	1.62	74	32-D-8	1.61	1.78
28	23-C-2	.96	1.99	75	32-D-8	1.77	1.60
29	23-F-2	.91	1.61	76	32-D-8	1.57	1.88
30	23-F-2	.32	1.48	77	32-D-8	1.14	2.46
31A	23-G-4	.57	1.41	78	32-E-8	1.01	1.66
31	23-G-4	.86	1.14	79	32-E-8	.59	2.04
32	23-G-3	1.02	1.66	80	32-E-8	.92	1.52
33	23-G-3	.89	1.24	81	32-F-10	.76	1.98
34	23-G-3	1.47	1.36	82	32-F-9	1.31	1.82
35	23-G-3	1.11	1.64	83	32-E-9	1.17	1.34
36	23-G-3	.99	1.62	84	32-E-9	1.04	1.86
37	23-F-4	.81	1.28	85	32-G-8		
38	23-F-4	.92	1.60	86	32-G-8		
39	23-G-2	1.17	2.54	89	32-G-10	.53	2.00
40	23-G-2	1.20	1.56	90	32-G-10		ca.2.00
41	23-G-1	1.30	1.68	91	32-G-9		
42	23-F-4	1.08	1.72	92	32-G-9		.80
43	23-C-1	1.58	1.64	94	32-F-8		

VI

Pottery from Strata VII–IV

The pottery shown in figures 1–17 came from the floors of the four strata of occupation at the largest field excavated at Tell es-Saʻidiyeh, 23-C/G-1/9 and 32-C/G-8/10. The layers of debris that accumulated when the mud-brick houses of Strata VII–IV were destroyed or fell into disuse were generally clearly defined and easily distinguishable. Ceramic vessels and sherds appeared on the surface of the floors of houses and sherds were often imbedded within the floor which had been built up during the occupation of the house. Above the floor there was generally a layer of the sterile clay of decomposed sun-dried mud brick. The deposition of the clay layer can readily be understood. When the roof of the house collapsed, either because of a fire or neglect through abandonment, the sun-dried bricks of the walls, as well as the clay of the roof, were dissolved by the rains, and the resulting mud accumulated upon the floor. When the area was prepared for rebuilding it was necessary only to level further the stubs of the remaining walls and to lay the first bricks of the new house upon this layer of accumulated clay or in a trench cut into it. Thus, it was not necessary generally to bring filling from another area; the fill was ready at hand and, fortunately for the excavator, relatively free from sherds or other occupational debris. The pottery shown on the plates of drawings is limited to that which clearly came from on or in the floors of the houses of Strata VII–V and their streets. The pottery from Stratum IV, a period when the area was not occupied by houses, was found either within the pits of that stratum or upon the surface from which the pits were dug.

An explanation of the way in which the examples of vessels illustrated on the plates were selected is in order. Whole or fairly well-preserved forms of vessels were set aside immediately upon excavation for cataloguing, drawing, and photographing. Of the 435 forms shown in figs. 1–17, 128 are objects which were catalogued and assigned field numbers. In addition to the well-preserved pieces, there are the smaller fragments of rims, handles, and bases that were selected as representative from the sherds brought from the excavation at the end of each day. These forms are designated in this publication as the Type Series (TS) for a particular stratum. The Type Series includes novel forms found within a stratum and which are characteristic of that stratum. Since an attempt was made deliberately to retain several examples of forms that occurred with high frequencies, the selection within the Type Series can be said to be in some sense quantitative.

Distribution of Vessels by Strata

The largest sample of forms in the corpus of pottery (see Table 1) is that from Stratum VII, which is 32 percent of the total; Stratum VI is documented by 24 percent of the total; Stratum V, by 26 percent; and the latest stratum, Stratum IV, by only 18 percent of the total. However, in comparing the amount of pottery from each of the floors of the four strata adjustments must by made for the different sizes of the areas occupied by the four strata. The areas which were excavated in Strata IV and V were each 1125 sq. m. Of this relatively large area only approximately 400 sq. m. were excavated through the two underlying layers of occupation, Strata VI and VII. Thus the floor space on which the ceramic material was found in Strata IV and V was approximately three times the size of that of Strata VI and VII. This difference in the size of the areas actually excavated serves to distort the picture given above of the proportional yields of pottery from the various levels. Strata VII and VI provided considerably more ceramic vessels in proportion to the size of the areas investigated than did Strata V and IV. The relatively small sample from Stratum IV can be explained by the particular use that was made of the area: it was a place for the storage of grain in bins and not the domestic quarter as it had been in the previous periods of occupation. The more difficult question is why there is such a marked quantitative difference,

TABLE 1
Distribution of Vessels

Stratum	VII no.	*%	VI no.	*%	V no.	*%	IV no.	*%	Total no.	**%
Bowls	41	30	17	16	29	26	29	37	116	27
Storage Jars	21	15	17	16	16	14	15	19	69	16
Cooking Pots	14	10	16	15	21	19	13	16	64	15
Kraters	18	13	15	14	16	14	8	10	57	13
Jugs	15	11	11	10	7	6	7	9	40	9
Juglets	4	3	13	12	11	10	—	—	28	6
Lamps	4	3	5	5	1	1	2	3	12	3
Pilgrim Flasks	3	2	1	1	2	2	1	1	7	2
Decanters	1	1	4	4	5	4	—	—	10	2
Tripod Cups	4	3	1	1	3	3	—	—	8	2
Miscellaneous	13	9	6	6	1	1	4	5	24	5
Total	138		106		112		79		435	
Percent of Total		32		24		26		18		

* Percent of the total number of vessels within the stratum.
** Percent of the total number of vessels within the corpus of Strata VII–IV.

after adjustment is made for the floor space, between Strata VII and VI on the one hand and the much larger area of Stratum V on the other. The latter stratum is represented by only approximately one-third the quantity of pottery found in each of the two earlier strata.

A tabulation of the catalogued pieces, apart from those belonging to the Type Series, reveals a more even distribution of pottery among the four strata when differences in floor space are taken into consideration. Of a total number of 128 catalogued vessels in the corpus Stratum VII had 13 percent, Stratum VI had 24 percent, Stratum V had 47 percent, and Stratum IV had 16 percent.

Distribution According to Types of Vessels

From Table 1 it can be seen that of the 435 vessels, which are represented either by complete examples or fragments from which the type of vessel can be identified, bowls constitute the largest constituent, 27 percent of the entire corpus from the four strata. Bowls are followed in the order of frequency by storage jars and cooking pots, which constitute 16 and 15 percent, respectively, of the total. Kraters constitute 13 percent of the total assemblage of ceramic vessels. These are followed by jugs, which make up 9 percent of the total, and juglets, which account for 6 percent. The remaining vessels, such as lamps, pilgrim flasks, decanters, tripod cups, occur only sporadically in quantities of from 3 to 2 percent of the total. Five percent of the total number of vessels is classified as miscellaneous.

The order of frequency for types within the 138 vessels from Stratum VII is similar to that found to prevail for the entire corpus. Bowls and storage jars occupy the first and second places. Next come kraters, jugs, and cooking pots, although the order is different from that found for the whole. The remaining vessel types, represented by only 3 percent and under of the total of 138 forms, are at the end of the list, although there are some changes in the order of occurrence from that found in the total corpus.

The order of percentages of types for Stratum VI is remarkably similar to that for the combined four strata. Bowls and storage jars have the first place, each with 16 percent; cooking pots and kraters follow, with 15 and 14 percent respectively. The positions of jugs and juglets are reversed from those of the general list. These classifications are followed by lamps, decanters, pilgrim flasks, and tripod cups, in that order. There is, therefore, a marked similarity between the order of frequency in types of Stratum VI and that of the collection as a whole.

In Stratum V bowls are the most frequently found vessels, constituting 26 percent of the total. Cooking pots (19 percent) and storage jars (14 percent) follow; kraters (14 percent) are in fourth place, just as they are in the composite order. Juglets (10 percent) and jugs (6 percent) follow, but in the reverse order of frequency found in the total corpus. The four smaller categories of vessels—decanters, tripod cups, pilgrim flasks, and lamps—occupy the bottom of the list as they do in the two earlier strata and in the list of totals.

The sample of vessels from Stratum IV is the smallest, consisting of 79 vessels. Three of the categories—juglets, decanters, and tripod cups—are not represented within this stratum. However, the sequence of percentages in which the remaining types of vessels occur conforms exactly to that of the corpus for the four strata. The absence of juglets, decanters, and tripod cups in this stratum may be explained either by the difference in the use to which the area was put during the time of the Stratum IV occupation or by the replacement of these forms of vessels by others at the time of Stratum IV. It is also possible that the absence of these relatively rare vessels is merely an accident of discovery.

Surface Treatment

Burnishing appears as a surface treatment of 23 percent, or approximately a quarter of the ceramic repertoire from the four strata (see Table 2). The percentages of burnished wares found in each of the strata are remarkably close. Strata VII and VI each have 22 percent; in Stratum V the percentage drops to 21; Stratum IV has the highest percentage of burnished ware, 27 percent. From this even distribution it is impossible to draw any conclusions as to the relative popularity of the use of this technique of surface treatment within Strata VII-IV.

The vessel most frequently burnished is the bowl. Slightly more than half, 54 percent, of the bowls recorded are wheel burnished, on both inside and outside, or on either the inside or the outside, or on one of the sides and on the rim of the other. From a figure of 54 percent of burnished bowls in Stratum VII the rate declines to 41 percent in Stratum VI, and then rises again to 59 percent in both Strata V and IV. Thus, one can say that there is but a slight increase in the use of this treatment of the surface of bowls from the earlier strata to the later.

The figures for the occurrence of burnishing on juglets are more erratic, but the sample of these vessels is relatively small. From 25 percent of burnished juglets in Stratum VII, the figure rises to 100 percent in Stratum VI; it then declines to 55 percent in Stratum V; and there are no juglets from Stratum IV. In addition to the use of burnishing on these two types of vessels there are occasional examples of a burnished jar, jug, krater, or storage jar. These are listed under "Miscellaneous" in the table of frequencies. No examples of the use of burnishing were found on cooking pots, lamps, pilgrim flasks, decanters, or tripod cups.

The Use of Slip

Slip is used as a surface treatment on 9 percent of the vessels from Strata VII-IV (Table 3). It appears predominantly on bowls (slightly more than half of the examples); jugs and juglets occasionally are slipped; only rarely is slip recorded for a krater, decanter, or a storage jar. No other types of vessels have slip applied to the surface.

When the use of slip within the assemblages of the

TABLE 2
Burnished Vessels

Stratum	VII		VI		V		IV		Total	
	no.	*%	no	*%	no	*%	no	*%	no	*%
Bowls	22	54	7	41	17	59	17	59	63	54
Juglets	1	25	13	100	6	55	—	—	20	71
Miscellaneous	8		3		—		4		15	
Total**	31	22	23	22	23	21	21	27	98	23

* Percentage for bowls and juglets is that of all bowls or juglets in the stratum.
** Percentage for the totals is of the the total number of vessels within the stratum.

TABLE 3
The Use of Slip

Stratum	No. of Vessels	% of Total
VII	13	9
VI	13	12
V	12	11
IV	3	4
Totals	41	9

individual strata is tabulated there appears to be a noticeable decline in its use in Stratum IV. There is 9 percent of the vessels with slip in Stratum VII. This rises to 12 percent in Stratum VII and drops to 11 percent in Stratum V. But in Stratum IV only 4 percent of the vessels are recorded as displaying slip. This decline in the use of slip in Stratum IV is particularly significant since it is in Stratum IV that the use of burnishing reaches its high point.

The use of paint as a decoration is extremely rare in the corpus of pottery from Strata VII-IV. Only 7 of the vessels shown on the plates of drawings bear paint; 5 of these are from Stratum VII; the other 2 are from Stratum V.

Types of Vessels Characteristic of Each of Strata VII-IV

In making an analysis of the entire corpus of ceramic material it became apparent that certain forms appeared only in one of the four strata, while others were found in two or more of the strata. Forms that were found exclusively within the assemblage of a stratum may be taken, barring the accident of discovery, as characteristic or diagnostic of that particular stratum. Other forms seem to have had a longer life and extended without appreciable change through two, three, or even four strata. The following division of the pottery into eight groups of diagnostic forms—Strata VII, VII–VI, VI, VI–V, V, IV, VII–V, and VII–IV—provides a means for establishing the position of the various strata, or groups of strata, within the stratigraphic sequence at other excavated sites of the region. For each of the 44 Types we have described the vessel, given the figure or figures in which it appears, and cited comparative material. A summary list of correspondence appears in Table 4 (p. 50).

Stratum VII

1. Bowl of fine, burnished ware; upright, simple rim, with external ridge where rim joins the body (figs. 2:21; 3:10). Although this type of bowl is represented by only two sherds, the unusual decoration of an external ridge below the rim is distinctive. The closest parallels are to be found at Heshbon, where the type is represented by numerous examples from the fill loci of Phase 1 (Bowl Type 13, *Heshbon*, pl. 3:161–80). The diameters of the Heshbon bowls measure within the range of .18 to .23 m.; our two bowls have diameters of .20 m. and .24 m. Wheel burnishing is common at Heshbon for this type, as is the decoration of red and black bands of paint (*Heshbon*, 36). Lugenbeal and Sauer have listed possible parallels from the Adoni Nur tomb in ʿAmman, Sâliyeh, and Dhiban, but conclude that none of these parallels is as certain as one would like (*Heshbon*, 37). Parallels to our bowls from sites in Palestine proper are Hazor IV (*Hazor* 1: pl. 69:30, Samaria ware burnished on the interior and exterior) and Hazor VA (*Hazor* 2: pl. 93:13, burnished on the interior). Mention should be made of a closed hemispherical bowl of thin ware found in Hazor VII (*Hazor* 3-4: pl. 180:9), but this example has black-brown decoration on the exterior.

2. Bowl with straight sidewall and simple rim (fig. 2:22, 24, 28, 29). The bowl is burnished on the outside, as in the examples fig. 2:22 and 24, or on both inside and outside, as in fig. 2:28 and 29. The base is not preserved in these examples but a complete vessel with an analogous rim (but unburnished) from Stratum VII (fig. 2:27) has a thick, flat base. A parallel is to be seen in Hazor V (*Hazor* 1: pl. 67:11), a bowl burnished on the exterior. The form is also known at Tell el-Farʿah 2 (*RB* 58:415, fig. 11:10; 60:569, fig. 8:10, a bowl with a red band painted on the rim). At Samaria this type of bowl was very common (*SS* 3: fig. 13:1-3; the bowl shown in pl. 13:1 is from locus E 207 = Period VI). It is said to have been rare in Periods I and II, but common by Period IV and continued so through Periods V and VI, and then to have gone out of use (*SS* 3: 141). Burnishing, however, is said to be rare on these bowls. Pieces from this type of vessel were used for fifty of the Harvard ostraca (*SS* 3: 141 and 469). From Megiddo III–II there comes a bowl of similar sidewall and rim, but wheel burnished (*Megiddo* 1: pl. 24:42; cf. pl. 24:40, 41, for examples without burnishing). It may be of some significance that this type goes out of use after Samaria Period VI and at our site after Stratum VII.

An unburnished example was found at Joya, Lebanon (Chapman, fig. 24:238). Similar bowls came from Dhiban (*Dhiban* 2: fig. 2:29) and Khaldé, Tomb 121 nos. 29, 30 (*Khaldé* 71).

3. Bowl with pedestal base (fig. 3:18). From the fragment of this form it is difficult to determine whether it belongs to a chalice or to a footed cup (such as *Megiddo* 1, 33:13, of Stratum III). It is also possible that the vessel was a lamp with a high-footed base (*SS* 3: fig. 27:6, from locus E 207 = Period VI).

4. Krater with neck ridge to which handles are attached (fig. 1:7). An early form of this krater appears in Hazor VIII (*Hazor* 2: 56:4). From Megiddo IV–III is a similar form (*Megiddo* 1: 28:88), which is thought to be a development of an earlier multi-handle form found in Stratum V (see *Megiddo* 1: 32:167).

5. Krater with everted rim and diagonally flattened lip (fig. 1:1–3, 5).

6. Ovoid juglet with tubular spout (fig. 5:9). A similar form was found in Hazor VI (*Hazor* 3-4: pl. 184:16).

7. Juglet with flat base (figs. 4:34; 5:7, 8). This rare form of a dipper apparently has as its successor the common form of juglet with a rounded base found in Strata VI and V.

8. Storage jar with externally thickened rim and groove on shoulder (fig. 4:26).

9. Bowl with plain upright rim and pierced lug handles (fig. 2:23).

10. Pilgrim flask, with two symmetrical sides to body (fig. 4:30, 33). Hazor VI produced a fragment of neck and handles of a pilgrim flask of similar profile, but only one view is shown in the drawing (*Hazor* 1: 52:25).

11. Pilgrim flask with asymmetrical body (fig. 5:17). This flask from Stratum VII could be related to the later form that appears in Stratum IV (fig. 11:17), in which the larger hemisphere is deeper.

Strata VII-VI

12. Tripod cup with perforations in the upper half of the wall (figs. 1:19; 5:11, 12, 21; 8:25). Examples of this type of the tripod cup are from Hazor (*Hazor* 3-4: pls. 171:16, 17 (XB); 208:34 (IX); 2: pl. 55:43, 44 (VIII); 2: 63:34 (VII); 3-4: pl. 180:13 (VII); 3-4: pl. 249:19 (VI); 1: pl. 54:18 (V)), Megiddo (*Megiddo* 1: pl. 23:22), Tell el-Farʿah (*RB* 58: 411, fig. 10:16; 62: 585, fig. 19:1). Other examples from Samaria, Gezer, Lachish, Jericho, Kamid el-Loz, Tell el-Ghassil have been listed and discussed by the writer in "On the Use of the Tripod Cup," *Ugaritica VI*: 427–34. Since the publication of this study of more than a hundred tripod cups, other examples have been published from Dhiban (*Dhiban* 2: fig. 16:15–18, from Tomb J 5), Tell el-Kheleifeh (*Kheleifeh* 32, fig. 3:5–12, Level IV = seventh and sixth centuries), and Buseirah (*Buseirah* 2: fig. 15:1; 3, fig. 7:18). This new material has not altered the conclusions of the 1969 study in *Ugaritica VI*, that this form seems to have had its origin in the Jordan Valley rift and the adjacent areas. The chronological priority of the "deep" perforated type of cup of Strata VII-VI over that of the "shallow" type found in Stratum V seems to be established by the stratigraphy of Tell es-Saʿidiyeh, even though one fragment of a deep type of cup is recorded from Stratum V (*Ugaritica VI*, fig. 1:5). One must conclude that this one example of the dominant type of the two earlier strata had survived into a period when the "shallow" type came into general use.

13. Jug with simple, incurving rim, grooved externally (fig. 7:23, 25).

14. Chalice (fig. 7:30). The profile of the cup of the chalice from Megiddo II (*Megiddo* 1: pl. 33:8) is fairly like that of our example, but unfortunately the base is not preserved. Another example from Megiddo, Stratum III, is analogous to ours in shape (*Megiddo* 1: 33:12), but it has yellow, light red, and black decoration. Two painted chalices of similar profile come from locus E 207 (= Period VI) at Samaria (*SS* 3: fig. 25:1, 4).

The pottery of Stratum VI seems to have fewer unique forms than does that of any of the four strata under consideration. Quantitatively the distinctive ware of this stratum is minimal. However, Stratum VI shares a number of distinctive forms with Stratum VII on the one hand and with Stratum V on the other.

Strata VI-V

15. Bowl of fine ware, wide base, straight side and simple rim (figs. 6:1; 10:1, 2). Examples of this type have come from Samaria, locus E 207 (*SS* 3: 18:6), Hazor VII (*Hazor* 1: 49:23), Hazor V (*Hazor* 1: 67:24), Tell el-Farʿah 2 (*RB* 60: 569, fig. 8:11), Sarepta C (*Sarepta*, pl. 38:3), and Tyre (*Tyre*, pl. 1:1, 2).

16. Burnished juglet with handle from shoulder to rim, usually of red to brown ware (figs. 7:4–12; 11:1,

5, 8). This common type of dipper is known from Megiddo IV–I (*Megiddo* 1: 2:55, 64, 65), locus E 207 at Samaria (*SS* 3: 23:11), Hazor VB (*Hazor* 2: 79:23), Beth-shan IV (*Beth Shan*, 70:13, 16), as well as from Tell Beit Mirsim A2, Lachish III, Arad VIII, Beer-Sheba II, and Beth-Shemesh IIc (*BASOR* 224: figs. 1:15; 2:15; 3:15; 4:15; 5:15).

17. Burnished black juglet, generally smaller than those listed above (figs. 7:1–3; 11:9, 10). The parallels are numerous; among them are examples from locus E 207 at Samaria (*SS* 3: 23:2, 3), Megiddo III–II (*Megiddo* 1: 2:48, 49), Tell el-Farʿah 2 (*RB* 60: 569, fig. 8:1), and Hazor VA (*Hazor* 2: 86:16, 17). It is also found at the eighth-century Judahite sites (*BASOR* 224: figs. 1–5).

18. Decanter with narrow neck and sharply profiled rim with two ridges (figs. 7:26–29; 11:11–13, 15). This form appears in two wares: a gray, metallic-hard ware (figs. 7:29; 11:11–13), and a softer tan to reddish brown ware, usually with thicker walls. Among the parallels are those from Megiddo IV–I (*Megiddo* 1: 2:66; 4:99–110; see p. 163, where the form is said to have appeared in profusion in Stratum III), Tell el-Farʿah 2 (*RB* 59: 571, fig. 9:7; 58: 415, fig. 11:23), Hazor IV–V (*Hazor* 1: 72:7), Samaria locus E 207 (*SS* 3: 22:1, p. 167), Beth-shan IV (*Beth Shan*, 71:7). In southern Palestine it appears at Lachish III, Arad VIII, and Beer-Sheba II (*BASOR* 224: figs. 2:13; 3:13; 4:13.)

19. Storage jar with three handles and cup/funnel (figs. 9:13, 14:13). This distinctive type of vessel is found in Strata IV–I at Megiddo (*Megiddo* 1: 12:61, 62), Stratum VII at Hazor (*Hazor* 3-4: 215:23), Beth-shan IV (*Beth Shan*, 72:3; cf. Beth-shan V, *Beth Shan*, 31:14), Tell el-Farʿah 2 (*RB* 59: 571, fig. 9:5), Samaria Periods IV–VI (*SS* 3: 31:1–3; 1a, 1b, and 3 are from locus E 207; see p. 192). Similar types from Lachish III, Arad VIII, Beer-Sheba II, and Beth Shemesh IIc are listed in *BASOR* 224: figs. 2:10; 3:10; 4:10; 5:10.

20. Krater with articulated neck and incurving rim, generally thickened on the exterior (figs. 8:7, 9, 11; 12:10, 12). The following parallels are noted: Hazor VI (*Hazor* 3-4: 215:8; *Hazor* 2: 68:5, 6, 9, 11), Hazor VA (*Hazor* 2: 94:7; *Hazor* 3-4: 226:14), Samaria Period VI and common in locus E 207 (*SS* 3: 21:7, p. 164), Tell el-Farʿah 2 (*RB* 59: 557, fig. 3:4), and Dhiban (*Dhiban* 2: fig. 1:41).

Stratum V

It is apparent from the following listing of ceramic forms that there was a change in the ceramic repertoire during the period of time represented by Stratum V. Forms unknown in the two preceding periods were introduced. The following forms were found only within Stratum V:

21. Hemispherical bowl of fine ware; upright, simple rim; burnished on exterior (fig. 10:3). This extremely thin bowl is found at Megiddo IV–III (*Megiddo* 1: 24:55), Hazor V (*Hazor* 1: 74:13), and in Period VI at Samaria (*SS* 3: 18:5; 10:12).

22. Bowl with direct, simple rim, and flat base (fig. 10:7). This example is burnished on the inside and over the rim. Parallels may be seen in a form common in Period VI and locus E 207 at Samaria (*SS* 3: 13:7), and at Dhiban, (*Dhiban* 2: fig. 1:73).

23. Bowl with simple, everted rim (fig. 10:22).

24. Shallow bowl with slightly concave side and simple rim; ring base (fig. 10:23). The form occurs at Samaria (there are three examples from locus E 207) in Period VI (*SS* 3: 13:11). It appears in Tell el-Farʿah 2 (*RB* 59: 569, fig. 8:8).

25. Bowl with thickened incurving rim and external ridge; flat base (fig. 10:16).

26. Deep, closed bowl with externally enlarged rim and rounded lip (fig. 10:27). This example is burnished on the inside and on the rim.

27. Krater with differentiated neck; rim externally thickened and flattened (fig. 12:7, 9, 14—the last with four handles). Hazor VA has an analogous krater, but with a somewhat thicker rim (*Hazor* 2: 83:10). See also *Hazor* 2: 68:9, from Stratum VI; *Hazor* 3–4: 183:10, from Stratum VI.

28. Jug with high neck, simple rim, and strainer spout (fig. 11:23). A fragment of a strainer appeared in Stratum VI (fig. 7:16) and could have belonged to this type of jug. Similar jugs have come from Hazor VA (*Hazor* 3–4: 228:1) and even from the earlier Stratum VI (*Hazor* 1: 52:20; 65:1), as well as from Megiddo V (*Megiddo* 1: 6:153).

29. Jug with a high neck and a high ring base (fig. 11:22).

30. Pilgrim flask with pinced mouth; decorated with painted bands on one side (fig. 11:18).

31. Asymmetrical pilgrim flask (fig. 11:17). A comparable example appears in Tell Keisan V (*Tell Keisan*, pl. 42:7).

32. Storage jar with broad shoulder at sharp angle to body; thickened rim (fig. 14:11).

33. Tripod cup, "shallow" and without perforations (fig. 10:28, 29). Similar examples have been found in tombs at ʿAmman, Sahab, Meqabelein, Irbid (*Ugaritica VI*: 427–28) and on the mound at Heshbon (*Heshbon*, pl. 5:280–85). See also *Hazor* 3–4: 182:22, for example from Stratum VI. Hazor VIII also has examples (*Hazor* 2: 54:20–22); eight others are found in the Sahab tomb (*Sahab*: 98, fig. 4:24–30).

Strata V–IV

34. Storage vessel of "hole" mouth type; incurving rim, enlarged externally and flattened (figs. 14:17, 18; 16:7, 9, 10; 17:31, 32). There is some variation in the shape of the rim but all are incurving. Burnishing appears on the rim, both inside and outside, of fig. 14:17; the outside of the fragment shown in fig. 16:10 is burnished. The type corresponds to Jar Type 1 at Heshbon (*Heshbon,* pl. 6–7: 333–75).

Stratum IV

35. Carinated bowl of "Assyrian ware" (figs. 15:12, 14; 17:8). Two examples are burnished on the outside only (figs. 15:12; 17:8, on rim) and one is burnished both inside and outside (fig. 15:14). This type of bowl appears at Tell el-Farʿah 1 (*RB* 59: 419, fig. 12:1–4) in Period VII at Samaria (*SS* 3: 11:22), at Buseirah (*Buseirah* 2: fig. 15:2), and at Tell el-Kheleifeh (*Kheleifeh*, 35, fig. 4:1, 2, 7, 8) and at Heshbon (*Heshbon,* pl. 5:273).

36. Bowl with upright sides and rim externally thickened; burnished on the inside and sometimes on the rim or the entire outside (figs. 15:5, 7, 10, 11, 13; 17:4, 7). Examples appear in Hazor IV (*Hazor* 1: 58:2; 2: 98:13; 3–4: 254:15) and at Samaria Period VII (*SS* 3: 11:1–7; only 1, 3, 5 are burnished). The type is characteristic of late Iron II sites in south Palestine (Miriam and Yohanan Aharoni. "The Stratification of Judahite Sites in the 8th and 7th Centuries B.C.E.," *BASOR* 224: 85–89, figs. 6:1; 7:1; 8:1).

37. Shallow bowl with rim externally thickened (figs. 15:16; 17:1). Compare *Heshbon,* pl. 4:223.

38. Bowl of heavy ware, grooved on the side (fig. 15:9). Compare Heshbon Bowl Type 25 (*Heshbon,* pl. 4:231–41).

39. Krater with rim enlarged, then flattened or depressed (fig. 15:15, 17, 19, 21).

40. Bowl with external ridge below the rim (fig. 15:23).

41. Lamp with flat base (fig. 16:18). Parallels may be seen in the Sahab tomb (*Sahab,* fig. 4: 82–86), Samaria (*SS* 3: 27:3), Megiddo III–I (*Megiddo* 1: 37:8), Lachish (*Lachish* 3: 286, Class L. 11, Type 660—sixth century), and Dhiban (*Dhiban* 2: fig. 23:21).

Strata VII–V

42. Bowl with carinated or angular profile, simple rim, usually burnished inside and outside (Stratum VII: fig. 3:5, 8, 9; Stratum VI: fig. 6:3, 8; Stratum V: fig. 10:9, 11). Parallels to this bowl are found in Hazor VI (*Hazor* 1: 51:26) and Hazor V (*Hazor* 1: 53:4; 54:8). The three examples of this type from Stratum VII exhibit a thickening of the sidewall at the point of carination. This feature is to be seen in two ninth-century examples, one from Hazor VIII (*Hazor* 2: 55:13) and another from Hazor VII (*Hazor* 3–4: 180:3).

Strata VII–IV

43. Cooking pot with thickened rim grooved externally (Stratum VII: fig. 3:22–25; Stratum VI: fig. 6:31–37; Stratum V: fig. 13:4, 9–15, 18–21; Stratum IV: figs. 15:25–28, 17:12). From the examples of bodies that have been preserved it is evident that its shape is squat and rounded without carination and has two handles. There is no whole example without handles. There are many variations in the form of the rim as to thickness and the position of the groove on the outside.

According to Amiran this type of cooking pot predominates at Hazor from Stratum VII onward and is not found earlier (R. Amiran, *Ancient Pottery of the Holy Land*, 227). The examples are numerous: Hazor VI (*Hazor* 1: 52:9–11; 2: 69:11; 3–4: 215:9), Hazor V (*Hazor* 1: 55:4, 7–10), Hazor VB (*Hazor* 2: 79:20), Hazor VA (*Hazor* 2: 85:1–5, 7–9; 3–4: 227:15–17), Megiddo IV–I (*Megiddo* 1: 39:1, 3–8, 10–12), Bethshan IV (*Beth Shan,* 69:16), Tell el-Farʿah 2 (*RB* 59: 571, fig. 9:3). At Samaria this form appears first in Period IV and becomes common in Period VI (*SS* 3:117, 191). For examples from Period IV see *SS* 3: fig. 6:39, 40; for locus E 207 (Period VI) see ibid., fig. 30:4–6, 20–24). See also *Heshbon,* pl. 6, no. 332; other generally simpler forms are characteristic of the Heshbon repertoire (*Heshbon,* pl. 6:314–25). Southern examples from Tell Beit Mirsim A2 and Lachish III are cited by Miriam and Yohanan Aharoni in "The Stratification of Judahite Sites," *BASOR* 224: figs. 1:3, 2:3.

44. Ridged-neck storage jar. (Stratum VII: fig. 4:1–4, 6; Stratum VI: fig. 9:7, 11, 12, Stratum V: fig. 14:1–5; Stratum IV: fig. 16:3). The ridged-neck jar is usually associated with an ovoid body (R. Amiran,

TABLE 4
Summary of Correspondences

Type	Samaria	Far'ah	Megiddo	Hazor
Stratum VII				
1				VA, IV
2	IV–VI	2	III–II	V
3	VI (?)		III (?)	
4			IV–III	VIII (?)
6				VI
10				VI
Strata VII–VI				
12		3-middle	IV–II	XB–V
Stratum VI				
14	VI		III–II	
Strata VI–V				
15	VI	2		VII, V
16	VI		IV–I	VB
17	VI	2	III–II	VA
18	VI	2	IV–I	V, IV
19	IV–VI	2	IV–I	VII
20	VI	2		VI, VA
Stratum V				
21	VI		IV–III	V
22	VI			
24	VI	2		
27				VI, VA
28		V		VI, VA
33				VIII, VI
Stratum IV				
35	VII	1		
36	VII			IV
41			III–I	
Strata VII–V				
42				VIII–V
Strata VII–IV				
43	IV–VI	2	IV–I	VII, VI, V
44	IV–VI, VII	2	IV–I	VI, V

TABLE 5
List of Types

Type	Fig.
1	2:21; 3:10
2	2:22, 24, 28, 29
3	3:18
4	1:7
5	1:1–3, 5
6	5:9
7	4:34; 5:7, 8
8	4:26
9	2:23
10	4:30, 33
11	5:17
12	1:19; 5:11, 12, 21; 8:25
13	7:23, 25
14	7:30
15	6:1; 10:1, 2
16	7:4–12; 11:1, 5, 8
17	7:1–3; 11:9, 10
18	7:26–29; 11:11–13, 15
19	9:13; 14:13
20	8:7, 9, 11; 12:10, 12
21	10:3
22	10:7
23	10:22
24	10:23
25	10:16
26	10:27
27	12:7, 9, 14
28	11:23
29	11:22
30	11:18
31	11:17
32	14:11
33	10:28, 29
34	14:17, 18; 16:7, 9, 10; 17:31, 32
35	15:12, 14; 17:8
36	15:5, 7, 10, 11, 13; 17:4, 7
37	15:16; 17:1
38	15:9
39	15:15, 17, 19, 21
40	15:23
41	16:18
42	3:5, 8, 9; 6:3, 8; 10:9, 11
43	3:22–25; 6:31–37; 13:4, 9–15, 18–21; 15:25–28; 17:12
44	4:1–4, 6; 9:7, 11, 12; 14:1–5; 16:3

Ancient Pottery of the Holy Land, 241). Fig. 9:11 has a pronounced shoulder set at a sharp angle to what appears to have been an ovoid body; see similar profile from locus E 207 at Samaria (*SS* 3: 21:5).

Examples of this storage jar appear at the following sites: Tell el-Far'ah 2 (*RB* 59: 571, fig. 9:6; cf. also an Iron II form in *RB* 55: 583, fig. 4:8), Hazor VI (*Hazor* 2: 71:11), Hazor V (*Hazor* 1: 68:3), Hazor VA (*Hazor* 2: 89:1), Samaria Period IV (*SS* 3: 6:14), Samaria locus E 207, Period VI (*SS* 3: 163, where it is said to have been the most common type in that locus), Samaria Period VII (*SS* 3: fig. 11:24), Megiddo IV–II (*Megiddo* 1: 15:76), Megiddo IV–I (*Megiddo* 1: 15:77), Beth-shan IV (*Beth Shan*, 70:5).

Notes on Comparisons with Sites in Other Areas

At this point of our study of the pottery from Strata VII–IV at Tell es-Sa'idiyeh, situated within the Jordan Valley, we shall seek to ascertain what relationships existed between the ceramic traditions at our site and those of roughly contemporary sites in other geographical areas. An effort has been made to look at other assemblages for forms analogous to ours for the purpose of assessing cultural relations and contacts. Four general areas have been considered: Transjordan, Phoenicia, South Palestine, and North Palestine. References have already been listed for parallel forms to the vessels included in the 44 Types. Included in the following discussions are some additional references to analogous forms for the figures on the plates which are not included in the Types. From these comparisons we shall seek to establish the position of Tell es-Sa'idiyeh within the pattern of the regionalism of the area during the time span of Strata VII–IV.

Transjordan

DHIBAN

In addition to the correspondences at Dhiban to our Types 12, 20, 33, and 41, it should be noted that, although many of the cooking pot rims found at Dhiban are without parallel at Tell es-Sa'idiyeh, the very common grooved rim of our site (fig. 3:20) appears also at Dhiban (*Dhiban* 2: fig. 1:17, 18). Both sites have lamps with rounded bases (compare *Dhiban* 2: fig. 15:5 with out fig. 5:13, from Stratum VII). Only a few storage jar types are common to the two sites, but *Dhiban* 2: fig. 1:1 may be compared to our fig. 4:21; and *Dhiban* 2: fig. 1:2, 3 resemble our fig. 4:15). The differences between the two assemblages are in general more pronounced than the similarities. Although the absence of certain forms in an assemblage may be accidental, it may be useful to list certain observations on missing types and quantitative assessments. The dipper juglet which is so common at Tell es-Sa'idiyeh (figs. 16:1–13; 21:1–15), is matched by only a single example from Dhiban (*Dhiban* 2: fig. 21:11). The decanter of Stratum VI (fig. 7:26–29) and Stratum V (fig. 11:11–13, 15) is not represented at all in either the pottery from the tell or among the vessels found in the tombs at Dhiban. On the other hand the so-called Cypro-Phoenician painted juglet, which Tushingham assigns to the eighth and seventh centuries (*Dhiban* 2: 89 and fig. 16:1–13), is without a single example at Tell es-Sa'idiyeh. Our pilgrim flasks (fig. 11:17–18, from Stratum V) are not found at Dhiban.

BUSEIRAH

We have mentioned above the similarities to our tripod cup, Type 12, and to the carinated bowl, Type 35. A further correspondence between the two sites may be seen in a form of rim belonging to a holemouth storage jar. Although the rim is preserved for our example from Stratum IV (fig. 17:31), it could well have belonged to a cylindrical jar like the fully preserved example from Buseirah (*Buseirah* 2: fig. 14:10). Except for the correspondences in a few nondiagnostic bowl forms, there would appear to have been little in common between the traditions of ceramic forms at Tell es-Sa'idiyeh and those at Buseirah.

A marked difference between the assemblages found at the two sites is to be seen in the manner of surface decoration. Paint, rarely used on pots at Tell es-Sa'idiyeh, is common on the Buseirah vessels, particularly in the form of red and black bands. The grooved rim of the cooking pot, so common in each of the four strata, is not illustrated in the plates of pottery forms from Buseirah. Kraters, common at our site in all four strata, are missing in the published Buseirah repertoire.

HESHBON

Among the forms coming from the fill loci of Phase 1 at Heshbon there are correspondences to types from Tell es-Sa'idiyeh, such as Types 1, 34, 35, 37, 38, and 43 mentioned above. In addition to these the following parallels are noted: fig. 15:4—*Heshbon*, pls. 1–2:1–93; fig. 15:30—*Heshbon*, pl. 5:309; fig. 17:2—*Heshbon*, pl. 9A:504–15; fig. 17:19—*Heshbon*, pl. 8:424; fig. 17:10—*Heshbon*, pl. 2A:142. It is to be noted that these correspondences with forms found at Heshbon are, with the exception of the bowl with a ridge around the rim (Type 1), from Stratum IV. Lugenbeal and Sauer have noted similar geographical differences between Heshbon and sites on the West Bank: "Thus, most of the typical West Bank forms are missing at Heshbon: black juglets, decanters, jugs, holemouth jars, profiled- or rilled-rim cooking pots, storage jars, heavy wheel-burnished bowls, stump-based lamps. On the other hand, the most dominant types discussed above are not represented on the West Bank, except in occasional instances" (*Heshbon*, 64).

TELL EL-KHELEIFEH

The perforated tripod cup, Type 12, is found at Tell el-Kheleifeh but the profiles of the wall and the rim of the Kheleifeh examples are different from ours. The "Assyrian" type bowl, Type 35, is found in Stratum IV, but it is decorated with bands of paint. Apart from these two types of vessels there are, as far as we can see from the published material, virtually no forms that are shared by the two sites.

UMM EL-BIYARA

The pottery from the excavations at Umm el-Biyara, near Petra, assigned by the excavator, Crystal-M. Bennett, to the seventh century (*Umm el-Biyara*, 402) contains only a few items that provide links with Tell es-Sa'idiyeh. The profile of the rim from a large jar with four handles (*Umm el-Biyara*, fig. 2:7) displays the same kind of external thickening as the fragment shown in our fig. 16:7, from Stratum IV. Also similar is a sherd in fig. 3:10 of the Umm el-Biyara publication. The bowl with an angular profile and externally thickened rim from Stratum V, shown in our fig. 10:21, resembles *Umm el-Biyara*, fig. 2:6; cf. also fig. 3:4. One further comparison may be seen between the bowl in our fig. 10:26 and *Umm el-Biyara*, fig. 2:10.

'AMMAN TOMBS

Tomb A at 'Amman (= "Group A") has four of the tripod cups without holes (*QDAP* 11: 70, nos. 10–13), but they are more elaborate in profile and in decoration than our examples from Stratum V. Nothing else that can be compared with our repertoire of pottery makes its appearance in this tomb, or in Tomb B. Similarly the Adoni Nur tomb in 'Amman has tripod cups (*APEF* 6: 48–72, esp. fig. 21:77–81), but they are of a type more like that found in Tomb A than that found in our Stratum V. 'Amman Tomb C (*ADAJ* 1: 37–40) has a repertoire of 39 vessels. With the exception of such nondiagnostic pieces as the straight-sided bowl with simple rim (fig. 1:1, 3) and the simple dipper juglet (fig. 1:20, 21), there are no forms similar to those found in Strata VII–IV at Tell es-Sa'idiyeh. One example of the tripod cup without perforations does appear (fig. 1:11), but the rim is sharply inturned.

SAHAB TOMB

Of the eight unperforated tripod cups of Type 33, all but two have an incurving rim (*Sahab*, fig. 4:24–30). The other two cups (fig. 4:22, 23) differ also in profile from the Tell es-Sa'idiyeh forms. The remainder of the pottery in the tomb seems to differ from that of our corpus and, with the exception of the Type 41 lamp mentioned above, there are no convincing similarities.

In addition to the pottery from the sites mentioned above there is Iron Age ceramic material which has been reported but not published from Tell el-Mazār (University of Jordan excavations, since 1977, directed by Khair Nimr Yassine) and Ṭabaqat Faḥl-Pella (The College of Wooster and The University of Sydney excavations, since 1979, under the direction of Robert H. Smith and Basil Hennessy). The site of Deir 'Allā should provide parallels to our types but only pottery from Phases A–L has been published in H. J. Franken, *Excavations at Tell Deir Allā*, 1969. Our repertoire belongs to later phases. Excavations carried out in Iron Age levels at Tell el-Rumeith have been reported (*RB* 70: 406–11; *RB* 75: 98–105) but no pottery has as yet been published.

From this survey of comparative materials at the Transjordanian sites of Dhiban, Buseirah, Heshbon, Tell el-Kheleifeh, Umm el-Biyara, as well as in the Iron Age tombs of 'Amman and Sahab, it is apparent that there are relatively few direct links between the ceramic tradition of the middle Jordan Valley and the sites on the Jordanian plateau to the East and to the South, reaching down to the Gulf of 'Aqabah. Of all the vessels found at Tell es-Sa'idiyeh, the tripod cup seems to be the form with most correspondences in Transjordan. As for other ceramic forms there is an occasional correspondence, but the differences far outnumber the similarities.

Phoenicia

When the pottery from Strata VII–IV is compared with that found at the Phoenician site of Sarepta there are a few correlations. Stratum C of Sounding Y at Sarepta, dated to ca. 850/825–650 (?) B.C. (*Sarepta*, 615), consists of Substratum C2 (the earlier) and C1, with a division between these two phases that has been placed at ca. 750/725 B.C. (*Sarepta*, 608). The most conspicuous example of what might be said to be a common form is the bowl of thin ware with simple rim, straight sides and a broad base, which has been mentioned in our description of Type 15. A similar form of the thin-ware bowl of this shape (F-1) appears in Substratum C1 at Sarepta (*Sarepta*, pl. 38:3), although these examples from coastal Phoenician are decorated with burnished red slip. This type of bowl has its highest frequency in Substratum C1.

Another correspondence is to be seen in a parallel to the large bowl with rim enlarged and flattened on top (fig. 2:8) found in Stratum VII at Tell es-Saʿidiyeh. In Substratum C1 at Sarepta there is an analogous vessel (*Sarepta*, pl. 37:3), but it lacks the exterior and interior burnishing found on the Tell es-Saʿidiyeh bowls of this form. Similar parallels to our fine-ware bowls appear at Tyre (*Tyre*, pl. 1:1, 2) in Stratum 1 (dated to ca. 700 B.C., *Tyre*, 67). At Khaldé III there is little that can be compared to the corpus from Tell es-Saʿidiyeh. The straight-sided bowls, nos. 29 and 30 from Tomb 121 (*Khaldé*, 71) have been cited under the description of Type 2. The wide use of paint as decoration on the Khaldé pottery is in marked contrast to the rarity of painted decoration found on our vessels (p. 46). At Tell Keisan, a Palestinian site with Phoenician affinities, there appeared in level 5 an asymmetrical pilgrim flask (*Tell Keisan*, pl. 42:7) comparable to the one from our Stratum V (Type 31, fig. 11:17), although ours is without the painted concentric circles found on the example from Tell Keisan.

The ceramic styles that prevailed in Phoenicia during the eighth and seventh centuries of the Iron Age do not seem to have exerted any major influence upon the potters at our site in the Jordan Valley. The few specific correspondences mentioned above—the thin-ware bowl, the bowl with straight sides, and the asymmetrical pilgrim flask—could have been derived at Tell es-Saʿidiyeh from Palestinian sites on the West Bank, at which they appear frequently. The occurrence at Tell es-Saʿidiyeh of the grooved-rim cooking pot throughout Strata VII–IV, the wide representation of decanters in Strata VI–V, and the presence of other characteristic forms that do not occur at Phoenician sites serve further to support the independence of the Tell es-Saʿidiyeh tradition from that of Phoenicia.

Southern Palestine

The study made by M. and Y. Aharoni of the ceramic forms found in Judahite sites which were occupied in the eighth and seventh-sixth centuries is useful as we seek to assess the relationship between Tell es-Saʿidiyeh and sites in the southern part of Palestine ("The Stratification of Judahite Sites," *BASOR* 224: 73–90). In the description of the Types we have listed some correspondences with the Aharoni pottery types for their eighth-century sites (Tell Beit Mirsim A2, Lachish III, Arad VIII, Beer-Sheba II, and Beth Shemesh IIc). They are juglets Types 16 and 17, decanter Type 18, storage jar Type 19, and the shallow cooking pot Type 43. The characteristic Judahite forms of the eighth century missing at Tell es-Saʿidiyeh are: the deep cooking pot with grooved or ridged rim (Aharoni's no. 4), the *lammelekh* storage jar (no. 6), hole-mouth storage jar with ridged rim (no. 8), *amphoriskos* (no. 11), and lamp with high base (no. 17). The differences between the Tell es-Saʿidiyeh assemblages and those of the Judahite sites are greater than the similarities. It is interesting that, with the one exception of the shallow cooking pot with grooved rim, Type 43, no obvious parallels to the eighth-century forms in the South occur at Tell es-Saʿidiyeh later than Stratum V, and most of the correspondences are found exclusively within Strata VI–V.

For the sites with strata belonging to the second half of the seventh to the beginning of the sixth century (Lachish II, Arad VII–VI, Tell Masos, Ramat Raḥel, En-gedi, Meṣad Ḥashavyahu) the only clear parallel to our assemblages is the bowl with externally enlarged rim, our Type 36, which is found exclusively within Stratum IV. The other characteristic forms from southern Palestine are missing at Tell es-Saʿidiyeh. Thus in the seventh and the first part of the sixth centuries the correspondences between our site and those of Judah are even fewer than they were in the eighth century.

Northern Palestine

SAMARIA

Very strong correspondences are to be found between our ceramic forms and those at Samaria. Fifteen types, Types 2, 14–22, 24, 35, 36, 43, and 44, have been found to have analogous forms in Periods IV–VII at Samaria. In addition to the items mentioned in the descriptions of Types five other correspondences should be mentioned. Our bowl from Stratum VII (fig. 2:8) has a parallel from Samaria locus E 207 (*SS* 3: fig. 13:16) and three bowls from Stratum VI (figs. 6:12; 6:10; 6:17) have parallels from locus E 207 (*SS* 3: figs. 13:17; 16:2; 20:1 respectively). Our jug shown in fig. 7:21 may be compared to the Samaria example shown in *SS* 3: fig. 22:6, also from E 207. All the parallels cited, with the exception of those to Types 35 and 36, forms which are peculiar to our Stratum IV, have examples in locus E 207, "an Israelite shrine" (*SS* 3: 137–39; see

137, n. 1, for list of 155 objects which came from E 207, drawn in figs. 13–31). The correspondences with the pottery at Samaria are distributed over the four strata, Strata VII–IV, with by far the greater number appearing in Strata VII–V. Some outstanding differences, however, between the two sites are to be seen in the absence of kraters at Samaria and the lack of the high-foot bowl (*SS* 3: 14:2–7, 10–13) at Tell es-Saʿidiyeh.

TELL EL-FARʿAH

Types 2, 12, 15, 17–20, 24, 35, 43, 44 found in Strata VII–IV at Tell es-Saʿidiyeh have parallels at Tell el-Farʿah. With the exception of the tripod cup Type 12 and the "Assyrian" bowl Type 35, all the parallels from Tell el-Farʿah appear in level 2, a stratum which is generally equated with Periods IV–VI at Samaria. The perforated tripod cup, Type 12, appears in both level 3 and the intermediate level. The other correspondence found outside of level 2 is the "Assyrian" bowl Type 35, from level 1. At Tell es-Saʿidiyeh this form is found exclusively in Stratum IV.

MEGIDDO

In addition to the Megiddo forms listed in descriptions of the types of vessels (Types 2–4, 12, 14, 16–19, 21, 28, 41, 43, 44) three other analogous pieces should be mentioned. Our bowl from Stratum VI shown in fig. 6:4 may be compared with that in *Megiddo* 1: pl. 25:59, which appears in Megiddo IV–II. A juglet from Stratum VI (fig. 7:22) has a parallel in *Megiddo* 1: pl. 3:74, from Megiddo IV–III. The lamp from Stratum V, shown in fig. 14:19 corresponds in type to a lamp from Megiddo III (*Megiddo* 1: 37:16). With the exception of the Megiddo counterpart to our Type 28, which appears in Megiddo V, the Megiddo material cited is to be found in one or more of the strata IV–I. Most correspondences come from Megiddo III (36%); Stratum II has 26%; Stratum IV, 21%; Stratum I, 15%. One noticeable contrast between the repertoires of the two sites is the presence at Megiddo of burnished mushroom-lip jugs (*Megiddo* 1: pl. 3:78–79) and red-burnished trefoil-mouth jugs (*Megiddo* 1: pl. 3:83–86).

HAZOR

From the summary of correspondences in Table 4 it is apparent that parallels have been found at Hazor for our Types 1, 2, 4, 6, 10, 12, 15–21, 27, 28, 33, 36, 42–44. However the distribution of these forms at Hazor extends all the way from Stratum XB through Stratum IV. The range can be narrowed somewhat if we exclude ten examples of alleged correspondences (bowl of Type 1 in IV, possible krater of Type 4 in VIII, tripod cup of Type 12 in XB–VII, bowl of Type 15 in VII, storage jar of Type 12 in VII, decanter of Type 18 in IV, tripod cup of Type 33 in VIII, bowl of Type 36 in IV, bowl of Type 42 in VIII and VII, cooking pot Type 43 in VII) the remaining 26 references cited are to vessels assigned to Strata VI and V. Although our Strata VII–IV seem to correspond in some degree to Hazor VI–V, it is difficult to refine further the relationship of the individual strata of the two sites. It is apparent, however, that the two sites share common ceramic traditions.

Summary

From the comparisons we have listed (see Table 4) in the preceding section it appears that connecting links are to be found most frequently with the sites of Samaria, Tell el-Farʿah, Megiddo, and Hazor. The relatively close proximity of these sites to Tell es-Saʿidiyeh (Samaria is 36 km. away; Tell el-Farʿah, 22 km.; Megiddo, 50 km.; and Hazor, 61 km), linked as they are by routes of travel, made communication easy. The geography, as well as the political unity that prevailed within the area during the latter part of the Iron Age, favored a homogeneity of styles and techniques in the production of ceramics. Theoretically the comparisons of pottery forms found within strata of the excavated sites within this limited area should provide a basis for establishing stratigraphic correlations among the five sites. It must be borne in mind, of course, that a stratum or period at one site may have represented a longer period of time than did a stratum at another. Strata are not to be fitted together precisely. From the Table of Correspondences (Table 4) and the preceding discussions of comparisons to the pottery found in Strata VII–V at Tell es-Saʿidiyeh, it has been apparent that many forms are comparable to those found in Periods IV–VI at Samaria, and especially in locus E 207, assigned to Period VI. The correspondences at Tell el-Farʿah appear, with the the one exception of the tripod cup Type 12, in level 2. At Megiddo the parallels, with the exception of those to our Type 28, are distributed over Strata IV–I, with the greatest number of correspondences occurring in Stratum III. At Hazor the evidence is more ambiguous. Although some forms like the tripod cup, bowls of Types 15 and 42, a decanter, a storage jar and a cooking pot, are present in earlier strata from XB to VII, on the one hand or in Stratum IV on the other, the majority of the parallels derive from Strata VI–V at Hazor. Types that make their appearance exclusively in Stratum IV correspond to ceramic forms in Period VII at Samaria, level 1 at Tell el-Farʿah, Stratum IV at Hazor, and at the Judahite sites of Lachish II, Arad VII–VI, Tell Masos, Ramat Raḥel, En-gedi, and Meṣad Ḥashavyahu. Thus, there seems to be a clear line of division in the alignment of parallels between Tell es-Saʿidiyeh Strata VII–V on the one hand and Stratum IV on the other. (In 1975 Thomas L. McClellan made use of the "whole or nearly complete vessels" found in Strata VII–V [then called levels 4–2] in a type-percentage seriation to determine the relation of the Tell es-Saʿidiyeh stratigraphy to that at other sites in Palestine ["Quantitative Studies in the Iron Age Pottery of Palestine," Ph.D. diss., University of Pennsylvania, 1975, 426–38]. The assemblages used were small: 22 vessels in Stratum VII; 34 in Stratum VI; and 38 in Stratum V. Although the samples were small, his resulting seriation, given in his figs. 71 and 72, gives the following order: Farʿah 3, Beth-shan VB, Beth-shan VA, Tell es-Saʿidiyeh VII = Hazor VIII, Samaria Period III, Samaria Period VI, Samaria locus E 207, Beth-shan IV, Farʿah 2, Tell es-Saʿidiyeh VI, Tell es-Saʿidiyeh V = Hazor VB.)

It is more difficult, however, to assign absolute dates to our strata than it is to find their correspondences at neighboring sites. Since the ancient name for Tell es-Saʿidiyeh is not known it is impossible to make use of historical sources for suggesting dates for destructions at the site. We must be content, then, with the utilization of the dates generally assigned to the strata at the sites which correspond to those at Tell es-Saʿidiyeh.

Before citing the dates suggested by the excavators at Samaria and Hazor a word should be said about the methods employed for linking the archaeological remains with absolute dates. The event of the capture of Samaria in 722 B.C., with the the deportation of the native population and the settlement of a new one, is recounted in biblical and Assyrian sources. The excavators at Samaria equated this disruptive event with the destruction which appeared at the site at the end of Period VI. A cultural discontinuity was observed in Period VII, which was the successor to the destroyed Period VI. The evidence consisted of a new type of bowl with rounded base, carinated side, and a high flaring rim (our Type 35). The bowl was found to have affinities with Assyrian ware, which was dated to the end of the eighth century (SS 3: 97–98). This ware and a burnished bowl with externally thickened rim (our Type 36), along with the disappearance of older forms found in Period VI, provided the evidence for discontinuity within the ceramic tradition. Biblical references to the founding of the city by Omri (placed at ca. 880 B.C.) and to the completion of the layout of the city by Ahab provided dates for Periods I and II. The archaeological periods between II and VI were assigned dates on the basis of the comparative stratigraphy at such sites as Tell Beit Mirsim, Megiddo, Tell Abu Hawam, and Beth Shemesh.

The account of the destruction of Hazor by Tiglath-pileser III in 732 B.C., mentioned in 2 Kings 15:29, has been used for fixing the date of the destruction found in Stratum V (Y. Yadin, *Hazor*, 1972, 190). Two references in the prophetic literature of the Old Testament to an earthquake, Amos 1:1 and Zech. 14:5, provide the basis for pegging the end of Stratum VI to about 760 B.C. (ibid., 113 and 181). The references to an earthquake in these passages do not provide a location for the area of the earthquake. The hypothetical character of these equations in which events mentioned in literary sources are joined to destruction levels found within the excavation cannot by overemphasized. Any conclusions about absolute chronology at Tell es-Saʿidiyeh must of necessity have the limitations of certainty which are inherent in the calculations of dates for Samaria and Hazor.

Periods IV–VI at Samaria have been dated to the eighth century (K. M. Kenyon suggested that Period V may have come to an end with Assyrian destruction of Samaria in 722 B.C. and that Period VI does not touch upon the seventh century—SS 3: 96–97); Strata VI–V at Hazor have been said to represent the occupation there in the eighth century down to 732 B.C. (ibid., 200); and level 2 at Tell el-Farʿah has been assigned by the excavator within the eighth century down to 723 B.C. (R. de Vaux in *RB* 62: 587). From an analysis of the pottery it has been seen that Strata VII–V correspond well to the span of occupation at Samaria Periods IV–VI, Tell el-Farʿah 2, and Hazor VI–V, or roughly to the first three quarters of the eighth century. This span of time, however, may seem a short period into which to compress three occupational periods, each with its distinctive city plan. Two observations may alleviate this apparent difficulty. First, Stratum V was destroyed by a general fire. That this catastrophe may have come not too long after the building of the houses of this occupation is suggested by the lack of obvious deviations from the standard plan and measurement of the 12 houses; over a long period of use private owners would have made alterations to fit family needs. It could well be that the buildings of Stratum V were destroyed not too long after they had been constructed according to a uniform plan. Secondly, the ceramic forms which we have from Stratum VII and which we have used to date this stratum are those found on floors of buildings which were abandoned at the end of the period of occupation. Thus our pottery serves to supply a date for the latter part of Stratum VII; its beginning and earlier history could have reached back into the ninth century. If, then, the end of Stratum VII and the beginning of Stratum VI is placed in the early part of the eighth century and its ending too far before the destruction of a short-lived Stratum V, then Stratum VI may well have spanned a half century or so.

Stratum IV, with its "Assyrian" ware, bowl with rim externally thickened to a triangular section, and flat-bottom lamp, has correspondences with Samaria Period VII, Tell el-Farʿah 1, and Hazor IV, strata which have been assigned to the latter part of the eighth and the early seventh centuries (*SS* 3: 97–98; Y. Yadin, *Hazor,* 1972, 200).

VII

The Stairway

The stairway that leads from the top of the tell to the water source at the bottom was discovered during the first season of excavations (fig. 182). Looking down from the north rim of the tell we were able to see two parallel walls running north–south on the north slope. When a sounding was made (Sounding 1) half way down the slope the steps of the stairway were encountered between the two walls. In further soundings (Soundings 2–7) we were able to trace the course of the north-south section of the stairway in 14-G/H/J-3/10 and 5-G/H-1/2. At the lower end of this stairway, there was a change of direction. The stairs continued, after a 90° turn to the right, in an easterly direction. The upper reaches of the north-south section of the stairway had been completely removed as the rim of the tell was eroded. Thus, no connection remained with any of the strata of occupation of the site. The stairway is situated about 8 m. to the east of a depression or trough in the surface of the north side of the tell (see contour map in Fig. 176, and figs. 105 and 106). This conspicuous trough was probably a drain for the city at one or more periods of occupation. Drainage from Strata VII–IV was from the south to the north and rain water would have to have been channeled through an opening in the city wall and allowed to run down the north slope of the tell to the wādī below. While the direction which the stairway takes is roughly north from the line of the city wall there is a slight inclination to the west in its downward course (see fig. 182). This variation is puzzling, since at the bottom of the main section of the stairway it turns eastward in order to reach the water source. It is possible that this less direct route for the stairway from the city to the water source was taken because of the existence at the time of building of a drainage channel from the city above.

We shall describe the stairway beginning from the lowest part we were able to excavate (the presence of a modern irrigation canal at the bottom of the tell made it impossible to excavate the lowest reaches.) The width of the stairway in the east-west section is only 1.65 m., compared to 2.25 m. for the stairs running north–south. The treads of the lowest 12 steps are relatively narrow and the angle of incline is the steepest to be found in the entire course of the stairs (fig. 111). Climbing from the lowest point reached in the excavation one comes by 12 steps to a landing, measuring 1.60 by 1.80 m. (fig. 111). After a turn to the left more steps with narrow treads (fig. 110) lead to a platform, 1.10 m. long, which seems to have supported the lower end of a mud-brick wall. Beyond the platform there is a sloping ramp, 2.75 m. long, and 10 broad steps or platforms (fig. 108), all sloping slightly upward, with a single narrow-tread step after the second platform. From this point onward, as one goes upward, the steps are fairly uniform in size; the angle of ascent, however, is more acute for these 63 steps. The total number of steps and platforms that have been preserved is 95.

The method that had been employed in the building of the stairway became clear from three soundings made outside of the east wall of the north-south section (Soundings 2, 4, and 5) and one outside of the west wall (Sounding 1). The builders had first cut a trench, about 4 m. wide and at least 2.50 m. deep, down the north side of the tell. They then proceeded to build a wall of wādī stones, averaging about 75 cm. thick, against each side of the cut. The inside faces of these walls had been carefully fitted to make a smooth surface for the sides of the stairway; the outer faces of the walls (those resting against the vertical cut) were irregular and rough. An idea of the size of the stones used for these walls may be gained from fig. 114, where there is a view of the upper courses of the two outer walls of the stairway. To judge from two or three stones to which the plaster still adhered (fig. 113) the inner faces of the walls were plastered with lime plaster. Most of the plaster, however, had disappeared.

The steps and the ramps were constructed of stones that were generally somewhat smaller than those used for the side walls. These stones were laid directly on the earth of the cut, without any foundation (see fig. 116, left center, where a balk reveals only one layer of stones for the steps; below is packed earth). The excellent state of preservation in which the treads were found (see fig. 107) is due to their having been set in clay mortar and protected from the action of the weather (see below).

An unusual feature of the stairway is the mud-brick

wall that runs for most of the length of the north-south portion (figs. 182, plan and 183, section). It consists of a single line of bricks, about 35 cm. wide, which divides the stairway into two passageways. Two segments of this dividing wall are missing, one in 14-J-4/5 and another in 14-H-10. Both were casualties of excavation: the former was removed by a supervisor, who dug the anomalous wall material after interpreting it as the fill for a trench; the other segment was dissolved by the water that drained into the sounding after a heavy rain. The brick dividing wall seems to have ended in the lower part of the north-south section of the stairs, about 4.50 m. before its end. The lowest course of brick was generally laid directly upon the steps; however, for the lowest 4 m. of the divider there was a shallow foundation of small stones laid upon the surface of the ramp and the platform on which it sits. The greatest preserved height of the wall is 1.25 m.

At the lower-end of the north-south section the stairway turns to the east. The north wall of the east-west section is 1.60 m. thick and constructed of heavy stones (figs. 111, 115, 182). About 1 m. outside of this wall there are the remains of what seems to have been a road (fig. 112), running northeast to southwest. It is possible that this road was one that led to an entrace to the city at the west. If the road was indeed an approach to the city gate then the heavy wall bordering the stairway on its north side would have served to protect, as well as to camouflage, the access to the city's water supply.

A dozen meters or so to the north of the stairway is the Wādī Kufrinjeh (fig. 109), which is fed at this point by several perennial springs. These would seem to have been the principal water source for the city on the top of the tell, since today there are no other observable springs in the vicinity. Obviously the stairway was constructed as a means of access to water; although we were unable to reach the lower end of the stairs it must have come to an end at a spring or at an underground pool supplied by springs.

It seems most likely that the stairway had been roofed over to form a tunnel that ran down the north side of the tell. First, it is obvious that without a covering the mud-brick wall built in the center of the stairs would not have survived long in the heavy winter rains of the Jordan Valley. In fact, as we have stated above, the water that filled one plot during the course of excavation in the winter of 1964 completely demolished the section of mud-brick wall in 14-H-10. Second, the fact that the stairway had been built within a deep trench and not on the surface suggests that the purpose may have been to conceal the stairs from view. If the stairway was roofed, as we suppose, then the function of the mud-brick wall is understandable: it served to support the roof beams and to keep them from sagging under the heavy load of roofing material and fill. The dividing wall could have served also to facilitate the movement of traffic up and down this access to the water source. The use of narrow bricks rather than rubble masonry which had been used in the thicker side walls, served to provide the necessary support for the roof with the minimum loss of space within the tunnel.

Thus, even though we do not, as yet, have the termination of the stairway at the water source, and the entranceway into the walled city is irretrievably lost through erosion, it seems reasonably certain that the remains which have been discovered are those of a covered stairway from inside the city wall to a protected water source at the north end of the tell. Moreover, it seems fairly certain that the stairway was roofed over and possibly camouflaged so that an enemy outside the city would not know of the existence of an access to a vital source for water in time of siege. The heavy wall at the north end of the stairway may have been designed to provide added protection against mining by an enemy proceeding along the road that led to one of the principal approaches to the city.

Date for Construction and Use

A sounding that was made at the top of the preserved portion of the stairs, in 14-J-2/3, disclosed that the trench cut for the tunnel had gone through what appears to have been a city wall (figs. 116 and 184C). The width of the wall is more than 2.50 m. and its line runs some 16.5 m. to the north of the line of the city wall of Stratum VII. Its base lies at a level of −252.28 m., which is about 7. m. below the base of the city wall in Stratum VII. The building of the tunnel, therefore, must be placed at sometime after the building of the city wall in 14-J-2/3, which is, as yet, undated.

It is obvious that the debris which was found within the tunnel came from the top and side of the mound. After the tunnel had ceased to be used, winter rains had washed occupation debris down the course of the stairway until it had been filled in completely. There were no discernible layers, or lenses, in the deposit of silt, stones, and pottery fragments. It is impossible to determine the source of the filling. It may have come from one of the occupation layers on top of the mound, or the material may have been carried down in the erosion which had cut vertically through the successive layers of occupation deposited on the tell. Baskets of pottery taken from this filling were examined and their major periods noted. But since this pottery was not found in any stratigraphical relationship, it served only to give an indication of the periods of occupation of that part of the mound that lay above the upper reaches of the preserved tunnel. A tally of the records of field observation on the samples provided the following distribution of datable samples: Early Bronze, 1; Late Bronze, 22; Iron I, 32; Iron II, 14. There were no forms belonging to periods later than the Iron II Age.

At the present stage in the excavations it is impossible to assign dates for the construction and use of the tunnel. From the composition of the fill within the tunnel it would seem that it was filled in before the Persian period in the occupation of the city, since no sherds from a period later than Iron II were observed. If our interpretation of the function of the tunnel is correct, that it was a measure of defense for a walled city, then it must have functioned sometime before the period of Stratum III, when it seems that the city ceased to be surrounded by a wall. (see pp. 77–78).

VIII

Stratum III

The stratigraphic sequence from Stratum VII through Stratum IV is well established. Stratum VI was built upon Stratum VII, Stratum V followed the occupation of Stratum VI, and Stratum IV was the successor to Stratum V. Stratum III, however, is an arbitrary designation for the lowest architectural complex that was reached in an area of the tell adjacent to that in which Strata VII–IV were found. Although an attempt was made to link these two areas by the excavation of four 5-by-5 m. plots lying between them, the work was not finished; there is no stratigraphic link between Stratum IV and Stratum III. From a study of the artifacts found in each of these strata we believe it is improbable that they overlap in time. It is quite possible that they were separated by one or more periods of occupation or even by a gap in occupation. If and when further excavation is done at the site it should be possible to provide a stratigraphic connection between Strata VII–IV on the one hand and Strata III–I on the other. For the present we shall make use of a continuous numbering for designating the levels of occupation at the site.

The Square Building

The large building in 31-D/J-4/9 (fig. 185) is almost exactly square in plan (the north-south axis was measured by a meter tape as 21.95 m. and its east-west axis as 22.05 m.) and consists of a central open court surrounded by rooms on its four sides. It was built on the summit of the tell, where there was a slope to the surface rising slightly from west to east. The north balk of 31-D-8 exhibits a rise of the ground level from west to east, and stone foundations in the west side of the building tend to be constructed of more courses than those in the east. Thus, it would seem that the building was laid out and the foundations laid before the surface had been completely leveled. The elevations that were taken for the tops of the foundations of the building vary by as much as 69 cm., and in some places the stone pavement of a room joins the wall above the line of the foundation, and in other places below it. Evidence for foundation trenches was found for the west wall of the building at both its north and its south ends.

The superstructure of the building was of brick. Both the brown and the greenish-gray (*qaṭṭārah*) materials appear, with apparently no consistent pattern of alteration. The size of the standard brick is 45 by 45 by 14 cm. (in Stratum V the bricks were mostly within the range of 48–56 by 32–38 by 10–12 cm.), and there is frequent use of two and one-half rows of these to form a wall 1.25 m. in width. The bricks of each layer are set so that the joins of one layer do not correspond to those of the layer above or below. Timbers of wood had been imbedded in the brick walls at the doorway between Rooms 101 and 102 on the inside of the west doorjamb.

The internal, connecting doorways of the building are, for the most part, clearly defined, but the means of access to the building from the outside are not clear. The most probable position for an entrance is on the west side, into Room 104. If this is indeed a major entrance it would provide a connection with a large courtyard to the west, which, while not adjoining the square building, is aligned with it. A second possibility for an entrance is at the southwest corner at the south end of the paved corridor Room 103; but here, unfortunately, the erosion of the south side of the tell has destroyed whatever evidence there may have been for a doorway at this point. A third possible entrance is on the east side of the building, directly opposite the proposed doorway at the west. A few stones of pavement overlying the foundation wall to the east of Room 109, and directly to the north of the drain, constitute what evidence there is for a doorway into the building from the east. None of these possible doorways from the outside constitutes what could be called a grand entrance. It would seem, therefore, that the plan for the building emphasizes security from intrusion rather than ease of access from the outside.

Room 101 (fig. 185)

The central feature of the building is a large, rectangular courtyard, measuring 9.55 m. from east to west and 7.80 m. from north to south. The entire surface of the court was paved with large and medium sized stones set fairly regularly in rows; uneven spaces were filled with smaller stones and pebbles (figs. 117 and 120). It is evident from the plan that there were at least two entrances: the one in the south wall connects with Room 102 by a doorway with the peculiar feature of an inset on the north side of the west doorjamb (fig. 123); the other provides access into Room 109 (fig. 130). It is possible that there were also other doorways, into Rooms 104 and 106, which had been destroyed when the reservoirs of the level above were built. The west, north, and east walls of the courtyard are fairly uniform in thickness, averaging ca. 1.25 m. and built of two and one-half rows of the standard bricks. The south wall, however, is 1.60 m. thick and is constructed of three and one-half rows of bricks. What function this added strength in the south wall was designed to perform it is impossible to say; it may be that the thicker wall was built to support a superstructure on the south side of the building.

The court was drained by a covered channel, which led from an opening in the floor at the southeast corner (figs. 118 and 119), ran under the floor of Room 109 and the east wall of the building, and ended on the side of the mound at a distance of some 3.50 m. beyond the limits of the building. The stones that cover the drain are at the same elevation as the top of the foundations of both the east and west walls of Room 109, and the mud-brick superstructure rests directly upon them. Lime plaster lined the collecting basin and the beginning of the canal under the east wall of the courtyard (and as far as it could be examined), but no plaster was found in the canal at its opening in 31-K-6.

On the floor of the courtyard there were no evidences of burning and few artifacts, except for bits of intrusive pottery which had been imbedded in the filling. Thus, the absence of household goods, the distances between the walls (too long to have been spanned without supports), and the drain for carrying off the rain water combine to make it almost certain that this room was an open courtyard.

OBJECT:

Lamp,
 S1186/P665 (fig. 18:4).

Room 102

Room 102 is bounded on the west by the corridor, Room 103, with which it connects by a doorway, and on the east by the west wall of Room 110 (figs. 122–124). Its main entrance is from the open courtyard, Room 101, to the north, the floor of which is 14 cm. higher than that of Room 102. The wall that juts out from the north wall of the room at the east end is puzzling (its foundation can be seen in fig. 121). It may be either a structural member of the tower to the east, or a divider that served to form a closet or small room. If the wall is taken as a secondary modification then the entranceway into Room 102 from the open courtyard to the north is in the middle of its north wall and the room is symmetrical.

The paving in Room 102 consists of stones slightly smaller than those found in the pavement of the open courtyard to the north. It was broken in an area along the south wall by the digging of a pit in a later period (fig. 124, right); four clay ovens were found on the floor of the pit. Another break in the pavement appeared immediately before the doorway opening into the courtyard (fig. 123). Although charcoal was found at the entrance leading to Room 103, where there was evidence for the destruction of that part of the building by fire and some ashes on the pavement in the northeast corner of the room, the remainder of the room had no trace of burning. Since there was no drain in the floor to carry off the rainwater, as there was in Room 101, it is likely that the room was roofed over.

OBJECTS:

Iron nail with bronze head,
 S1088/M275, L. 14.9 cm., D. of head, 3.2 cm.
Fibula,
 S1075/Br57 (fig. 18:11).
 S1031/Br56, fragment, L. 6 cm.
Loom weight,
 S1047/M259, spherical, D. 3.6 cm. P.

Room 103

This well-paved room (fig. 125) could only have been a corridor within the complex of rooms and courtyard. It is certain that it opened into Room 104 by a doorway measuring slightly less than the width of the corridor itself; the doorsill was the stone foundation of the main east-west partition wall of this part of the building. A second opening led into Room 102 to the east (fig. 124), but here the sill was a continuation of the paving of the corridor. A unique feature of the construction of this doorway consisted of a charred wooden beam, 17 cm. wide, found between the pavements of Rooms 103 and 102; along the floor beside the doorjambs of this doorway were spaces for beams comparable to the one which had been charred (fig. 185).

The south end of the corridor lies at the south edge of the present tell, where the evidence for the original plan of the building had been destroyed by erosion and by the digging of a pit at the southwest corner. Pierre Proulx, the supervisor in this area, noted that there were remnants of what may have been three steps within the line of the south wall of the building; these could have belonged to an entrance to the corridor at this corner. The east wall of the corridor consists of two and one-half rows of mud bricks, but, unlike most of the other walls of the building, it does not have a stone foundation. It does not run parallel to the other north-south walls of the building but veers slightly to the west in its course from north to south. Plaster was noted on the east and west walls of the corridor, as well as on the north doorjamb of the entrance leading into Room 102.

Throughout Room 103 there was evidence of heavy burning. On the floor were charred beams, hard packed clay with impressions of reeds, and 11 pieces of baked clay tiles, averaging from 2.5 to 3 cm. in thickness. In contrast to other rooms in the building there was a considerable assemblage of artifacts on the floor. In addition to the objects listed below, the supervisor mentions six loom weights, which were not catalogued.

OBJECTS:
Jar,
   S1054/P616 (fig. 18:2).
Cosmetic palette,
   S1024/St70, white stone, two incised lines on exterior just below rim, H. 2.6 cm, D. 7.7 cm. P. (fig. 168:9).
Iron weapon,
   S1036/F46, L. 8.2 cm., W. 2 cm. P.
Anklet,
   S1027/Br52 (fig. 18:8).
Spindle whorl,
   S1017/M251 (fig. 18:14).
Loom weight,
   S1044/M256, oblong, two holes, 7.8-by-5.7-by-4.2-cm. P.
   S1043/M255, two oblong weights, 8-by-6-by-5-cm., and 6-by-3.5-by-3.2-cm. P.
   S1042/M254, two fragmentary, oblong. P.
   S1063/M264, oblong, 5.5-by-3.2-by-1.9 cm. P.
Eleven tiles,
   S1067/M267, 2.5–3. cm. thick. P.

Room 104

Room 104 is a long, narrow room with a tightly packed mud floor. It was entered on the south from Room 103, through a doorway, the sill of which was raised ca. 5 cm. above the paved floor of Room 103 (fig. 125) and seemed to be a continuation of the stone foundation for the main east-west partition wall. Although the bricks of the west wall of this room were destroyed, the stone foundation was intact. Running over these foundation stones at the southwest corner of the room there was a hard-packed floor, about 1.25 m. in width, which was thought to have indicated that there had been an entrance to the building from the west (fig. 126). Additional evidence for an entrance at this point is the presence of two large stones in the foundation of the west wall (one stone appears in fig. 185, the largest stone in the portion of wall that is within 31-E-6; the other was 1.25 m. to the south, but was not drawn on the plan). A third doorway led from Room 104 into Room 105 to the north. What remains of the east wall of the room—most of it had been destroyed by the cutting of the reservoirs of Stratum I—is plastered.

This room, like Room 103 to the south of it, had been destroyed by fire. Ash and charcoal (^{14}C sample P-1446) were found on the floor and blackened plaster on the east wall, extending as high as 65 cm. above the floor in some places. Two fragments of roof tiles were found within the room, along with the inscribed limestone incense altar (see below). Pottery was noticeably absent from the debris. The area had seen temporary occupation after the destruction of the building of Stratum III and before the building of the house of Stratum II above it. Since no walls could be found to be associated with the two pits and the packed layers it is probable that the area was but a temporary shelter after the destruction of the building of Stratum III.

OBJECTS:

Incense burner,
  S1181/St82/S14 (figs. 18:6;174:1–6)
Bronze pin,
  S1146/Br70, L. 15.9 cm., Th. 0.3 cm.
Tile,
  S1066/M266, Th. ca. 3 cm., L. 19 cm. P.
  S1065/M265, Th. ca. 3 cm. L. 21 cm. P.

Room 105

Room 105, a small rectangular room paved with large stones, corresponds in plan to Room 108 at the northeast corner of the building. It is entered from Room 104 through a doorway, which has a slight step upward. A door socket was found at the east side of the opening in what seemed to have been its original position. The doorway leading to Room 106 has a threshold of stones, which appear to be the foundation for the north-south wall rather than a paving. The jambs for the two doorways were plastered, although no plaster was noted for the other surfaces of the walls. In the northeast corner of the room there was found a clay storage container, conical in shape, containing a few sherds, animal bones, and shells.

OBJECTS:

Bronze needle,
  S1268/Br84 (fig. 18:10).
Bronze ring,
  S1215/Br78, D. 1.8 cm., Th. 0.33 cm.
Stopper,
  S1201/M289, with string impression on top (fig. 18:15).

Room 106

Several large pits sunk from an upper level had destroyed the floor of this room. Joanna Fink McClellan, who supervised its clearance, noted that its east wall did not have the usual stone foundations and suggested that it might not have been a part of the original plan of the building. First, it is too small to have been of any effective use, except as a kind of closet to Room 105, to which it has its only connection, unless there was a doorway into the large courtyard that had been removed by the builders of the reservoirs of Stratum I. Second, the east wall of Room 106 destroys the general symmetry of the building, especially that of the north part of the structure. This hypothesis of a secondary adaptation of the plan could not be tested adequately since pits dug into the north wall of the building had made it impossible to see if the bricks of the north-south wall had been bonded into those of the north wall.

Room 107

This long, narrow room had been disturbed by several periods of later use, as had also Rooms 108 and 109 at the northeast corner of the building. Later stone foundations had been laid along the north-south axis of the room, and a strip of paving running east-west was found on the floor. The only door to the room is that leading from Room 108. It had a threshold of packed earth, and there was evidence along the southern east-west wall that the room had originally had a floor of packed earth. The foundation of the east wall had two courses of stones.

OBJECTS:

Amber bead,
  S1159/J65 (fig. 18:13).
Fibula,
  S1160/Br72 (fig. 18:9).
Juglet,
  S1190/P669 (fig. 18:3).
Bronze kettle,
  S1269/Br85 (fig. 18:7), stratigraphy uncertain; possibly intrusive to Stratum III.

Room 108

Room 108 (fig. 128), which is similar in size and plan to Room 105 at the northwest corner of the building, had a door opening into Room 107 and probably another leading into Room 109 to the south, although a later pit had cut into the east end of the south wall where there had possibly been a doorjamb. Subsequent building was evidenced in stone foundations for a later wall set directly upon the remnants of brick that formed the southern east-west wall of Room 108 (fig. 129). The floor of the room seemed to have been made of hard packed earth.

Room 109

In addition to the probable opening from Room 109 into Room 108, there appears to have been a door leading from Room 109 into Room 101; the pattern of stones in the foundation of the west wall at its north end suggests a sill for the doorway (fig. 131). In the east wall of Room 109, just to the north of the channel for draining the courtyard, there are paving stones that run across the foundation for the east wall (fig. 118); they may constitute what is left of the sill of an east entrance into the building at this point. It was apparent from two features that the room had been modified and reused in later periods: first, a later foundation wall rests firmly on the brick wall that forms the east side of the building and secondly, the stone pavement shows signs of having been plastered, a feature that does not appear on any other pavements of the building. The room was paved except for a border 50 to 60 cm. wide beside the west wall. The pavement ends abruptly at the border in a row of upright stones running parallel to the west wall (fig. 130). A loose fill lay between the stones and the wall. It has been suggested that this unpaved strip may have been the foundation for a stairway leading from Room 109 to a tower to the south of it. One would expect some entrance to a tower from inside the building, but this corridor is rather narrow for the purpose. Another possibility is that the upright stones belonged to a bench.

OBJECTS:
Basalt mortar,
    S1105/St75 (fig. 18:5).
Ring of silver (?),
    S1217/J67 (fig. 18:12).
Tile,
    S1203/M291, Th. 2.3 cm., L. 23.3 cm. P.

Room 110

The southeast corner of the building, Room 110 on the plan, seems to have been reinforced by a doubling of the thickness of the south wall of the building and an additional north-south wall built through the middle of the room (fig. 132). The two small rooms on each side of the dividing wall have no entrances and no well-established floors. The most attractive suggestion for the function of this construction at the southeast corner of the building is that it was a tower, rising above the height of the remainder of the structure. As such it would have provided a lookout station as well as a last line of defense in case an enemy gained access to the building. The possibility of an entrance to the tower by means of a narrow stairway along the west wall of Room 109 has already been suggested. It is obvious that there was no entrance to the tower from the outside of the building.

Function and Date of the Building

The relatively meager list of objects catalogued from the rooms of the square building of Stratum III would suggest that the building evidenced little use or that the building was emptied of its contents before its abandonment or destruction. It thus stands in marked contrast to the large building of Stratum II whose floors were literally strewn with broken pottery and other objects. The inventory of catalogued objects from this building is not only small but it is unusual as to the distribution of types of objects. Ceramic vessels are limited to a single jar, a juglet, and a lamp. A spindle whorl, seven loom weights, and a needle would suggest the activities of spinning, weaving, and sewing and basalt mortar may have been used in milling. Articles of personal adornment and cosmetics—three fibulae, a bead, two rings, an anklet, and a cosmetic palette—and such incidental objects as a nail, a pin, a stopper, and a weapon of iron, a kettle, and an incense burner can indicate little more than that the building evidenced human occupation. The tiles, of which only 14 examples were found, constitute a much smaller sample than one would have expected from the roof of such a large building.

Another puzzling feature is the absence of stone pavements in some rooms, particularly Rooms 104, 106, 107, and 108. Room 105 is well paved, but its counterpart at the northeast corner of the building, Room 108, is not. The pavement of Room 105 stops abruptly before it reaches into the adjoining room, Room 106. Furthermore, it was observed that the pavements of the rooms and the court exhibited no sign of having been repaired. There were indeed damaged portions of pavement, but all of this damage could be explained as having been done when pits were dug from the upper level.

A third puzzling circumstance is the localization of fallen roof material in the area of Rooms 103 and 104 (Room 109 had one broken tile) and its absence elsewhere in the building. Charred roof beams were found on the floors of these two rooms at the southwest corner of the building and in the doorway leading into Room 102, but elsewhere they were noticeably missing. In addition, these two rooms produced 13 pieces of kiln-baked tile (presumably roofing, since they were found in the context of burned material and charred beams).

How does one best explain these anomalies? It is possible that only the southwest corner of the building caught fire and was burned and that the fire did not spread into the remainder of the building. The remainder of the structure was then sacked and stripped of its contents, including the roof tiles that were salvaged for use elsewhere. In time the roof beams collapsed and decayed, leaving no traces. Another possibility is that the building was never completed and, (despite the modifications mentioned above) the partly finished building was abandoned before all the pavements had been laid. Only the southwest corner had been roofed over and this had been burned and the building project was abandoned. It is impossible to tell whether one or another of these explanations account for the state of ruins as we found them.

The plan of the building is that of the so-called "open-court building," long recognized as characteristic of Assyrian architecture and reproduced with modifications in Palestine (Ruth B. K. Amiran and I. Dunayevsky, "The Assyrian Open-Court Building and its Palestinian Derivatives," *BASOR* 149:25–32). Our building shares many characteristics of the series of Late Assyrian and Neo-Babylonian examples cited by Amiran and Dunayevsky (ibid., 29), particularly the plan of an open court with rooms and halls around it on all four sides. However, when our building is compared with the plans of the second series of examples given by Amiran and Dunayevsky belonging to the Persian period, there are some differences in the plan. For, with the exception of the Lachish Residency, the cited examples show a plan of a courtyard surrounded on three sides by rooms (ibid., 30).

Similar in plan and size to our square building is a fortress in the central Negev at Ḥorvai Mesora, measuring 20 by 20 m. (R. Cohen, "The Iron Age Fortresses in the Central Negev," *BASOR* 236:70, fig. 7:4). The building is obviously a fortress and has been dated to the tenth century. Other fortresses of the type have been found at Ḥorvat Ritma (21 by 21 m.) and on a hill near 'Atar Horoʿa (ibid., figs 7:2 and 7:3; *Tel Aviv* 4:116–17, fig. 4; Z. Meshel suggests a date for the Ḥorvat Ritma building of the eleventh to the ninth centuries B.C., p. 125).

The fortresslike structures found in the Negev are similar enough in plan to suggest that our building was designed to achieve security. In addition to the features to provide protection there are other characteristics of the architecture that evidence a generosity in the use of space for a large courtyard with its adjoining room to the south. The general impression is one of affluence. The parallels of the fortresses of the Negev, however, obviously cannot provide a basis for the dating of our structure.

Among the artifacts found within the building the inscribed incense burner is the most distinctive and the most likely to be datable (see Note, pp. 66–68). Parallels to it from South Arabia, Palestine, and Mesopotamia range in date over a span of several centuries and do not serve to fix our example within anything like a narrow span of time (see James B. Pritchard, "An Incense Burner from Tell es-Saʿidiyeh, Jordan Valley," in *Studies on the Ancient Palestinian World*, ed. J. W. Wevers and D. B. Redford [Toronto, 1972], 9–17). The short inscription incised on the burner contains forms of the lapidary Aramaic script that were used from the late sixth to the fourth centuries. F. M. Cross, however, would place the inscription, on the basis of the forms of the letters, in the period of ca. 525–475 B.C., or about 500 B.C. in round numbers (ibid., 8, n. 13).

Dates for five ^{14}C samples of charcoal and grain from the floor of the square building and from the floor encountered in a sounding immediately below the floor of the square building are as follows:

^{14}C DATES OF STRATUM III SAMPLES

Sample No.	Age BP (5568 Half-Life)	RIC Calibrated Date (1 sigma)	RIC Calibrated Date (2 sigma)
P-1446 Charcoal from 31-E-6	2230 ± 50	405–180 B.C.	410–160 B.C.

^{14}C DATES OF SAMPLES FROM SOUNDING BELOW FLOOR OF STRATUM III

Sample No.	Age BP	RIC Cal. (1 sigma)	RIC Cal. (2 sigma)
P-1445 Grain from 31-E-7	2140 ± 60	255–145 B.C.	390–5 B.C.
P-1443 Charcoal from 31-E-7/8	2310 ± 100	440–375 B.C.	760–170 B.C.
P-1442 Grain from 31-E-7/8	2420 ± 50	620–410 B.C.	775–395 B.C.
P-1448 Grain from 31-E/F-7/8	2490 ± 60	785–550 B.C.	795–415 B.C.

Since the evidence for the date of the square building in Stratum III is limited to only one ^{14}C sample with an age of 2230 ± 50 (5568 half-life) the date ranges of 405–180 B.C. (1 sigma) and 410–160 B.C. (2 sigma) we have included the results of the analyses of four samples of grain and charcoal found on the floor of a building lying immediately below (about 1 meter) the floor of the square building in 31-E/F-7/8. Within the small area of the sounding it has not yet been possible to gather evidence for whether or not there was a gap in occupation between the end of the period represented by the materials from the sounding and the construction of the square building of Stratum III. The difference, however, between the ^{14}C dates would suggest that in this part of the tell there may have been a gap in occupation.

If P-1445 is omitted because of statistical inconsistency by the Chi-square test the average age provided by the other three samples is 2410 ± 90 (5568 half-life), which corresponds to date ranges of 635–400 B.C. (1 sigma) and 790–260 B.C. (2 sigma) according to the international calibration. If the two short-lived samples (P-1442 and P-1448 are averaged, the result is 2460 ± 50 with date ranges of 640–420 B.C. (1 sigma) and 785–405 B.C. (2 sigma).

Conclusion

The massive proportions of the square building of Stratum III indicate that it was designed primarily for defense. Since it would appear that the city was without the protection of a city wall it would have been necessary to provide such an important building with its own security. The arrangement of rooms around a central court is that of the so-called "open-court building," of which examples are known from the Persian period in Palestine. The structure cannot be dated precisely from architectural parallels; nor can the artifacts generally be used for dating. Only the five-letter Aramaic inscription on the incense burner offers a clue for date. The letters would appear to be compatable with the forms used from the late sixth to the fourth century. This date provided by comparative paleography falls within the range of the ^{14}C dates for the three samples from the floor immediately under the building of Stratum III. The lack of more precise figures from the ^{14}C analyses and the dearth of datable artifacts from the building make it prudent to withhold judgment on absolute dates until further excavations can provide data on the layer of occupation immediately below Stratum III and clarify the relationship between the two. For the moment it is, perhaps, enough to say that the square building belongs to the Persian period.

Note: Incense Burner (S1181/St82S14; figs. 18:6; 174:1–6 = Sides A–F)

This elaborately decorated incense burner was found on the floor of Room 104 of the square building of Stratum III. It was cut from a block of soft limestone that had measured at least 7 cm. long, 6.7 cm. wide, and 7 cm. high. The sides were tapered toward the base, which now measures 5.7 by 6 cm., and the stone between four legs, one at each corner of the base, had been removed. A basin, about 1 cm. deep, was hollowed out at the top; its sides were slightly bevelled inward and a rim of slightly less than 1 cm. was left around the perimeter. The sides of the burner had been polished by an abrasive, which had left diagonal marks that are still visible on side D (see fig. 174:4).

The sides of the burner are covered with a pigment or paint. Sides D and F are red and sides C and E are black. The bottom (B) is painted with two bands, approximately 1.3 cm. wide. The one extending between sides C and E is black, conforming to the color of the two sides; that connecting sides D and F is red, as are these sides. The longer band overlays the shorter. The coloring is abraded in places, but enough remains to indicate the original painting of the stone surface.

A second stage of the decorative process was the incising of the rim of the top, the sides, and the base with geometric designs cut with a sharp instrument through the paint into the soft stone so that the white of the incisions stand out against the red and black backgrounds. The top is decorated with eight circles, each with a smaller one inside, around the rim (A). These were crudely drawn, without a compass, but evenly placed, one at each corner and one at approximately the middle of each side. These concentric circles match in size and design the thirteen circles that appear on the four sides of the burner.

The decoration on the sides of divided into three registers or zones that continue around the four faces in continuous friezes. The upper register, averaging 2 cm. in width, is a reserved band bordered above and below with a zigzag line that provides a sawtooth decoration as a border. The teeth of the "saw" are incised diagonally. Horizontal lines at the top and bottom serve to contain the upper register.

The second register consists of a narrow band of vertical lines contained by two horizontal lines, one at the top and one at the bottom, running around the four sides. The vertical lines are arranged in groups of from four to nine strokes forming panels separated by blank spaces. There seems to be no pattern in the alternation of the number of strokes in the individual panels.

The third and widest register is the most complex. On the opposing sides C and E the design consists of a series of lozenges, each with a pair of concentric circles in the center. The space between lozenges is hatched with diagonal lines. Four lozenges appear on side E, and five on side C. The third register on the other two sides (D and F) is decorated differently. On these sides, in the intervals between three "column" decorations of vertical and horizontal hatching, are two x-like designs hatched diagonally. At the meeting point of the two bars of the cross, or x, there is a pair of concentric circles matching those of the third register on the other two sides and those incised on the rim. The entire third register is contained by two horizontal lines that extend around the four sides.

The feet are incised with double zigzag lines, but the resulting triangles are not hatched as are those in the upper register. The zigzag design is bordered at the top by one horizontal line that runs around the incense burner, and two lines are incised at the bottom of each foot. From the arrangement of the design it is apparent that the lines incised on the four feet were cut after the material between the legs had been cut away.

The crossed bands painted on the bottom (B) of the burner are incised with zigzag lines with smaller triangles or chevrons filled in. The band across the longer axis runs over that of the shorter. Each band is bordered by two lines.

The final stage in the decoration was the addition of the two crude drawings (D and F) and the inscription (C). It is obvious from the position of the animal on side D, mostly in the upper register but with feet extending through the second and into the third register of the carefully planned geometric design, that this graffito was an afterthought and not part of the original plan. The drawing was probably meant to portray a horse, since the mane is represented by lines extending upward from the neck and a loop is attached to the head to indicate an ear. The four legs are represented by simple lines.

In the upper register of side F there appears a crude graffito of what may have been intended as a composite figure. Its horizontal position was probably determined by the long and narrow shape of the space available in the upper register, which could not accommodate this type of figure if drawn vertically. In the lower part of the figure one can see an attempt to represent a human body, with right arm raised and the left extended downward. The legs are not differentiated and no feet are represented. The upper part of the figure appears to be the head of an animal, or possibly a bird, since the six lines extending from the head suggest feathers. Yet another possible interpretation is that the head is that of a snake. But, despite the uncertainty over the head, it seems reasonably clear that the figure is a composite creature, perhaps intended to serve an apotropaic function.

The inscription has been incised in the reserved space of the upper register of side C with a broader instrument than that used in the cutting of the geometric designs and one more comparable to that used for cutting the figure in the upper register of side F. The letters are cut to a uniform depth, except for the enigmatic stroke to the right of the vertical of the second letter (from the right). The reading, if the script is lapidary Aramaic, as Frank M. Cross, Jr. has suggested, is *lzkwr*, "Belonging to Zakkūr." The reading has the advantage that all the letters fit nicely into the period of the late sixth to the fourth centuries B.C. and the name Zakkūr is well attested (See M. Noth, *Die israelitischen Personennamen*, 1928, 187, for the use of *zkr* in names; and H. Donner and W. Röllig, *Kanaanäische und aramäische Inschriften*, 1962–64, 2:205–06, for listing of names.) Forms comparable to our *l, k, w, r,* are to be found in the Saqqarah stela (M. Lidzbarski, *Handbuch der nordsemitischen Epigraphik*, 1898, 448, pl. 28:1), which is dated to 482 B.C. Also analogous is the script of the Tēmā stela (*CIS* 2:113), which has in line 13 a clear form of our *z*. The Assuan stela (*CRAI*, 1903, pl. opp. 270) has good examples of our *r* and *w*. For the *w* there is also the Tobiah inscriptions at ʿArâq el-Emîr (E. Littmann, *Greek and Latin Inscriptions*, sec. A, I, 1914, 1–4). I am indebted to Professor Cross for these and other useful references. For a comparative study of incense burners from South Arabia, Palestine, Cyprus, and Mesopotamia see James B. Pritchard, "An Incense Burner form Tell es-Saʿidiyeh, Jordan Valley," *Studies on the Ancient Palestinian World*, 9–17; Nelson Glueck, "Incense Altars," *Eretz Israel* 10:120–125; and M. O. Shea, "The Small Cuboid Incense-burners of the Ancient Near East," *Levant* 15:76–109.

IX

Stratum II

Stratum II consists of a building in 31-A/E-5/8 (figs. 133, 136, and 186), part of which was constructed upon the remains of the square building of Stratum III. The west wall of the latter, in 31-E/F-4/9, lies slightly to the east and below the east wall of the building of Stratum II, in 31-E-5/8. From the overlap of these two buildings it is clear that Stratum II was the immediate successor to Stratum III.

The rectangular building of Stratum II, measured 13.30 by 21.20 m. The external walls of the building averaged 90 cm. in thickness, as did the longer of the east-west partition walls. Other partition walls were 65 cm. thick. The mud-brick walls were laid upon stone foundations, which for the east-west outside walls and for the partition wall to the west of Room 201 were built of four or five courses of stones. The foundations for the other partition walls within the building were generally only two (rarely three) courses deep.

An unusual feature of construction came to light when the mud-brick walls were removed from their foundations. When the builders had completed the stone foundation they laid a layer of reeds crosswise to the length of the wall in a layer of mud plaster (fig. 149); upon these reeds the first course of bricks was laid (For the use of layers of reeds between courses of brick, see Herodotus, 1. 179). This construction was observed in the east-west walls of Room 202 and in the north-south wall separating Room 203 from Room 204.

The mud bricks seems to have been of two sizes. The larger measured 40 by 40 by 15 (?) cm.; the smaller, 20 by 40 by 15 (?) cm. The smaller partition walls, those of a 65 cm. width, consisted of a row of larger bricks placed beside a row of the smaller size. The joins of one row were staggered with those of the other. The 90 cm. walls were built in courses that alternated between two rows of the larger bricks and a course of two smaller bricks with one larger brick in the center.

There was evidence that the brick walls of the rooms had been plastered; but nowhere (except in the south wall of Room 206) did the plaster that coated the mud bricks extend downward over the stone foundation to the floor level. Either the plaster had fallen from the stones of the foundation or the stone foundation had been exposed to view within the rooms.

The building had been destroyed by fire, as evidenced by ash and charred roof material almost everywhere on the floor. Pieces of charred reeds were found on the floor of 31-B-6 (fig. 150) and were identified as possibly the giant reed *arundo donax* (identified by B. F. Kukachka, Forest Products Laboratory, Forest Service, U. S. Department of Agriculture). The reeds had rested upon wooden beams, whose burnt remains were frequently encountered on the floors. The best evidence came from the floor of Room 203, where many large fragments of charred beams were found on the floor lying generally along the east-west axis. One segment of a beam was more than 10 cm. in diameter and was preserved for more than a meter of its length (fig. 151). B. F. Kukachka examined the sample and reported that it was fig (*ficus*), and could be the sycamore (*ficus sycamorus*). The distance for the east-west span of the room is 4.75 m. No evidence for central supports within the room was discovered.

The accumulation of the debris of destruction as it was deposited upon the floor of the building was seen in the north balk of 31-C-7. Upon the floor of hard packed earth and patches of stone pavement there was a layer of ca. 15 cm. of charcoal, pieces of broken brick, and sherds from pots. Above this there was a thin, water-laid layer, sometimes 5 cm. thick, of a soft, pink, plaster-like material spread evenly over the entire surface. Superimposed upon it was a layer of brick debris containing some pottery, which in turn was overlaid by a layer of orange-pink, soft material and a fine layer of black ash. Over these accumulations there was a thick layer of charred beams and roof fall mixed with black soil.

This elaborate and complex accumulation of debris in layers may possibly be explained as a deposit laid by heavy rains shortly after the burning of the building. The lower of the pink layers of soft material was laid down by the action of water on the remains of ash and brick after the burning. Later a second heavy rain could have been responsible for depositing the upper layer of orange-pink material; eventually the charred roof material, which had not become solidified because of the support which the beams had provided, was packed into the position which it eventually came to occupy. No hard surfaces within the debris were encountered until the lowest hard, smooth surface of the floor was reached. If this explanation of the layering is correct then all the pottery found must belong to the time of destruction.

Room 201

The largest room of the building is Room 201. The doorway in the north wall, measuring 1.60 m. in width, was wider than any of the connecting doorways inside the building; it must have been the principal entrance. Other openings appeared into Rooms 202 and 203. Evidence that the room had been roofed over consisted of fragments of burnt roof beams throughout the area, and especially in the doorway at the north side, where ash and charcoal extended over the threshold. The roof of the room, which measured 5.10 m. across, could hardly have been without some central support, but no evidence for columns or posts was found. The south wall of this room had once collapsed and been repaired by a buttressing stone wall built again the south side of the building. Further evidence for the damage to this corner of the building was found at the southeast corner, where there is a 10 cm. gap between the stone foundation of the north-south wall and the east-west wall (not shown on plan).

Room 202

Room 202 is actually a corridor that provided access from Room 201 to five rooms to the west but not to Room 206, which was entered from Room 207. The brick of the north wall of the corridor had been almost entirely removed by the cutting of the trench for a cross wall of the Stratum I structure above it (fig. 139; see figs. 134 and 140 for photographs of the corridor after the mud-brick wall had been removed from the stone foundations).

Room 203

This room had two entrances, one from the large room to the east, and another from the corridor. It was the only room in which there remained considerable stone paving (figs. 137 and 148).

Room 204

This is the smallest of the rooms in the building; the opening to it from the corridor, Room 202, is exactly in the center of its south wall. The north-south mud-brick walls were found standing to a height of over a meter (fig. 137; for photographs taken after the mud-brick walls have been removed see figs. 135 and 146).

Room 205

In the northwest corner of the building was Room 205, which opened into the west end of the corridor. Its floor was slightly lower than that of the corridor (fig. 139), and a shallow pit had been cut into its southwest corner (fig. 135). Its south and east walls were found standing to a considerable height (fig. 139).

Room 206

The room at the southwest corner of the building, Room 206, is almost square, measuring 4.30 by 4.40 m. It is the only one of the smaller rooms that does not open into the corridor; its one doorway connects with Room 207 to the east of it. A large segment of its south wall and a smaller part of its west wall have been eroded (fig. 143), but it was assumed that the walls were continuous and without openings to the outside. Five stones appear near the center of the room and are assumed to have belonged to a temporary structure.

In view of the otherwise uniform and symmetrical plan of the entire structure and particularly the use of 90 cm. walls for the outside and a 65 cm. wall for most of the partition walls, it is surprising to find that the north walls of Rooms 206–208 are 90 cm. in width. The provision for added stress along this line may suggest that there was a second story to the building. There was, however, no evidence for a stairway or other means of access to an upper level.

Room 207

A doorway from the corridor opens into Room 207 (figs. 142 and 134). The mud-brick walls were standing, except where they had been removed by the builders of Stratum I.

Room 208

Room 208 was entered from the corridor through a doorway at its northwest corner (fig. 148). Its walls were standing to a height of over a meter, except in the places where they had been cut for later foundation trenches.

OBJECTS FROM STRATUM II
(for locus see Catalogue):

Bowl,
  S1005/P604 (fig. 18:16)
  S876/P499 (fig. 19:7)
  S832/P470 (fig. 19:13)
Bottle,
  S936/P543 (fig. 18:17)
  S934/P541 (fig. 19:32)
  S935/P542 (fig. 19:33)
Jug,
  S896/P514 (fig. 18:18)
  S988/P568 (fig. 18:20)
  S870/P496 (fig. 19:27)
  S933/P540 (fig. 19:29)
  S895/P513 (fig. 19:31)
  S816/P457 (fig. 20:17)
  S939/P547 (fig. 20:18)
Jar,
  S871/P497 (fig. 18:19)
  S890/P508 (fig. 19:20)
  S894/P512 (fig. 19:26)
  S851/P487 (fig. 20:16)
Lamp,
  S1022/P613 (fig. 18:22)
  S815/P456 (fig. 19:21)
  S937/P545 (fig. 19:22)
  S938/P546 (fig. 19:23)
  S1001/P600, 31-D-7, gray ware, L. 9 cm., H. 2.5 cm., W. 5 cm., like fig. 19:22. A
Juglet,
  S932/P539 (fig. 19:19)
Cooking pot,
  S833/P471 (fig. 20:6)
Stopper,
  S1046/M258 (fig. 18:23)
Human figurine,
  S942/Pfig14 (fig. 18:24)
Bone point,
  S948/B21 (fig. 18:25)
Adze,
  S952/F31 (fig. 18:26)
Arrowhead,
  S888/F28 (fig. 18:27)
Spike,
  S873/F27 (fig. 18:28)
  S872/F26 (fig. 18:29)
  S949/F29, 31-A-7, iron, L. 10.5 cm., D. of head, 3.6 cm., two pieces. P
Iron instrument,
  S950/F30 (fig. 18:30)
Fibula,
  S947/Br45 (fig. 18:31)

Lead plate,
S946/M228, 31-B-5, fragment 8 by 7 by .1 cm. of plate. P

Pierced stone,
S856/St63, 31-B-6, D. 5.5 cm., H. 3.6 cm., rounded.

While the assemblage of artifacts from Stratum II is not large, it is considerably larger than that found in the square building that preceded it. The most noticeable difference between the two assemblages is that 24 ceramic vessels were catalogued from Stratum II, while only two were found in Stratum III. We have listed below a table of frequencies for vessels and, for comparison, the frequencies of the same categories of vessels found in Stratum V.

It can be seen from a comparison of the categories of vessels found in the two assemblages that there is a striking contrast between the repertoire from the rectangular building of Stratum II and that found in the domestic area of Stratum V. The three categories of vessels most frequently encountered in Stratum II are jugs, lamps and jars, which constitute 66 percent of the total vessels. Yet, in Stratum V these vessels make up but 11 percent of the total. On the other hand the bowls, juglets, and cooking pots found in Stratum II make up 21 percent of the total, compared to a proportion of 63 percent of the total assemblage in Stratum V. Bottles, which are fairly frequent in Stratum II, do not appear in the houses and streets of Stratum V. On the other hand, kraters, storage jars, and decanters, so well represented in Stratum V, are not found at all in Stratum II.

CATEGORIES OF CATALOGUED VESSELS

	Stratum II		*Stratum V**	
	No.	%	No.	%
Jugs	7	29	6	6
Lamps	5	21	4	4
Jars	4	16	1	1
Bowls	3	13	21	21
Bottles	3	13	—	—
Juglets	1	4	22	21
Cooking pots	1	4	22	21
Kraters	—	—	10	10
Storage jars	—	—	9	9
Pilgrim flasks	—	—	2	2
Decanters	—	—	5	5
Total	24		102	

*See p. 32.

Notes on Ceramic Forms from Stratum II

Lamps

Of the five lamps found in Stratum II, three belong to a well-known type that can be dated with relative precision (fig. 19:22 and 23; and S1001/P600, not illustrated). They are molded lamps, with a watchlike shape in profile, a long tubular nozzle, and a low flat or slightly concave base. The most distinctive feature is a projection from the side of the body (left side for fig. 19:22, 23; and right side for S1001/P600). On the upper side of two of the projections there appears a design of volutes (fig. 19:22 and S1001/P600). The top of the most elaborately decorated lamp, S1001/P600, is molded with lines extending as rays from the filling hole and a herringbone design in the area where the nozzle joins the body. Rays also decorate the top of fig. 19:22; but the top of the lamp in fig. 19:23 is plain except for three lines.

According to Richard Howland, this type of lamp was imported into Athens in the middle years of the third century B.C. and reproduced there (*Agora* 4: 143, Type 45A). Similar examples in the Benachi collection in Alexandria suggest that Egypt may have been the source for the form (ibid., pl. 55, Benachi 3). Fourteen examples of this type were found at Umm el-'Amed, south of Tyre (*Umm el-'Amed*, fig. 86d–f, h), and are dated by the excavator to the first half of the second century B.C., or even to the end of the third. At Tarsus, a single example of this type was found and placed in Group IV (*Tarsus* 1: no. 39; from a Hellenistic-Roman Unit, midsecond to ca. midfirst century B.C.). For examples found in Palestine see C. A. Kennedy, "The Development of the Lamp in Palestine," *Berytus* 14: 67–115, Type 2, no. 484; *Gezer* 3: pl. 183:16 (without projecting knob); *SS* 3: fig. 87:3; G. A. Reisner et al., *Harvard Excavations at Samaria* 1: 320, fig. 191:15a. Four examples were found at Sarepta (see forthcoming final report).

Fusiform Unguentaria

The fusiform unguentarium or spindle bottle shown in figs. 18:17 and 19:33 belongs to a type found in Palestine in the first half of the second century B.C. (P. W. Lapp, *Palestinian Ceramic Chronology, 200 B.C.—A.D. 70*, 197). But it appears in various parts of the eastern Mediterranean as early as the end of the fourth century B.C. (see P. Kahane, "Pottery Types from the Jewish Ossuary-Tombs around Jerusalem—I," *IEJ* 2: 131–39 for a listing of examples published before 1952).

Fish Plate

The fish plate of metallic-hard red ware (fig. 19:7) is a locally made dish common in the Hellenistic period in Palestine. At Samaria (*SS* 3: fig. 37:2) an imported example of similar form was found, as well as 43 sherds of out-turned rims, most of which were thought to have belonged to fish plates. See P. W. Lapp, *Palestinian Ceramic Chronology*, 206–207 for other Palestinian examples.

^{14}C Dates for Samples of Charcoal from Stratum II Building

Sample No.	Age BP (5568 Half-Life)	RIC Calibrated Date (1 sigma)	RIC Calibrated Date (2 sigma)	Sample No.	Age BP (5568 Half-Life)	RIC Calibrated Date (1 sigma)	RIC Calibrated Date (2 sigma)
P-1095 31-C-7 Room 203	2100 ± 60	190–15 B.C.	380 B.C.–A.D. 15	P-1447 31-B-6	2230 ± 50	405–180 B.C.	410–160 B.C.
P-1097 31-D-8 Room 203	2180 ± 50	390–165 B.C.	400–30 B.C.	P-1098 31-B-6	2270 ± 50	410–370 B.C.	525–175 B.C.
P-1096 31-D-8 Room 203	2200 ± 60	395–170 B.C.	405–45 B.C.				

Note: All samples had NaOH pretreatment.

The average age for the five samples is 2200 ± 60, converts to date ranges of 395–170 B.C. (1 sigma) and 405–45 B.C. (2 sigma).

Summary

The large building of Stratum II seems to have had only one major period of use. The outside walls (see fig. 141 for the west wall; fig. 142 for the south wall; fig. 144 for the east wall; and figs. 145–147 for the north wall) run continuously without any breaks or additions; only a slight repair is apparent at the east end of the south wall, which has been mentioned above. From the plan (fig. 186) it is apparent that the north wall was extended eastward, possibly to enclose an additional area. However, any structure that may have existed in this area to the east of the building would have been destroyed by the builders of the two reservoirs belonging to Stratum I. The differences between the assemblages of artifacts found in this stratum and those found within the domestic area of Stratum V are significant. The absence of mortars, pestles, and baking ovens would suggest that bread was produced elsewhere (see fig. 152 for ovens found outside the building). The total lack of storage jars and the presence of but one cooking pot point to the conclusion that the cooking area lay outside the building. These observations on the nature of the contents of the building, as well as the large size of the structure, would support the view that the building served some public function, such as that of a fortress or an administrative outpost.

X
Stratum I

The latest building remains upon the summit, or the highest part of the mound, were in 31-B/F-6/8, and consisted of a stone foundation for a rectangular building, measuring 9.25 by 10.40 m. and two plastered receptacles for water (fig. 187). Unfortunately both the floors and the superstructure of the rectangular building had been completely eroded, and it was impossible to obtain any reliable evidence either for the date of the construction or for the period of use of these structures. The relationship between the rectangular building in 31-B/D-6/8 and the plastered reservoirs in 31-E/F-6/8 could not be established precisely since the two elements were not connected stratigraphically (no common floor levels). However, the parallel alignment of the two structures and the similarities in width and method of construction of their respective walls suggest that they were built as parts of a single plan. It can be seen from fig. 187 that the east wall of the rectangular building is 6 m. distant from the west wall of the twin reservoirs and runs parallel to it. Furthermore, the one-meter foundation walls for the rectangular building appeared to have been built of the same kind of wādī stones as those found in the major outside walls of the plastered reservoirs. One may assume, therefore, that the two structures had once been connected in a single complex, possibly by walls now robbed or eroded, and that the water that drained from the roof of the building may have been collected in the two reservoirs to the east of it.

A more certain relationship is that of the rectangular building of Stratum I to the building below it. The north wall of the Stratum I building was built directly upon the foundation for the north wall of the large building in Stratum II, that is upon the north walls of Rooms 203 and 204. In fig. 153 the two rough courses of the foundation wall of the rectangular building can be seen lying on the top of the well-built foundation wall of the earlier building. The lines of the north walls of the two buildings correspond so exactly that one must rule out the possibility of coincidence in the positioning of the later wall. Furthermore, the east-west middle wall of the rectangular foundation for the Stratum I building was placed directly over the east-west wall to the north of the corridor in the Stratum II building (fig. 186). The builders utilized these two foundation walls of the earlier building, but they did not follow the plan further. Rather they cut foundation trenches (fig. 155 for a trench in 31-B-7, looking east) for other walls, sometimes directly through earlier well-built mudbrick walls (fig. 154, where the west face of the west wall of the rectangular building is seen just behind the doorway between Rooms 205 and 202 of the earlier building in 31-B-6). It would seem, then, that the rectangular building of Stratum I was laid out at a time when the ruins of the earlier building had not been covered over completely.

Reservoirs

The northern of the two reservoirs (fig. 187) was square in plan, measuring ca. 2.50 by 2.50 m. The upper portion of the walls had been destroyed and there was no evidence for a channel by which the water had been introduced. A stairway of nine steps along the west and the north walls (fig. 156) led to the bottom, which was 2.80 m. below the highest point of the existing wall structure. The steps, the walls, and the floor were plastered with lime plaster, much of which was found adhering to the stone walls.

It was also evident that lime plaster had been used as mortar in the building of the stone walls that surrounded the reservoirs.

The southern reservoir (figs. 157 and 158) was similar in size and shape to the one to the north, except it had no steps. The walls sloped slightly inward as they approached the bottom. The floor was only 5 cm. lower than that of its neighbor to the north. As can be seen from fig. 158, the plaster was of such good quality that it had survived in almost watertight condition. There was no connection between what remained of the two reservoirs. The presence of a stairs in one of these two otherwise identical reservoirs indicates that the two served different functions. One may suppose that the reservoir with steps was a bath that could be approached with ease even though the water line had declined. The pool without stairs was for storage. Whatever the function of the twin reservoirs, the arrangement is not unique. An example of a stepped bath beside a reservoir is to be found in the Herodian building at Tulul Abu el-'Alayiq at Jericho (James B. Pritchard, *The Excavation at Herodian Jericho, 1951, AASOR* 32–33: 9–10). Here, a basin (Room 9), measuring 2.35 by 3.61 m., was equipped with six steps. Beside it (Room 10) was a rectangular cistern, measuring 4.62 by 3.95 m. The probable date for the construction of the building to which these two basins belonged is the reign of Herod I, 37–4 B.C., (ibid., 57). More recent excavations at this site have disclosed earlier and somewhat closer parallels for adjacent pools (E. Netzer, "The Winter Palaces of the Judean Kings at Jericho at the End of the Second Temple Period," *BASOR* 228: fig. 1, no. 1, and fig. 3), which are dated probably to the time of Alexander Jannaeus (103–76 B.C.). This pair of adjacent basins are plastered; one has a stairs, which after the first four steps downward turns 90° to the right and continues with another step to the bottom. The basin seems to be about 3.5 m. square (another example of a stepped basin appears in ibid., fig. 7, where the steps are narrower).

Pottery from Stratum I

The assemblage of pottery from Stratum I (figs. 19:1–6, 8–12, 14–18, 24–25, 28, 32, 34–36; 20:1–5, 7–15) consists of ware found upon the surface and within the first layer of soil in Area 31. The deposit of material within the layer called Stratum I had been disturbed in modern times by grave diggers who had made use of the area for a cemetery. Thus the assemblage is mixed. It serves to suggest dates for the fill upon which the square structure and two basins of Stratum I were constructed and possibly to indicate periods of later sporadic occupation of the site.

Hellenistic forms are most frequent. There are three examples of the bowl with incurved rim (fig. 19:10–12). Although the base is missing for these bowls, it is likely that they belong to the well-documented type found in Palestine during the second and first centuries B.C. at Samaria, Qumran, 'Alayiq, and elsewhere (P. W. Lapp, *Palestinian Ceramic Chronology, 200 B.C.-A.D. 70,* 172 for references). The shape corresponds to the echinus bowls at Corinth, which were produced from the second quarter of the fourth century down to the destruction of the city in 146 B.C. (*Corinth* 7: iii, 29–33, nos. 15–34). It was known at Athens (*Hesperia* 3: 217–318, nos. A14–A18) and found in the Middle Hellenistic Unit context at Tarsus (*Tarsus* 1: 214–15, nos. 50–59).

Several pieces from Hellenistic molded bowls appear (fig. 19:14–16, 18), one of which (fig. 19:18) has a complete base with an elaborate design. In the center is a star-shaped medallion surrounded by imbricate leaf pattern contained in a circle. The adjacent pannel is decorated by nine veined leaves that extend upward. The upper part and rim of the bowl are broken away. For the Megarian bowls from Samaria see *SS* 3: 272–81 and the conclusion of Crowfoot that the Megarian ware at Samaria belongs to the second century with continuance, "though in slight quantities," throughout the first century B.C. (*SS* 3: 274). Fig. 19:32 is the upper part of a fusiform unguentarium like the examples from Stratum II (figs. 18:17, 19:33).

The assemblage of pottery from Stratum I is not homogeneous. Within this collection from the surface of the mound is the lower part of a jar that is well known from the late Byzantine and Umayyad periods in Palestine, fig. 20:14. Examples of this ribbed, white painted jar have been cited by James A. Sauer in *Heshbon Pottery, 1971,* Andrews University Monograph 7: 37–38, 43, as coming from Nebo, Khirbet Kerak, Beth-shan, Jerusalem, Bethany, 'Amman, Jericho, and Mefjer. More recently the ware has been found at Pella, a site not far to the north of Tell es-Sa'idiyeh (R. H. Smith, *Pella of the Decapolis,* 1:pl. 30:86 for a similar base; 45:281, for the white painted design).

Surface Remains

The most conspicuous architectural remains visible on the surface at the beginning of the excavations in 1964 were traces of the stone foundation for a wall that ran approximately east-west along the north rim of the tell (fig. 159). Upon the assumption that this outcropping was a city wall, the area just inside it was chosen for the first soundings to be made at the site. Eventually a segment of this foundation for a city wall was disclosed in 23-A/G-8 for a distance of 32 m. (figs. 160 and 188). It consisted of from two to three courses of stones of a wall, averaging 1.50 m. in width. The faces were constructed of large, round stones carefully set; the core between the two faces was packed with smaller stones. The line of the wall runs straight until it reaches 23-A-8, where there is the beginning of a curve toward the south. A foundation trench that had been cut when the wall was built could be traced on the inside, but there was no evidence for one on the outside. In the course of the second season of excavations it was discovered that this exposed segment of the city wall continued eastward along the north edge of the tell for at least another one hundred meters. A stretch of this continuation can be seen in fig. 159, where it extends across the deep, washed-out portion of the north side of the tell immediately above the stairway. Thus it would appear that the wall was built after the erosion had produced the depression in the north side of the tell (see p. 58).

A stone buttress, ca. 1 m. square, had been built against the outside of the wall in 23-G-9 (fig. 188). About 18.50 m. to the east there is another similar protrusion from the wall, but it had been considerably damaged. Other buttresses could be recognized at regular intervals along the line of the fragmentary city wall in its course eastward.

The relation of the city wall to the building levels on the tell has been mentioned in the descriptions of Houses 1 and 2 of Stratum V (p. 15). The line of the city wall is parallel to the east-west walls of the houses of Stratum V, but it varies considerably in orientation from the houses of the underlying levels.

To all appearances before excavation the smaller wall in 23-A/E-7 running parallel to the city wall was the inner shell of a casemate structure (fig. 188). Upon excavation it became apparent that this was not the wall's function. The lowest course of this 50-cm. wall is considerably higher than the top of the city wall to the north of it and well above the filling that covered the rooms of Stratum V. It should, therefore, be interpreted as a terrace wall built after Stratum V had been destroyed. Although there are no walls that can be assigned definitely to Stratum IV, this wall could have been a part of an enclosure for the large threshing floor and grain storage area of that period. The north-south wall in 23-E-8 appears on the plan to connect the two east-west walls, but it is more likely a secondary wall since it consisted of only one course of two rows of stones.

Rectangular Enclosure in 32-D/G-9/10

Only 5 to 14 cm. below the surface there appeared the north wall and parts of both the east and west walls, measuring 55 cm. in width, of a rectangular enclosure (figs. 161 and 189). The remainder of the east and west walls and the entire south wall seem to have been robbed. The only feature discovered within the enclosure was the stone-lined pit, 1.05 m. deep, found in 32-F-9 (fig. 162). Within the pit was a sample of wheat and legume (Appendix C, sample no. 9).

Corner of Building in 32-F/G-8

The east-west wall of a building (fig. 189) was exposed on the surface at its west end; the east end, in 32-G-8, lay only 17 cm. below the surface. No satisfactory floor level for the structure could be found. Further details about the house must await the excavation of the adjacent plots to the east and to the south.

Summary and Conclusions

Systems of Defense

The earliest city wall encountered at Tell es-Saʿidiyeh was in Sounding 3, 14-J-2/3, an area to the south of the uppermost steps of the stairway (fig. 116). From a section (fig. 184c) it appears as a mud-brick wall, more than 2.50 m. thick, belonging to a stratum lower than any which has been reached elsewhere in the excavation of the tell. Its base is ca. 7 m. lower than the base of the city wall that surrounded the city of Stratum VII. It runs along a line which is some 16.5 m. north of the projected course of the city wall of Stratum VII; thus, the defense system in this earlier period of the city's history enclosed a larger urban area that did the wall of Stratum VII. Since the wall had been in existence at the time of the cutting of the trench for the tunnel it is older than the construction of the stairway to the spring.

The first city wall that can be related to a city plan is the fortification of Stratum VII. From the plan of the preserved segment of more than 9 m. of this mud-brick structure lying to the north of the street and houses of this stratum, it is evident that its orientation is the same as that of the street and houses. The outer face of the wall had been eroded, but enough is preserved to show that it had once been at least 3.50 m. thick. The mud bricks, 46 cm. long and 36 cm. wide, were laid upon a foundation of unworked stones. It is probable that this city wall continued to be used as the fortification for the city of Stratum VI, although because of the erosion at the north of the tell there remained no stratigraphic connection between the architectural remains of Stratum VI and the city wall.

Of the wall that surrounded the city of Stratum V only its stone foundation remained, but its course could be traced for a distance of about 132 m. along the north rim of the mound. The mud-brick superstructure had been completely eroded. The wall averages 1.50 m. in width and it had a series of buttresses or projections, 1 m. by 1 m., at regular intervals on the outside. There is no evidence for any later circumvallation of the tell. The surface remains of this fortification are assigned to Stratum V because the orientation of the grid of streets and houses of Stratum V, differing as it does from that of the earlier strata, is the same as that of the city wall. Furthermore the alignment of the remaining pavement of House 2 corresponds to that of the city wall, from which it is separated by only the width of the north wall of the house.

The position of the gateway or gateways into the city can only be guessed from the general topography of the top of the tell. At the northeast the fragments of what appear to have been foundations for a city wall and a depression in the surface, which may have been formed by the erosion of this area through an opening in the city wall, make it probable that there had been a city gate at the northeast. A similar depression at the northwest of the tell may mark another entranceway into the city. Furthermore the precipituous north and south sides of the tell would have served to make entrances from these sides difficult.

Closely connected with the city's defense system was the stairway built along the north slope of the tell and leading from the city on the top of the tell to the water source at the bottom. It was a protected, and possibly secret, means of access to water. The stairway lay below the surface of the side of the tell; its median mud-brick wall provided a support for the roof; and the massive north wall at the end of its north-south segment served to protect those who made use of the tunnel from an enemy who might approach the city along the road that ran along the north side of the mound. One can only speculate about the nature of the entrance to the tunnel from the city since the upper section of the stairway had been completely destroyed by erosion. From the observation that the foundation of the city wall, which we have assigned to Stratum V, runs without interruption across the line that the tunnel probably took, it seems certain that the tunnel was constructed earlier than the city wall of Stratum V and after the building of the earliest city wall, which had been cut by the trench for the tunnel.

Urban Housing

The houses in Strata VII, VI, and V were all small domestic units in which the usual activities of preparing food, cooking, and weaving took place. Nine houses could be identified within the 400 sq. m. area of Stratum VII. In plan they were rectangular and, with the exception of House 64, consisted generally of two rooms. The houses were relatively small; four that could be fully measured had an average area of 18.25 sq. m. The arrangement was haphazard, with houses placed along narrow streets, one of which was equipped with a plastered gutter. Baking ovens, millstones, loom weights, bowls, dippers, storage jars, and other ceramic forms were frequently found on the floors of these houses, attesting domestic use. The only anomaly in the pattern of use is the three-room House 64. There, along with the more common household equipment, was a plastered platform on which rested a tripod cup lying in ashes. Two other cups were found on the floor, along with four lamps, and nine shells. Thus in addition to the more common household activities there were performed nonutilitarian activities.

Built upon the remains of the abandoned houses of Stratum VII were the six housing units of Stratum VI. These houses are slightly larger in area than those of the earlier stratum. They generally have but one room; and, as in Stratum VII, the plan for the streets and the houses beside them was irregular and casual.

Significant architectural changes and a more regular plan for the city made their appearance in Stratum V. Twelve row houses had been constructed at one time. A unit of six identical houses with their entrances on one north-south street was duplicated by another block of six houses, with their backs to those of the first unit, and their doors opening on to another north-south street. These houses were identical in plan; each had a row of columns dividing the large front room, and a smaller room to the back. The average size of the houses, 40.42 sq. m., is more than twice that of the houses of Stratum VII. The roof of packed clay overlay a layer of reeds placed over wooden beams, which spanned the walls. In addition to these two blocks of row houses there were others built along similar lines but differently placed along the streets.

The artifacts from the houses of Stratum V lay within the ash of their destruction. As in the houses of Strata VII and VI, the activities suggested by the objects found were domestic: grinding flour, baking, and weaving. An analysis of the assemblages found within these houses shows that the area occupied by Stratum V was given over completely to domestic housing.

After the destruction by fire of the houses of Stratum V the area was levelled off and used for the storage of wheat and barley. Ninety-eight circular pits, averaging 1.73 m. in diameter and .93 m. in depth, were found within the 1125 sq. m. of Stratum IV. Two brick-lined bins, 4.50 by 4.80 by 1 m. and 3.77 by 4.95 by 1 m., provided additional storage space for grain or possibly straw. While there were probably temporary shelters—a few postholes remained—there were no buildings within the area of the pits and bins, and it is impossible to determine whether or not the city wall of Stratum V was standing at this period.

Public Buildings

A large bastionlike building, 21.95 by 22.05 m., with rooms arranged around an open court was found in what we have called Stratum III, although there is as yet no stratigraphic connection between this building and the sequence of constructions in Strata VII–IV. The paved court was provided with a covered drain and most of the rooms of the building were paved with cobbles. The bricks used in the walls were square in plan (45 by 45 cm.) and timbers were built into some of the brick walls as a feature of the construction. Evidence for the roof is ambiguous: clay tiles (14 pieces) were found within Rooms 103, 104, and 109, but in Room 103 roof clay with reed impressions and charred roof beams lay on the floor. The building, covering 484 sq. m., is built of thick walls; it is of elegant proportions and situated on the summit of the mound on the south edge overlooking the valley of the Ghôr. The side of the tell falls away sharply at the south wall of the building and it is unlikely that there had been a city wall there at the time of Stratum III.

The assemblage of artifacts from the building is significantly different from that of the private houses of Stratum V. Most noticeable is the absence of baking ovens (the four ovens of Room 102 belonged to a later period) and of ordinary household ceramic utensils. A few objects associated with spinning, weaving, and sewing and objects of personal adornment were in evidence, as well as a limestone incense burner inscribed with its owner's name, Zakkūr.

A later building was constructed in Stratum II over the remains of a part of the square building of

Stratum III. Rectangular in plan, the building, measuring 13.30 by 21.20 m., consists of a large east room, from which a corridor provides access to five smaller rooms to the west. The external walls—mud brick on stone foundations—average .90 m. in thickness and the partition walls are even narrower (some are .65 m. wide). The full-sized bricks are square in plan, as they were in Stratum III, but they measure only 40 by 40 cm. The brick walls of the rooms were plastered. The roof consisted of wooden beams (fig or sycamore) covered with reeds that provided a base for the packed clay roof. A novel feature of the walls was a layer of reeds set between the stone foundation and the first course of brick laid upon it; possibly the layer provided a means of protecting the friable mud bricks against damage from ground water that would have been present among the foundation stones. A comparison of the equipment found on the 282 sq. m. of floors of the building with that of the smaller domestic houses of Stratum V makes it apparent that the daily activities of the preparation of food, so evident in Stratum V, took place elsewhere; there were no mortars, pestles, storage jars, ovens. Rather the equipment consisted principally of jugs, lamps, jars, bowls, and bottles (p. 72). One might guess from the objects found that the building was an administrative or other government center.

While the scant building remains found in Stratum I cannot properly be termed public in function, they are certainly not domestic housing units. Only the foundation of a rectangular building, measuring 96.20 sq. m. remains. To the east are the two plastered reservoirs, one equipped with a stairway, of a type known in Palestine from the first century B.C.

Dates for the Strata

There were occupations on the tell from the beginning of the Iron IIC period (about 800 B.C.), or slightly before, down through the Persian and Hellenistic and into the Roman period. From the evidence obtained from the main trench in Area 23-32, it appears that the occupation was continuous, without any major breaks, from Stratum VII through Stratum IV. But, as we have seen, it is impossible at this stage of the excavations to establish a stratigraphic connection between Stratum IV and Stratum III. Although the building of Stratum II partly overlays the square building of Stratum III, there could well have been a gap in the sequence. There is a possibility also of there having been a period of time between the final use of the building of Stratum II and the construction of the basins and building of Stratum I. Thus, for the present we do not have the evidence for a continuous use of the summit of the tell through the periods that correspond to our Strata III–I.

We have seen from the comparisons of the pottery from Strata VII–V with the assemblages from Hazor VI–V, Tell el-Farʿah 2, and Samaria Periods IV–VI, that there are significant similarities (pp. 54–56). These parallels would serve to place our Strata VII–V roughly within the first three quarters of the eighth century B.C., if the excavators' dates for the strata and periods at Hazor, Tell el-Farʿah, and Samaria are accepted. But since the pottery from the floor of Stratum VII may be associated with the end of the period during which the buildings were used, it is quite possible that Stratum VII may have been built as early as the last quarter of the ninth century B.C. Although there were no ^{14}C samples from Strata VII and VI, Stratum V did provide us with eight statistically consistent dates. For the 1 sigma calibration the average is a range of 820–765 B.C., based on a 5568 half-life (p. 33). If allowance is made for the possibility of the use of old timbers for the roofs of the houses of Stratum V, or the chance that the sample happened to come from the outer layers of the tree, then the date of the middle of the eighth century for Stratum V would fit into the span represented in the ^{14}C dates.

The area of the large trench was put to a specialized use during the period represented by Stratum IV. We have seen that the pottery forms found in and around the pits of the granary displayed a marked discontinuity with the preceding ceramic tradition at the site and had frequent parallels in Hazor IV, Tell el-Farʿah 1, and Samaria Period VII, strata which have been assigned to the end of the end of the eighth and the beginning of the seventh century B.C. The script used in the Phoenician inscription on the jar of Stratum IV (S100/S10, p. 86) has been dated to the end of the seventh century. It is quite impossible to gauge the length of occupation in the storage area, but pits were frequently dug into others that had been filled in. Thus, there is the possibility that Stratum IV represents a long period of time.

The dearth of datable artifacts found associated with the square building of Stratum III forces us to rely upon the results of the analysis of the ^{14}C samples from the Stratum and a floor immediately below it. The one ^{14}C sample from Stratum III provided a date range of 410–180 B.C. (1 sigma calibration); and the two short-lived samples of grain from the floor of a building directly below Stratum III have yielded the dates of 640–420 B.C. (1 sigma and based on 5568 years half-life).

The other stratum from which there are ^{14}C samples is Stratum II. Five statistically consistent dates for samples of carbon of charred wood and charcoal have provided the range of 395–170 B.C. (1 sigma; making use of 5568 years half-life). The most diagnostic pottery from the building of Stratum II are three lamps of a well-known type generally assigned to a period as early as the middle of the third century (p. 72) and as late as the first century B.C., and the fusiform unguentaria, usually dated to the first half of the second century at Palestinian sites (p. 73), but appearing elsewhere in the Mediterranean as early as the end of the fourth century. The dates suggested for the artifacts seem to be generally comparable with the ^{14}C dates for Stratum II. The building can be reasonably placed within the Hellenistic period.

In summary we may suggest general and tentative dates for Strata VII–IV and periods for Strata III–I.:

	^{14}C Dates
Stratum VII: ca. 825–790 B.C.	
Stratum VI: ca. 790–750 B.C.	
Stratum V: ca. 750–730 B.C.	820–765 B.C.
Stratum IV: ca. 730 (?)–600 B.C.	
(Below Stratum III:)	640–420 B.C.
Stratum III: Persian Period	420–180 B.C.
Stratum II: Hellenistic Period	395–170 B.C.
Stratum I: Roman Period	

Appendix A

Summary of Incomplete Soundings

Excavations were begun in 14-E-1/2 during the 1964 campaign in an attempt to determine the northern limits of the occupation of the tell. No walls or floors were encountered; nor was virgin soil reached in these two plots.

In 23-D-9/10 a one-meter trench was cut for determining the line of the city walls at the north of the tell. Although this sounding reached a depth of 4 m. at the dividing line between 23-D-8 and 23-D-9, there was no evidence for the defense systems associated with any of the levels extending from Late Bronze to the Iron II periods. It was apparent from the floor levels encountered that the northern limits of occupation on the mound extended to the north of this area.

Four plots, 32-H/K-8 and 31-A-8, were begun toward the close of the 1965 season for the purpose of correlating the strata of the main north-south trench in Areas 23 and 32 with those found on the summit of the tell in Area 31. Although some work was done, the actual connection was not established, principally because excavations on the summit had not reached the depth of Stratum IV of the principal excavation in Areas 23 and 32. Since the balks within the four soundings were not removed, the actual connections of the walls within them could not be seen. The results of the work in these four plots can best be interpreted after the excavation on the summit has been extended to lower levels.

In 23-G-7 a sounding was made in the floor of Stratum VII. Since this was the only area in which what could be called Stratum VIII was discovered the pottery has been reserved for publication when more of this stratum becomes available.

A more extensive sounding was made in 31-E/F-6/7, below the floor of the square building of Stratum III. A room was discovered which contained jars of grain, which is identified in Appendix C. Four ^{14}C samples were collected and analyzed (p. 000). The publication of the artifacts from the room has been deferred until a larger area can be excavated.

The material found below Stratum II in 31-A/D-5/8, excavated in 1966, has been reserved for publication at a time when this area can be extended. At the present, however, it seems likely that at the time of Stratum III this was a service area that was used for the storage of supplies and for cooking. A mud-brick wall, 88 cm. in width, enclosed a courtyard, about 13.50 by 14 m. Within it were 11 clay ovens and 9 pits dug from the floor. Below Stratum III three more floor levels were recorded, but the stratigraphic relation of these to other occupation levels on the tell is yet to be established.

Early in the 1964 season a sounding was made in Area 17 in order to determine the strata of occupation on the lower tell. It was soon apparent that the northeast section of the mound had been inhabited in the Early Bronze Age and then used as a cemetery in the Late Bronze and Iron I periods. The plan of the remains in this area has been published in *The Cemetery at Tell es-Sa'idiyeh, Jordan,* 1980, fig. 2. With the exception of the mud-brick walls of Tombs 101, 102, 108, 117, and the Byzantine (?) stone wall running east-west through 17-K-5 and 16-A-5, all the walls shown on the plan belong to the Early Bronze Age occupation of the site. Most of the stone walls shown on the plan seem to have been foundations for mud-brick walls, although the east-west wall in 17-K-6, which stands 1.52 m. high, seems to have belonged to a superstructure. The curved wall in 17-H/J-6/7 consists of a stone foundation with a mud-brick superstructure upon it. The walls of the Early Bronze period average about 60 cm. in width. Floors were generally of beaten earth, but in 16-A-6 there is a stone pavement. Although there was a succession of floor levels, the same walls were used throughout the occupation of this sector of the tell. From what has survived the erosion of the tell there seems to have been but one general period of occupation. Virgin soil was reached in 16-A-7 and in 17-H-7/9.

A sounding of 4 by 9.30 m. made in 17-H-7/9 reached the *qaṭṭārah* of the virgin soil. In a cut about 1 m. deep made in this material it was observed that there was a fault of 14 cm. in the striations that mark the deposits of the *qaṭṭārah* in the balk of the cut (fig. 163). Since the fault could not be traced in stratified occupational deposits it was impossible to suggest a date for the shift in levels.

Appendix B

Notes on a Section Through Strata VII–IV in Area 23–32

The section shown in fig. 181 is the east balk of the main excavation in Areas 23 and 32. It includes all the section drawings made before the end of the 1966 season for the east side of 23-G-2/8 (except for a segment of Stratum IV in 23-G-3; but photographs of the balk appear in figs. 63 and 66), as well as two available sections for Stratum IV in 23-G-1 and 32-G-10. The face of the balk shown in this section is not perpendicular; it has a 50 cm. step or inset between Strata VII–VI and V–IV, marked by a dot-and-dash line that is labeled "50 cm. inset." Thus, the line of the section for Strata VII and VI (figs. 177 and 178) runs 1 m. to the west of the east side of 23-G-2/8; and the section for Strata V and IV (figs. 179 and 180) runs only 50 cm. to the west of the east side of 23-G-1/8 and 32-G-10. The 50 cm. westward extension of the balk was left to reduce the hazard of a collapse of the scarp during the excavation of the lower strata. Most of the drawings and the actual writing of the first draft of the following notes were done by Magnus Ottosson and Thomas L. McClellan.

32-G-10

Pit 89 had been cut into two heavy layers of ash separated by brown clay, all of which was laid down over the Stratum V wall. The upper layer of burning can be traced in 23-G-1 and possibly in 23-G-2. To the north there is another pit (not recorded on the plan of fig. 180), which was cut earlier than Pit 89, since the tip line of the upper burning runs into the pit. Above the burning which lay in the bottom of this pit was a layer of soft, gray whitish substance that could not be identified.

23-G-1

In this section there was obviously another pit cut from Stratum IV, which missed detection when the plan of fig. 180 was drawn. On the south rim of the pit there was evidence of burning. The north rim of the pit must lie somewhere within the balk standing to the north. The filling of the pit is described as consisting of gray fill, broken bricks, and charcoal flecks.

23-G-2

The compact bands, actually of plaster, at the top of this section must represent the latest use of Stratum IV. The small pit to the south was cut from a later level and probably removed the traces of Stratum V, since the area in the plan of fig. 179 is blank at that point. The stones to the left, however, could be the inside facing of the wall of House 11 beside the clay oven shown in the plan. Below, the lines of pebbly soil belong to the north-south street of Stratum VI. Under the street is a fairly even layer of reddish brown soil or silt, which may represent a gap in the occupation of the site between Strata VII and VI. The absence of brick material in the filling of House 66 of Stratum VII suggests the possibility that during the period of desertion the mud bricks dissolved into loose earth.

23-G-3

The section of Stratum IV is missing in this segment. The mud-brick wall appears to be the lower courses of the wall for Houses 9 and 11 of Stratum V. To the south of this wall and at the top of the 50 cm. offset, evidence for the floor of House 11 appears in the thin line of dark gray or black soil, with which the stones to the south are to be associated. The stones imbedded in the wall of House 11 are probably the remains of the stone pavement inside the house. It is to be noted that there is no stone foundation for the wall of the Stratum V house; the wall had been built directly on the soil made of decomposed brick which separates it from Stratum VI.

The street of Stratum VI is absent in much of the section of 23-G-3, although it reappears to the north. From the plan for Stratum VI (fig. 178) it can be seen that the street veers to the west at this point and consequently the east side of the street was not caught in the section. Two large stones that mark the end of the street at the south of 23-G-3 are the curbing.

Below the street of Stratum VI and at the interruption of the street there is a band of dark reddish, siltlike soil, which is probably wash that accumulated when the site was deserted after the occupation of Stratum VII. Below this dark reddish band there is another wider layer of rather hard soil, and below it there is a layer of light gray, ashy soil, which overlays a wall of House 64.

23-G-4

The highest portion of this section is that of Stratum IV, a flat surface laid on material filled with broken bricks, probably fallen from the east wall of Houses 7 and 9 of Stratum V. Below the Stratum IV filling is the street of Stratum V. The large stones of the street are the west curbing. Below a layer of brown soil made from decomposed brick the street of Stratum VI reappears in its course northward. Below the Stratum VI street and the silt level on which it rests there are a mass of debris and the walls of houses of Stratum VII. It is again apparent that the ruins of Stratum VII were abandoned for a time before Stratum VI was built. The section is incomplete in the area of House 62.

23-G-5

Stratum IV is represented by Pit 22, which seems to have been filled in two stages, first from the north and later from the south. Under the floor of the pit there is some local burning lying immediately upon the upper level of the street of Stratum V. This burned material could have come from the houses to the west in Stratum V, when they were destroyed by fire. The abrupt step-down in the lowest level of the street is unexplained. Below a level of loose earth lies the street of Stratum VI, containing some large stones that probably belonged to its original construction. To the north, the layer of deposits on the street is thinner. Stratum VII is represented by a portion of the east wall of House 60.

23-G-6

In this area Stratum IV has been eroded and only the filling from the destruction of Stratum V remains. The street of Stratum V continues through most of the section and then veers to the west so that it is no longer cut by the section line. Immediately below the lines of pebbles there is a stub of a house of Stratum VI, of which there remained only the west wall and the north wall that returns to the east. What appears in the section as a door is merely a segment of the wall at its north end, which runs west of the section line (the plan does not show this). The Stratum VI street disappears as it takes a jog to the west and was not intersected by the line of the section. In the gap between the north-south and the east-west walls of a structure (not on plan) of Stratum VI lying mostly to the east of the excavated area there is a white floor line. The two stones to the south of the floor line probably belong to the east curb of the street, rather than to a stone foundation for the wall. It is difficult to interpret this section below Stratum VI. There is a series of stones at the lowest level that are part of the Stratum VII street near its north-south and east-west intersection.

23-G-7

Tip lines are to be seen running north from the east-west wall of Stratum VI, consisting possibly of disintegrated mud bricks washed down during a rainy season. The street of Stratum VI reappears in a section that shows several large stones in its construction. Below the street there is a thin layer of reddish brown clay, possibly the silt which separates Strata VI and VII. The Stratum VII street lies below with burning on top of it. Immediately below the foundation for this street is the wall of a house of Stratum VIII, which was reached in the closing days of the 1966 excavation.

23-G-8

Erosion is apparent in this area, as can be seen from the tip lines. To the north is the city wall of Stratum VII, and immediately to the south of it is the adjacent paved area. The two large stones at the south may have belonged to a retaining wall for the street of Stratum VII, or they may belong to a terrace wall that separates the north-south street from the paved area to the north. If the latter is the case then the street would have to take a turn to the right at this point. The limits of the excavation to the east made it impossible to test this hypothesis. The upward swing of the tip lines from the street of Stratum VI, as they approach the city wall, suggests that the city wall of Stratum VII served also to fortify the city in the following period.

Appendix C

Identification of Grains and Seeds

Grain samples were sent to the Crops Research Division, Agricultural Research Service, United States Department of Agriculture, Beltsville, Maryland, in June of 1968 for identification. The following observations were made by Dr. C. R. Gunn, of Plant Introduction Investigations, and Dr. G. A. Wiebe, Leader, Barley Investigations.

Provenience	Stratum	Sample no.	Contents
23-D-1	V	22	50% two-row barley hulled 50% wheat
23-D-1	IV, Pit 59	15	75% two-row barley hulled 25% wheat 1 seed, date(?)
23-E-3	IV, Pit 3	7	two-row barley hulled
23-E-3	IV, side Pit 3	6	two-row barley hulled
23-F/G-3/4 House 9	V, in cooking pot	19	two-row barley hulled
31-A/B-6		5	wheat and ½ kernel barley
31-E-7	III	16	wheat and one kernel barley
31-E-7/8	below III	14	two-row barley, 1 legume seed
31-E-7/8	below III	21	two-row barley hulled
31-E-7/8	below III	20	cruciferae
31-E-8	below III	3	few seeds each of wheat and two-row barley, cruciferae, lepidium or allied genera
31-E-8	below III	4	two-row barley hulled
31-E-9	III (?)	18	vicia eroilia wild
31-E/F-7/8	below III	1	wheat and cicer
31-J-7	III (?)	12	wheat and two kernels two-row barley hulled
31-J-7	III (?)	11	wheat and three kernels two-row barley hulled
32-F-9	IV, or later	9	wheat and legume

Appendix D

Notes on Inscriptions, Seals, Figurine, etc.

1. JUG WITH PHOENICIAN INSCRIPTION

The upper part of a small jug, with handle (S1000/S10, fig. 175:3a–d) was found in Pit 80, 32-E/F-8, of Stratum IV. The ware is tan throughout and contains a few small white grits; on the surface is a buff slip. The inscription, incised after firing, appears around the shoulder of the vessel. Professor A. Lemaire has published the following reading in *Rivista di studi fenici* 10: 11–12, pl. 6:

$\mathring{k}$ly šmm. ʾš 1ḥ$\mathring{r}$ . . .

"Vessel of oil belonging to ḤR . . ."

Lemaire proposed a date, on the basis of paleography, toward the end of the seventh century B.C.

2. OSTRACON WITH ARAMAIC INSCRIPTION

An ostracon (S889/S3, fig. 175:1) with six lines of Aramaic script written with black ink on a sherd of tan ware, with a tan and gray core, containing many mixed white grits, was found in Stratum IV of 32-G-8.

The following transcription, translation, and notes have been supplied by Professors Jonas C. Greenfield and Joseph Naveh. The drawing has been done by Ada Yardeni.

1]xx[
2 š ʾ]$\mathring{r}\mathring{n}$ krn 300[+ ?
3 pqyd lʾḥrn zẙ ʾ̊l̊k̊ . .[
4 4(?) ynwḥy šmh . .[
5 ʾḥrn. . . . kl[
6 lyd . . . [

1   xx
2 barley kors 300 [+ ?
3 deposited with (?) PN or another who is over (?)
4 4(?) his name is YNWḤY or called YNWḤY
5 PN or another (?)
6 for . . .

Notes:

A barley receipt. In line 2, probably more numerals after "300." This is a large amount. Line 3: Perhaps, a PN Aḥuna or just "to someone else who is in charge of . . ." Line 4: There are four strokes and another indistinct stroke. Line 5: If the second word could be read then the problem of ʾḥwn/ʾḥrn might be solved. Line 6: Probably a sum/quantity was handed over to someone.

3. ARAMAIC OSTRACON IN TWO PIECES

A sherd inscribed with six lines of Aramaic letters in black ink (S1143/S13, fig. 175:2) had been broken anciently. One piece was found in 31-C/D-5, and the other in 31-A/B-6. The stratum has not as yet been correlated with the general system of statigraphy. The ware is red-brown in color, has a gray core, and contains some mixed white grits. The transcription, translation, and notes are again the work of Professors Greenfield and Naveh; the drawing is by Ada Yardeni.

1 š]ʾry ʾ zy[
2 ʾn]zy ʾ mn .[
3]l̊wy$\mathring{h}$ . . .[
4 20]6 lšbd [. .
5]r plḥ šʿrn krn[
6]ʾ šwn š$\mathring{r}$[n

1 the barley of . . .
2 goats (?) from .

3 ... lwyh ...
4 26 to/for lšbd .. (with superscript r)
5 ???? barley kors ..
6 .. equal to barley ...

Notes:

We have no way of knowing how much is missing at either side of the ostracon. Since other ostraca mention barley and animals we have opted for the restoration 'nzy'. Line 3: Probably a personal name; the rest is too indistinct for reading. Line 4: šb$_d$ could be the beginning of a personal name. Line 5: a number is expected after kors. Line 6: Perhaps "worth," after "barley" restore krn ..., "kors + numeral."

TWO CYLINDER SEALS

1. The cylinder seal of brown stone (S978/S5, fig. 173:1), found in 32-E-8, Stratum V, has a length of 3.5 cm. and a diameter of 1.3 cm. The design consists of an important personage seated in a simple, high-backed chair, with a cup in the right hand, and with an elongated left arm extended toward an offering table. Upon the table, which matches the lower part of the chair in design, are four loaves of bread (?) surmounted by a fish. Behind the principal figure, and standing at a slightly higher level, is a figure with an upraised right arm and elongated right arm extending downward at the side. The figure wears a pointed cap and a long garment, the front part of which is represented in outline only. Beside the offering table is a stylized tree, shown with seven branches at each side. A crescent appears in the upper part of the scene slightly above the fish and the tree. Although close parallels to this scene are now known, the theme of a person seated before a table with food is known from the sarcophagus of Ahiram (James B. Pritchard, *The Ancient Near East in Pictures Relating to the Old Testament*, 1969, no. 458; hereafter *ANEP*), and on funerary stelae from Zinjirli (*ANEP*, 630) and Nerab (*ANEP*, 635). On each of these tables there appear loaves of bread, fashioned in a crescent shape, similar to those shown on our seal. In a relief from Zinjirli on which a man and a woman partake of a ceremonial meal, there is an offering table on which are four loaves and a fish (*ANEP*, 633).

2. Another seal (S977/S4, fig. 173:2) of tan and mottled calcite, measuring 2.6 cm. in length and 1.2 cm. in diameter, was found in 31-A-8, but in a context which has not as yet been assigned to a particular stratum. The representation is that of a bearded human figure seated in a small chair with a curving back. He raises a cup, to which a griffin turns back his head. The griffin's legs point toward a plant. Beyond the plant is a bull with its head turned back as if to look at or nibble the plant. The bull is shown as though dancing on his hind legs, while the griffin would seem to be supported by its tail and one leg. A second and somewhat larger plant or bush and an oval form or rhomb terminate the scene.

FIGURINE OF A SEATED PREGNANT WOMAN

A figurine of a pregnant woman seated on a chair or throne (fig. 169:6–7) was found in 31-C/D-5 within a context which is probably to be correlated with Stratum III, although the relationship of the locus to the square building has yet to be determined. Traces of reddish-brown paint appear on the front of the figure and on the headdress. This type of figurine has long been known from sites in Syro-Palestine and Cyprus. Although the representation is generally assigned to the Persian period, a precise archaeological context is lacking for most of the examples. An example has come from both the first and second levels at Kharayeb, in south Lebanon (*BMB* 11: pl. 2:1; 26: pl. 7:4). One has been found at Byblos (M. Dunand, *Fouilles de Byblos* 2: pl. 168:9047), and two are in the Musée du Louvre (L. Heuzey, *Catalogue des figurines antiques de terre cuite*, 1923, nos. 193, 194, fig. 6:3). This figure was popular at Sarepta, where fragments from numerous examples were found among the votive objects within the shrine (James B. Pritchard, *Recovering Sarepta, A Phoenician City*, 1978, 144–45, fig. 140). Examples have come from the Palestinian sites of Tel Sippor (*'Atiqot*, English Series, 6: 12, pl. 6:19, 20), Tell Abu Hawan (*QDAP* 4: 16, no. 25, and 17, no. 26, both from Stratum II), Makmish (*IEJ* 10: pl. 11A, B), Tell es-Safi (F. J. Bliss and R. A. S. Macalister, *Excavations in Palestine during the Years 1898–1900*, 1902, 138, pl. 70:10), Beth-shan (G. M. FitzGerald, *Beth-Shan Excavations 1921–1923*, 1931, pl. 24:3, left) and Achzib (*IEJ*, 9, p. 271). A number of these figurines have found their way into collections of Cypriot objects (N. Breitenstein, *Danish National Museum, Catalogue of Terra-cottas* ..., 1941, nos. 42–43, fig. 5; L. P. di Cesnola, *A Descriptive Atlas of the Cesnola Collection of Cypriote Antiquities* 2: pl. 4:23, 25–26; A. S. Murray et al., *Excavations in Cyprus*, 1900, 114, fig. 165:8–9). W. Culican has discussed the "Dea Tyria Gravida" and listed examples of the figurine in *Australian Journal of Biblical Archaeology* 1, no. 2: 35–50. See also: E. Stern, *Material Culture of the Land of the Bible in the Persian Period 538–332 B.C.*, 1982, 272, n. 57, for additional references to this type of figurine.

METAL OBJECTS

The bronze ladle, S1147/Br71 (fig. 172:1) was found in an as-yet-undefined stratum of 31-A/B-7. The handle ends in a hook or loop, at the end of which is a bird's head, possibly that of a swan or a duck. Protruding from the rim of the cup of the ladle are two projections near the point where the handle is attached to the cup. These would have served to hold the ladle securely to the outside of the vessel with which it was used if it were turned upside down and hooked over the rim. Similar ladles are known from Palestine, Cyprus, and Greece (*Gezer* 3: 135:15; *Beth-pelet* 1: pl. 27:817, 829 and pl. 47:716, 817; *Gerar*, pl. 24:AL196; Sarepta S2399 and S2561 in the forthcoming final report; D. M. Robinson, *Excavations at Olynthus* 10: 194–98, pl. 50:613, for examples said to have been found near the site of Olynthus and dated to the fifth or early fourth century B.C. by the author; see ibid., 195–96, n. 25, for a listing of examples of this type of ladle; *Swedish Cyprus Expedition* 2: pl. 45:4 for example from Marion Tomb 25:16, and pl. 154:5 for another from Marion Tomb 34:43).

FIBULAE

Five fibulae were found in Strata VII, V, III, and II. The earliest is of iron (fig. 5:22) and has a plain arched bow and fits into Stronach's Near Eastern Type I.1 (David Stronach, "The Development of the Fibula in the Near East," *Iraq* 21: 181–206), which is said to be common from about 800–600 B.C. (ibid., 190). Examples of this type of fibula have been found at Lachish (*Lachish* 3: pl. 58:22, 24), Gerar (*Gerar*, pl. 18:12), Gezer (*Gezer* 3: pl. 134:4), and elsewhere. A fibula from Stratum III (fig. 18:11) seems to be of the same type, although there is a difference in the manner of attaching the pin to the bow.

The two examples from Stratum V, although quite different, have a triangular bow. Fig. 14:33 has a large button at the end of the pin. There is some decoration on the part of the bow that has the clasp, but it has been almost destroyed by corrosion. The second fibula from Stratum V, fig. 14:32, is smaller and has an iron pin and is decorated on the bronze bow. These two examples should be classified as Near Eastern Type III in Stronach's scheme, a type that was used from the eighth century B.C. to the first century A.D. (Stronach, *Development of the Fibula*, 193–94). The one fibula from Stratum II is shown in fig. 18:16. It belongs to the triangular bow type and bears some decoration at the spiral end of the bow. For a later study of the fibula in Cyprus and the Near East see: Judy Birmingham, "The Development of the Fibula in Cyprus and the Levant," *PEQ*, 1963, 80–112.

Figures

Note on the present location of pottery:
All examples of forms from the Type Series (TS) are in the University Museum of the University of Pennsylvania, Philadelphia, as are the entries marked "P" at the end of the description. An "A" is used to designate objects which are now in the National Museum, Amman, Jordan. "S" indicates that the object was stored in the expedition house at Tell es-Sa'idiyeh, which was destroyed in 1968.

Figure 1 (Stratum VII)

	No.	Type	Provenience	Field No.	Description
Krater					
	1	5	23-F-8	TS	Tan ware; tan core; many mixed black grits.
	2	5	23-F-7	TS	Tan ware; grayish tan core; many small black grits.
	3	5	23-G-8	TS	Tan ware; tan core; many small and medium black grits.
	4		23-G-4	TS	Red-brown ware; tan core; many mixed black and white grits.
	5	5	23-F/G-3	TS	Brown ware; brown core; some small black and white grits.
	6		23-F-2	TS	Tan ware; tan core; many mixed black and white grits; red-brown slip on rim.
	7	4	23-F-7	TS	Red-brown ware; gray core; many mixed white grits; burnished on rim.
	8		23-F-8	TS	Red-brown ware; red-brown core; many small and medium black and white grits.
	9		23-F-6	TS	Tan ware; tan core; many small black grits.
	10		23-F-5	TS	Tan ware; tan core; many mixed black and white grits.
	11		23-F-7	TS	Tan ware; tan core; many mixed black and white grits.
	12		23-F/G-7/8	TS	Red-brown ware; gray core; many mixed black and white grits.
	13		23-G-8	TS	Tan ware; tannish gray core; many small black grits.
	14		23-F-7	TS	Red ware; tan core; many mixed black and white grits.
Bowl					
	15		23-F-7	TS	Tan ware; tan core; many small black grits; finely burnished inside and outside.
Krater					
	16		23-F/G-7/8	TS	Red-brown ware; red-brown core; many small and medium black grits.
	17		23-F-8	TS	Red ware; tan core; many small and medium brown and white grits; burnished outside.
	18		23-F-4/5	TS	Tan ware; tan core; some mixed black grits.
Tripod cup					
	19	12	23-F-7	TS	Red-brown ware; red-brown core; many small and medium black grits.
Mold					
	20		23-F-2	TS	Brown ware; gray core; some mixed white grits.
Lamp					
	21		23-G-3	TS	Tan ware; tan core; many small black and white grits; carbon deposit on nozzle.
Krater					
	22		23-G-8	TS	Brown ware; gray core, gray inside; many mixed black and white grits.

FIGURE 1

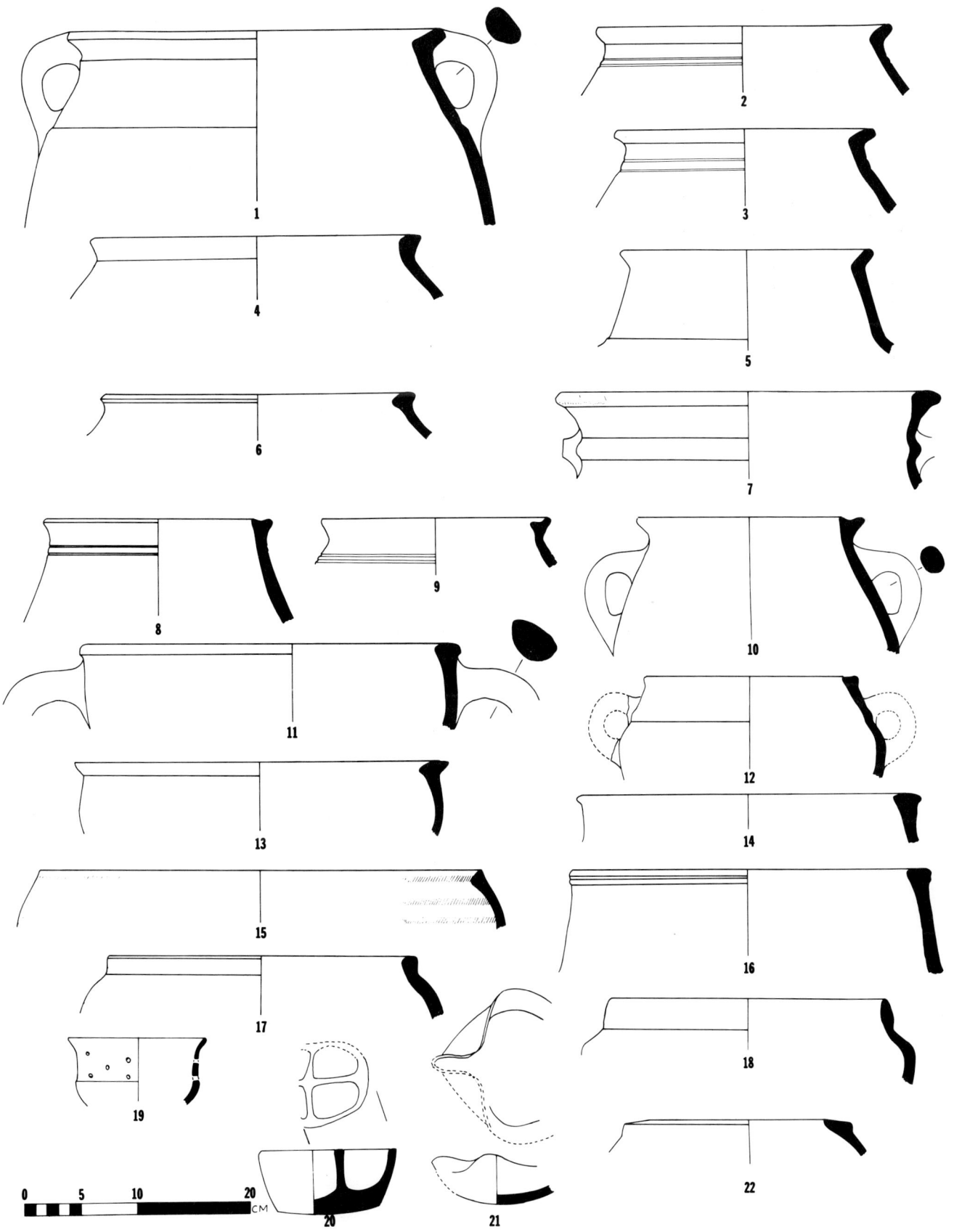

Pottery from Stratum VII.

Figure 2 (Stratum VII)

	No.	Type	Provenience	Field No.	Description
Bowl					
	1		23-G-8	TS	Buff ware; tan core; many small black and white grits.
	2		23-F-5	TS	Brown ware; gray core; many mixed black and white grits.
	3		23-G-8	TS	Red-brown ware; gray core; many mixed white grits.
	4		23-F-5	TS	Buff ware; brown core; a few small black and many small white grits.
	5		23-F/G-3	TS	Tan ware; tan core; some small black and white grits.
	6		23-F/G-7/8	TS	Red-brown ware; red-brown core; many mixed black and white grits; hand burnished outside and on rim.
	7		23-F-5	TS	Tan ware; tan core; mixed black and white grits; burnished outside.
	8		23-F-2	TS	Buff ware; buff core; many mixed white grits; red-brown slip on inside, rim and dripping down outside; burnished inside and out.
	9		23-F/G-3	TS	Tan ware; tan core; many mixed black and white grits; burnished inside and out.
	10		23-F-5	TS	Tan ware; gray core; many mixed white and some black grits.
	11		23-G-8	TS	Tan ware; tan core; some small white grits; burnished on rim and outside.
	12		23-F/G-3	TS	Tan ware; tan core; some mixed black and white grits.
	13		23-F-5	TS	Red ware; tan core; many small black and white grits; burnished inside on rim.
	14		23-F/G-3	TS	Tan ware; tan core; many small black and some white grits.
	15		23-F-5	TS	Tan ware; tan core; many small and medium black grits; burnished inside and out.
	16		23-F-7	TS	Tan ware; tan core; many mixed black, white and brown grits; red-brown slip inside and out.
	17		23-F/G-4/5	TS	Tan ware; tan core; many small black grits; self slip.
	18		23-F-2	TS	Tan ware; tan core; some small black grits; red-brown slip inside, on rim and below.
	19		23-F-7	TS	Buff ware; buff core; many mixed black and white grits.
	20		23-G-8	TS	Tan ware; gray core; many large brown, black and white grits; burnished on rim.
	21	1	23-F/G-3	TS	Tan ware; tan core; many black and white very small grits; burnished outside.
	22	2	23-G-4	TS	Tan ware; tan core; mixed black, brown and many small white grits; burnished outside.
	23	9	23-G-4	TS	Red ware; gray core and inside; many mixed white and some black grits.
	24	2	23-G-4	TS	Tan ware; tan core; many mixed black and some white grits; burnished outside.
	25		23-G-4	TS	Red ware; brown core; many small black and white grits; red-brown paint outside and inside rim.
	26	2	23-F/G-7/8	TS	Red ware; tan core; many small black and white grits; red-brown slip on outside; burnished inside and out; very finely on inside.
	27		23-G-3	TS	Tan ware; tan core; many mixed black and white grits.
	28		23-F/G-4/5	TS	Buff ware; buff core; many mixed black and white grits; red-brown slip all over; hand burnished inside and out.
	29	2	23-F/G-4/5	TS	Tan ware; tan core; many small black and white grits; burnished inside and out.

FIGURE 2

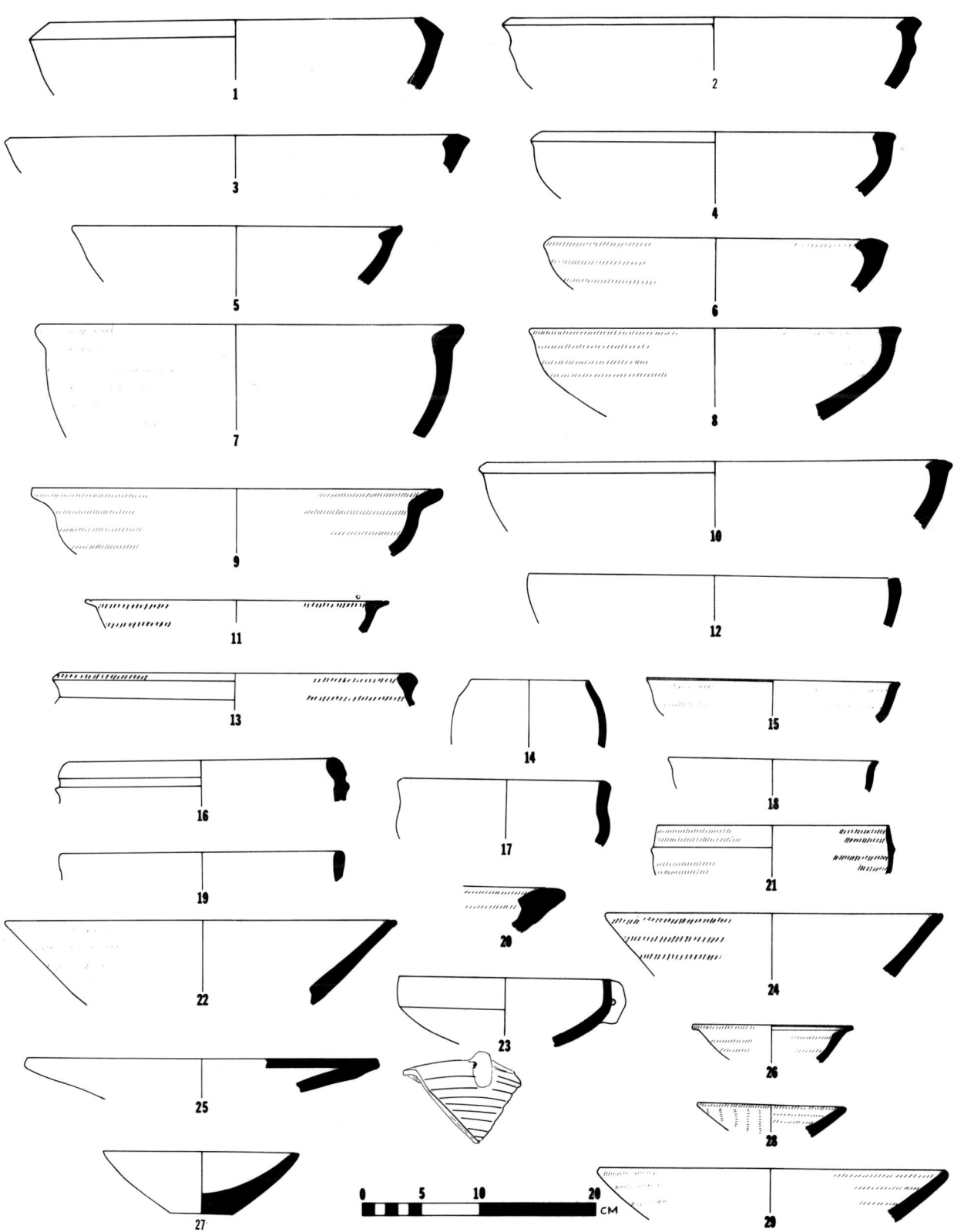

Pottery from Stratum VII.

Figure 3 (Stratum VII)

	No.	Type	Provenience	Field No.	Description
Bowl					
	1		23-F-6	TS	Buff ware; buff core; some small black and white grits; self slip; burnished inside and out.
	2		23-F-7	TS	Buff ware; gray core; many mixed black and white grits.
	3		23-G-8	TS	Brown ware; brown core; many small and some medium black and white grits.
	4		23-F-8	TS	Tan ware; tan core; many small black and white grits; burnished inside and out.
	5	42	23-F-7	TS	Tan ware; tan core; many small and medium black and white grits; burnished inside and out.
	6		23-F-6	TS	Red-brown ware; gray core; some mixed black and white grits.
	7		23-G-4	TS	Tan ware; tan core; many small black and white grits; ring burnished inside and out.
	8	42	23-F-2	TS	Buff ware; brown core; small black and white grits; burnished inside and out.
	9	42	23-G-5	TS	Tan ware; tan core; many mixed brown, black and white grits; red-brown slip inside and outside down to the carination; burnished inside and out.
	10	1	23-F/G-4/5	TS	Tan ware; tan core; many small and medium black and white grits; burnished inside and out.
	11		23-G-3	TS	Tan ware; tan core; many small black and white grits.
Base					
	12		23-G-8	TS	Tan ware; tan core; some mixed brown, black and white grits.
	13		23-F-7	TS	Buff ware; buff to tan core; some small and medium black and white grits.
	14		23-F/G-7/8	TS	Red-brown ware; red-brown core; many mixed black and white grits.
	15		23-F-5/6 House 59	TS	Red-brown ware; gray core; many small and medium black and some white grits.
	16		23-F/G-4/5	TS	Tan ware; tan core; many small black and white grits.
	17		23-F/G-7/8	TS	Tan ware; tan core; many small black and white grits; burnished inside and out.
	18	3	31-G-5	TS	Lost in transit.
	19		23-F/G-4/5	TS	Red-brown ware; tan core and tan inside; many small and medium black and some white grits; burnished outside.
Cooking pot					
	20		23-F-7	TS	Red-brown ware; gray core; many mixed white and some crystalline grits.
	21		23-F/G-3	TS	Brown ware; gray core; many mixed black, brown and some crystalline grits.
	22	43	23-F-6	TS	Brown ware; gray core; mixed black and some crystalline grits.
	23	43	23-G-8	TS	Red-brown ware; brown core; mixed brown, and some crystalline grits.
	24	43	23-F/G-7/8	TS	Red-brown ware; gray core; many mixed white and some crystalline grits.
	25	43	23-G-8	TS	Red-brown ware; gray core; many mixed black and white and crystalline grits.
	26		23-G-8	TS	Red-brown ware; gray core; many mixed white and some black and crystalline grits.
	27		23-F/G-3	TS	Brown ware; red-brown core; many mixed brown and crystalline grits.
	28		23-F-8	TS	Tan ware; tan core; many small and medium black and white grits.
Jug					
	29		23-F-2	TS	Red-brown ware; red-brown core; many mixed brown and white grits.
Cooking pot					
	30		23-F-3	TS	Brown ware; gray core; many mixed white, crystalline and some black grits.
	31		23-F/G-7/8	TS	Red-brown ware; red-brown core; tan on inside; many mixed white and crystalline grits.
	32		23-F-4/5	TS	Dark brown ware; gray core; many mixed white and crystalline grits.
	33		23-F-8	TS	Red-brown ware; gray core; many mixed white and some black and crystalline grits.
	34		23-F-7	TS	Brown ware; brown core; many mixed white and crystalline grits.

FIGURE 3

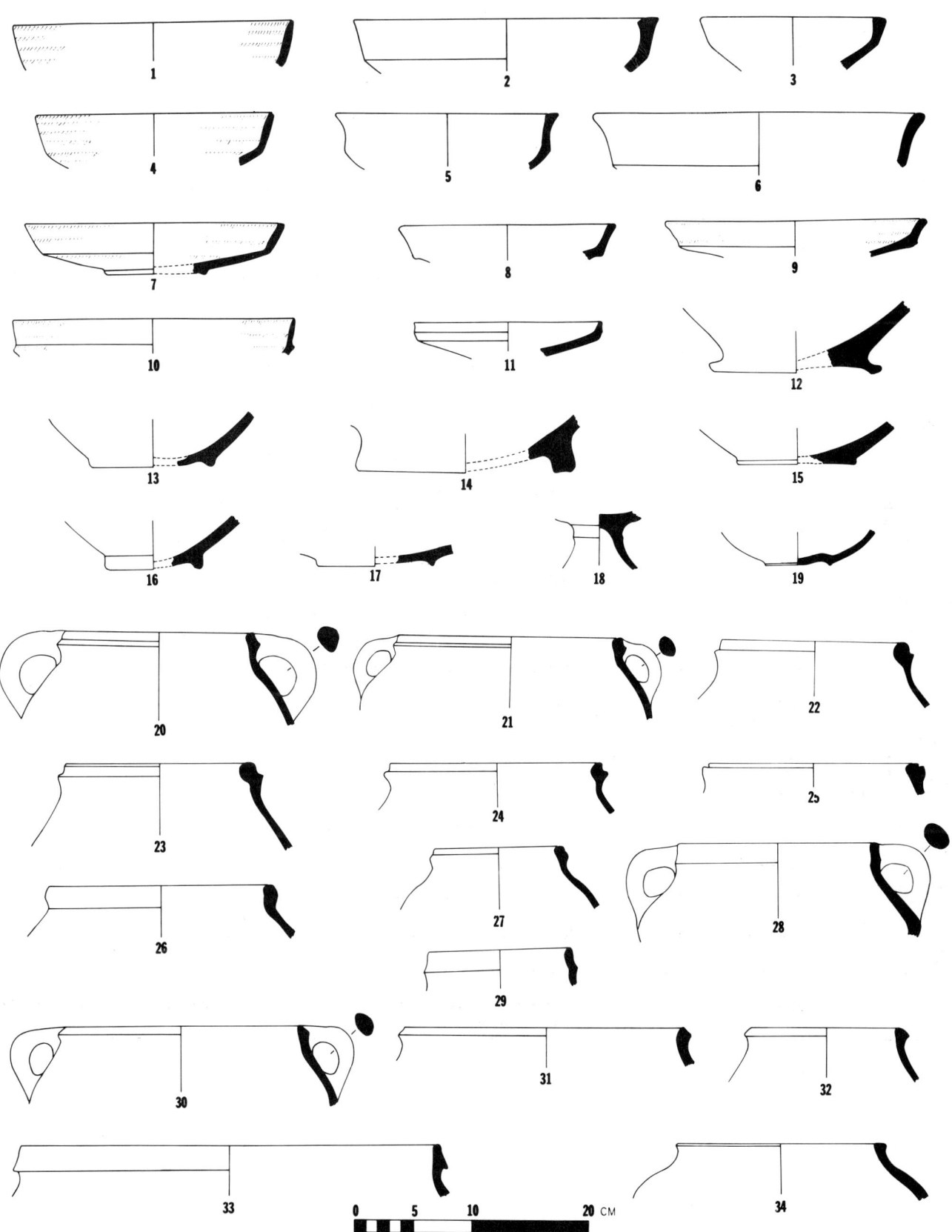

Pottery from Stratum VII.

Figure 4 (Stratum VII)

	No.	Type	Provenience	Field No.	Description
Storage jar					
	1	44	23-F-3	TS	Buff ware; buff core; many mixed black and white grits.
	2	44	23-F-7	TS	Buff ware; buff core; many mixed black grits.
	3	44	23-F-8	TS	Brown ware; gray core; many mixed black and white grits.
	4	44		TS	Lost in transit.
	5		23-F/G-7/8	TS	Tan ware; tan core; small black and white grits.
	6	44	23-F-5/6 House 59	TS	Red-brown ware; gray core; many mixed black and white grits.
Jug					
	7		23-G-8	TS	Buff ware; buff core; many mixed white and some brown and black grits.
Storage jar					
	8		23-F-6	TS	Buff ware; buff core; many mixed white and some brown and black grits.
Jug					
	9		23-F-7	TS	Buff ware; buff core; many mixed brown, black and white grits.
	10		23-F-6	TS	Red ware; gray core; many mixed black and white grits.
Storage jar					
	11		23-F-8	TS	Red ware; red core; many small black and white grits.
	12		23-F-7	TS	Red ware; tan core; many mixed black and white grits.
	13		23-F-5/6 House 59	TS	Tan ware; tan core; many black grits.
	14		23-F/G-7/8	TS	Red-brown ware; tan core; some mixed black grits.
	15		23-F-7	TS	Red-brown ware; tan core; many mixed black and some white grits.
Jug					
	16		23-F-7	TS	Tan ware; tan core; many mixed black grits
Storage jar					
	17		23-F-6	TS	Tan ware; tan core; many mixed black and white grits.
	18		23-F/G-7/8	TS	Gray ware; gray core; some small black grits.
	19		31-C-5	TS	Discard. Recorded provenience is questionable.
	20		31-C-5	TS	Discard. Recorded provenience is questionable.
	21		23-F-5	TS	Tan ware; tan core; many small black and some white grits.
	22		23-G-8	TS	Buff ware; buff core; many mixed black, brown and white grits.
	23		23-F-7	TS	Buff ware; brown core; many mixed black and white grits.
Jug					
	24		23-F-7	TS	Red ware; gray core; many small and medium black and white grits.
Storage jar					
	25		23-F-6	TS	Buff ware; brown and gray core; many mixed black, brown and white grits.
	26	8	23-F-7	TS	Red-brown ware; gray core; many mixed black and some white grits.
Juglet					
	27		23-F-7	TS	Red ware; red core; many mixed white grits; hand burnished.
Jug					
	28		23-F/G/6 E-W Street	TS	Tan ware; tan core; many small black and mixed white grits.
Decanter					
	29		23-G-6	TS	Tan ware; gray core; many mixed white and some black and brown grits.
Pilgrim flask					
	30	10	23-G-4	TS	Tan ware; brown core; many small black and some white grits.
Spout					
	31		23-F-2	TS	Red-brown ware; red-brown core; many mixed black grits.
Jug					
	32		23-G-4 pit	TS	Brown ware; brown core; many mixed black grits; buff slip.
Pilgrim flask					
	33	10	23-G-4	TS	Tan ware; gray core; many mixed brown, black and white grits.
Jug					
	34	7	23-G-4 pit	TS	Red-brown ware; tan core; some mixed black and white grits.
Handle					
	35		23-G-8	TS	Tan ware; tan core; mixed black grits; hand burnished.
Jar					
	36		23-F-8	TS	Tan to white outside; gray inside; gray core; few small white grits; finely burnished; bands of brown paint on body.

FIGURE 4

Pottery from Stratum VII.

Figure 5 (Stratum VII)

	No.	Type	Provenience	Field No.	Description
Jar					
	1		23-G-4 House 60-62	S1191/P670	Tan ware; tan core; many small and some large black and white grits; six horizontal bands of brown paint; finely burnished. Carbon deposit on body. P.
Jug					
	2		23-G-2 House 64	S1222/P680	Tan ware; tan core; many mixed black and white grits; red-brown slip. P.
	3		23-G-4	S1225/P683	Red-brown ware; tan core; many mixed black and white grits.
	4		23-G-2 House 64	S1223/P681	Red-brown ware; tan core; many mixed black and white grits. P.
	5		23-G-4 House 62	S1219/P677	Tan ware; tan core; many mixed black grits. P.
	6		23-G-3 House 64	S1260/P697	Red-brown ware; tan core; some small and medium black and white grits.
Juglet					
	7	7	23-F-7 House 55 (or 53)	S1155/P649	Buff ware; tan core; some mixed white grits. P. Fig. 164:4.
	8	7	23-G-2 House 64	S1220/P678	Tan ware; tan core; many mixed black grits. P.
Jug					
	9	6	23-G-4 House 60–62	S1198/P674	Buff ware; some mixed black grits; tan to red-brown slip. P.
Juglet					
	10		23-G-3 House 64	S1257/P695	Red-brown ware; tan core; many mixed black and white grits; traces of tan slip and four horizontal red-brown bands; burnished. P.
Tripod cup					
	11	12	23-G-3 House 64	S1221/P679	Tan ware; tan core; many mixed black and white grits; red-brown paint on rim and in zone ca.35 mm. down inside and out.
	12	12	23-G-3 House 64	S1199/P675	Tan ware; tan core; many mixed black and white grits. S.
Lamp					
	13		23-G-3 House 64	S1183/P662	Tan ware; tan core; many small black grits; carbon on nozzle. P.
	14		23-G-3 House 64	S1185/P664	Buff ware; gray core; many small and medium black and white grits; carbon deposit. P.
	15		23-G-3 House 64	S1182/P661	Red-brown ware; red-brown core; many small and medium black grits. S.
Spindle whorl (?)					
	16		23-F-5	S1151/M284	Frit, faience? White/blue. P.
Pilgrim flask					
	17	11	23-G-4 House 60–62	S1237/P692	Red-brown ware; many mixed black and white grits; incised concentric circles on sides. P.
Arrowhead					
	18		23-F-5 House 59	S1153/F62	Iron. P.
	19		23-G-3 House 64	S1265/F79	Iron. Corroded.
	20		23-G-8	S1152/F61	Iron; point broken. P.
Tripod cup					
	21	12	23-G-3 House 64	S1187/P660	Red ware; mixed black and white grits; some holes not punched through. P.
Fibula					
	22		23-G-2 House 66	S1207/F65	Iron; in two pieces. P.
Bead					
	23		23-G-2 House 64	S1246/J69AB	Frit; light green, luminescent. P.
	24		23-G-7 House 51	S1253/J70	Frit; white. P.
	25		23-G-2 House 64	S1245/J68	Frit; light blue; luminescent. P.
Cup					
	26		23-F-2 House 65	S1144/St79	Alabaster.

Figure 7 (Stratum VI)

	No.	Type	Provenience	Field No.	Description
Juglet					
	1	17	23-F-2 House 43	S1096/P637	Black ware; gray core; many mixed white grits; burnished vertically. P. Fig. 164:9.
	2	17	23-F/G-7/8 House 33	S1095/P636	Black ware; gray core; many small black and white grits; burnished vertically. P.
	3	17	23-F/G-5 House 37	S1090/P631	Black ware; brown core; many small white grits; black slip; burnished vertically. P. Fig. 164:5.
	4	16	23-F-5 House 37	S1081/P628	Red ware; red core; many small black and white grits; burnished vertically. P. Fig. 164:8.
	5	16	23-F-5 House 37	S1080/P627	Tan ware; tan core; many small and few large white grits; burnished vertically. P.
	6	16	23-G-3/4 House 41	S1053/P615	Red-brown ware; red-brown core; many small and medium white grits; burnished vertically. P.
	7	16	23-F-5 House 37	S1059/P621	Brown ware; brown core; many mixed black and white grits; burnished vertically. P.
	8	16	23-F/G-5 House 37	S1092/P633	Red-brown ware; red-brown core; many mixed black and white grits; burnished vertically. P. Fig. 164:6.
	9	16	23-F-5 House 37	S1079/P626	Red-brown ware; red-brown core; some small white grits; burnished vertically. P.
	10	16	23-F-5 House 37	S1060/P622	Tan ware; tan core; many small and some large white grits; burnished vertically; fired unevenly. P.
	11	16	23-F-5 House 37	S1058/P620	Tan ware; tan core; many small and medium black and white grits; burnished vertically. P.
	12	16	23-F-4 House 39	S1021/P612	Tan ware; fired red-brown on one side; many mixed black and white grits; burnished vertically. A. Fig. 164:7.
	13		23-F/G-7/8 House 33	TS	Red ware; red core; some small black grits; traces of vertical burnish.
Jug					
	14		23-F-4	TS	Tan ware; brown core; some small black and medium white grits.
	15		23-F-4	TS	Tan ware; tan core; many mixed black and white grits.
	16		23-G-4	TS	Tan ware; gray core; some large and medium black and white grits; red-brown slip.
	17		23-F-8 House 31	S1161/P651	Red ware; tan core; some mixed black grits. P.
Pilgrim flask					
	18			TS	Tan ware; gray core; mixed white grits.
Jug					
	19		23-F-5	TS	Buff ware; buff core; many small black and white grits; red-brown slip.
Base					
	20		23-G-4	TS	Red ware; light gray core; many small and medium black grits; red-brown slip continuing over bottom of disk base; burnished on outside.
Jug					
	21		23-F-4/5 House 39	S1056/P618	Brown ware; red-brown core; many mixed white grits. S. Fig. 165:4.
	22		23-F-3/4 House 41	S1162/P652	Red-brown ware; red-brown core; some mixed black grits. P.
	23	13	23-F-5	TS	Red-brown ware; red-brown core; many mixed white grits.
	24		23-F-2 House 43	S1136/P647	Red ware; tan core; many mixed black grits; some white grits. Fig. 165:5.
	25	13	23-F-5 House 37	S1094/P635	Red-brown ware; red-brown core; many small and some large white grits and possibly sand. P. Fig. 165:3.
Decanter					
	26	18	23-F-4/5 House 39	S1057/P619	Tan ware; many mixed white and some black grits. P. Fig. 166:3.
	27	18	23-F-3 House 41	S1023/P614	Brown ware; gray core; many mixed white grits; buff slip? A. Fig. 166:4.
	28	18	23-F-4/5 House 39	S1055/P617	Red-brown ware; red-brown core; many small black and white grits; buff slip(?); incised lines on shoulder. S. Fig. 166:5.
	29	18	23-F-5 House 37	S1093/P634	Gray ware; gray core; many small and large white grits; two incised lines on shoulder. P. Fig. 166:6.
Chalice					
	30	14	23-F-5 House 37	S1078/P625	Tan ware; tan core; many small and medium black and white grits. A. Fig. 166:8.
Lamp					
	31		23-G-7 House 35	S1099/P640	Red-brown ware; brown core; many mixed white grits. P. Fig. 168:1.
	32		23-F/G-7/8 House 33	S1098/P639	Tan ware; brown core; many mixed white grits. P. Fig. 168:2.
	33		23-F/G-7/8 House 33	S1100/P641	Red-brown ware; red-brown core; many mixed white grits. P. Fig. 168:3.
	34		23-F/G-6/7 House 35	S1097/P638	Red-brown ware; red-brown core; many mixed white grits. P. Fig. 168:4.
	35		23-F-5 House 37	S1082/P629	Tan ware; gray core; some small black and white grits. P.

FIGURE 6

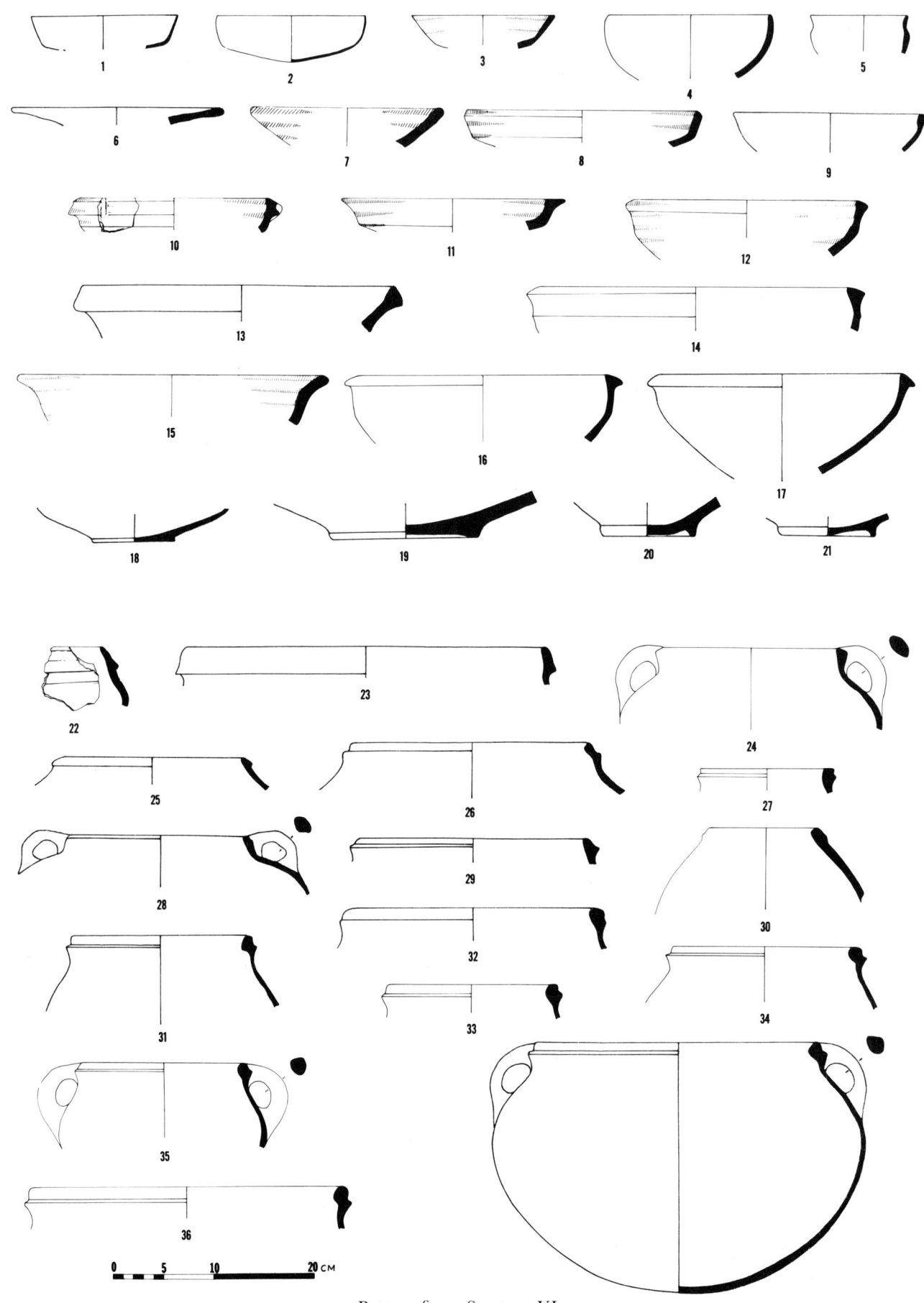

Pottery from Stratum VI.

Figure 6 (Stratum VI)

	No.	Type	Provenience	Field No.	Description
Bowl					
	1	15	23-F-5	TS	Brown ware; fired buff on outside near rim; gray core; some medium white grits; metallic hard.
	2		23-F-4 House 41	S1019/P610	Red-brown ware; red-brown core; some mixed black and white grits. A. Fig. 164:1.
	3	42	23-F-2	TS	Tan ware; many small black and some white grits; red-brown slip; burnished inside and out.
	4			TS	Red ware; tan core; some black and many mixed white grits.
	5		23-F-4	TS	Tan ware; tan core; many small black grits.
	6		23-F-7	TS	Buff ware; some small white grits.
	7		23-G-2	TS	Tan ware; tan core; many small and few large black grits; red-brown slip; burnished inside and out.
	8	42	23-D-1	TS	Tan ware; tan core; many small black and few small white grits; burnished inside and out.
	9		23-F-4	TS	Tan ware; tan core; few medium white and many small black grits.
	10		23-F-4	TS	Buff ware; many small black grits; red-brown slip; burnished inside and out.
	11		23-F-2	TS	Brown ware; many mixed black and white grits; burnished inside and out.
	12		23-F-4/5	TS	Tan ware; tan core; red-brown slip, burnished inside and out; many mixed black and white grits.
	13		23-F-2	TS	Brown ware; tan core; many mixed black grits; red-brown wash (?).
	14		23-G-7	TS	Tan ware; tan core; mixed black and some white grits.
	15			TS	Red ware; tan core; many small black and white grits; burnished inside and out.
	16		23-F-7	TS	Tan ware; brown to gray core; many mixed black and white grits.
	17		23-F-7	TS	Tan ware; tan core; many mixed black and some white grits; red-brown slip on rim.
Base					
	18		23-F-5	TS	Red ware; brown core; many small black and few white grits.
	19		23-G-4	TS	Tan ware outside; gray core; mixed small black and white grits.
	20		23-G-2	TS	Tan ware; tan core; mixed black and few white grits.
	21		23-G-3	TS	Red-brown ware; gray core; many mixed black and white grits.
Cooking pot					
	22		23-D-1	TS	Dark brown ware; gray core; many mixed white and crystalline grits.
	23		23-G-7	TS	Dark brown ware; gray core; many small white and crystalline grits.
	24		23-G-2	TS	Brown ware; gray core; many mixed white and crystalline grits.
	25		23-F-4	TS	Red-brown ware; red-brown core; fired gray in inner core; many mixed white and crystalline grits.
	26		23-F-5	TS	Brown ware; brown core; many mixed white and crystalline grits.
	27		23-G-4	TS	Gray ware; dark brown core; many mixed white and crystalline grits.
	28		23-F-4	TS	Brown ware; gray core; many mixed white and crystalline grits.
	29		23-G-7/8	TS	Brown ware; gray core; mixed black, white and crystalline grits.
	30		23-F-4	TS	Brown ware; gray core; many mixed white and crystalline grits.
	31	43	23-F-5	TS	Red-brown ware; red-brown core; many mixed white and crystalline grits.
	32	43	23-F-6	TS	Brown ware; brown core; many mixed white and crystalline grits.
	33	43	23-F-5	TS	Red-brown ware; brown core; many mixed white and crystalline grits.
	34	43	23-G-3	TS	Red-brown ware; gray-brown core; many mixed white grits.
	35	43	23-G-5	TS	Red-brown ware; red-brown core; many mixed white and crystalline grits.
	36	43	23-F-5	TS	Brown ware; gray core; many mixed white and crystalline grits.
	37	43	23-F-5	TS	Red-brown ware; brown core; many mixed white and crystalline grits.

FIGURE 5

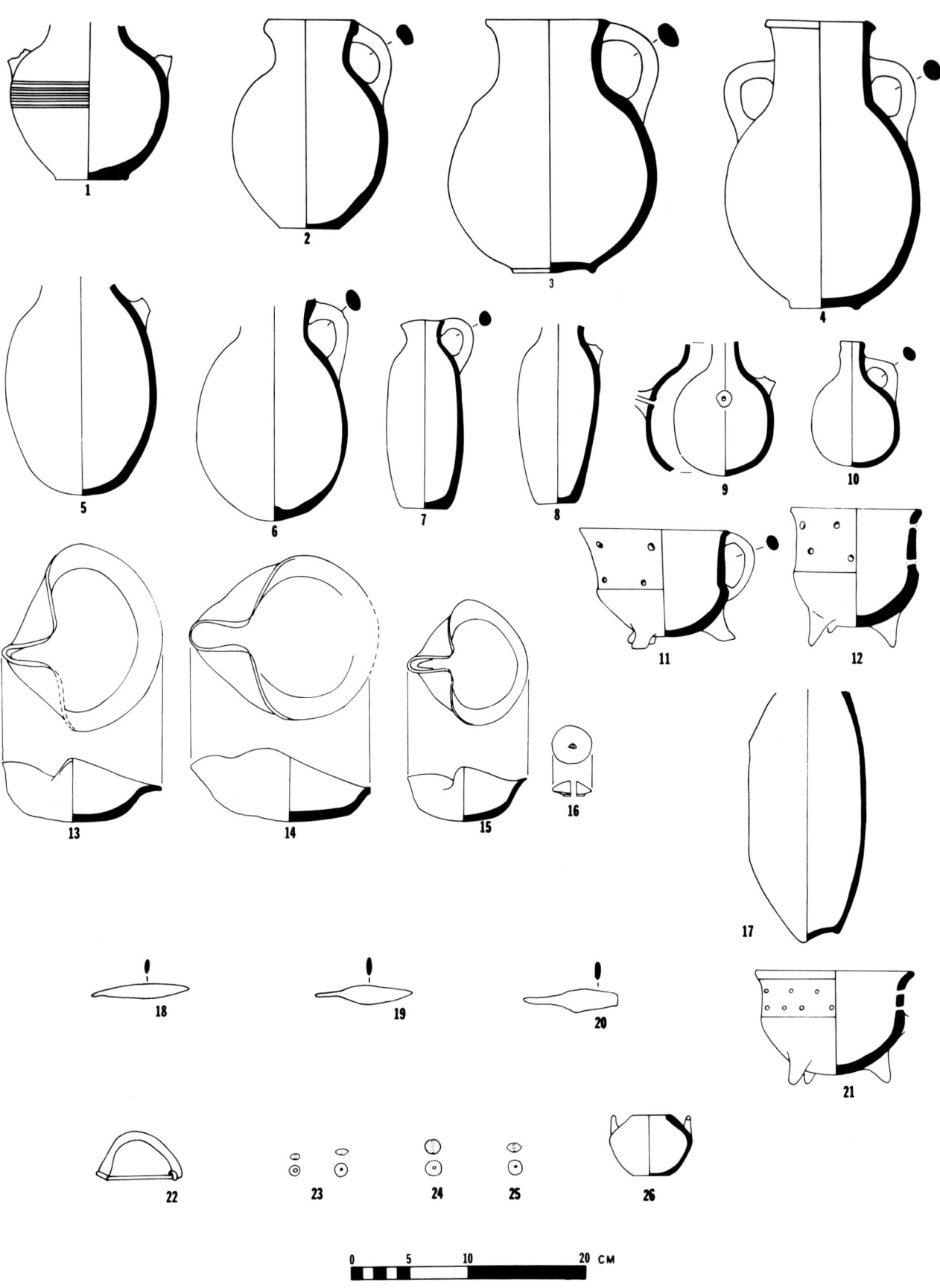

Pottery and other objects from Stratum VII.

FIGURE 7

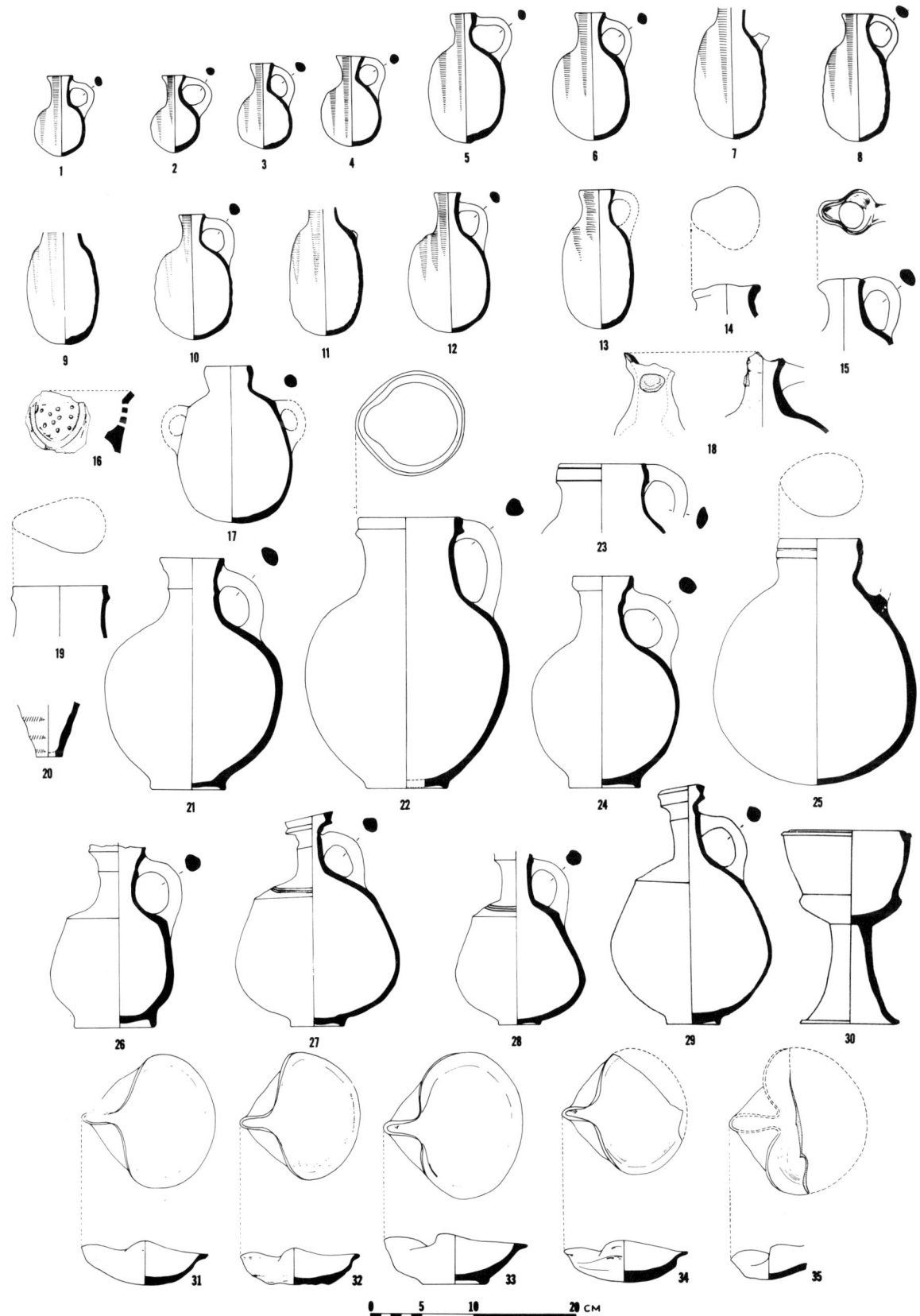

Pottery from Stratum VI.

Figure 8 (Stratum VI)

	No.	Type	Provenience	Field No.	Description
Krater					
	1		23-G-3	TS	Red-brown ware; gray core; many mixed black and white grits.
	2		23-D-1	TS	Red ware; red-brown core; many small and few medium black and white grits.
	3		23-F-4	TS	Tan ware; tan core; some black and mixed white grits.
	4		Street	TS	Tan ware; brown core; some small black and white grits; incised lines below rim.
	5		23-F/G-5 House 37	TS	Red ware; red core; many mixed white grits.
	6		23-G-2	TS	Red-brown ware; gray core; many mixed black and white grits.
	7	20	23-F/G-7/8 House 33	TS	Red-brown ware; gray core; many mixed black and white grits.
	8		23-F-5	TS	Red-brown ware; gray core; many mixed white grits.
	9	20	23-F-5	TS	Red-brown ware; gray core; small and medium white grits.
	10		23-F-5	TS	Brown ware; brown core; many mixed black and white grits.
	11	20	23-G-7	TS	Red-brown ware; gray core; many mixed white grits.
	12		23-G-2	TS	Tan ware; gray core; some black and many mixed black and white grits.
	13		23-G-7	TS	Red-brown ware; tan core; many mixed white grits.
	14		23-F/G-7/8 House 33	TS	Tan ware; red-brown core; some medium white grits.
	15		23-F/G-5 House 37	TS	Red-brown ware; tan core; many small black and white grits.
Ring					
	16		23-F-5 House 37	S1077/Br59	Bronze; some corrosion. P.
Arrowhead					
	17		23-F/G-8 House 31 (or 33)	S1145/F60	Iron; much corrosion. P.
Knife					
	18		23-F/G-2/3 House 43	S1109/F52	Iron; three rivets. A.
Tripod bowl					
	19		23-G-3	TS	Foot only; red ware; gray core; many mixed black and white grits.
Spatula					
	20		23-F/G-4/5 House 39	S1074/B33	Bone; polished but worn. P.
Mold					
	21		Street E of House 33	S1133/M282	Tan ware; tan core; some large and small black and white grits. Red-brown residue in places. P.
Cup with lid					
	22		23-F/G-5 House 37	S1084/M274	Faience; white; traces of green glaze on outside; lid and handles punctured for fasteners. Beads found inside. A. Fig. 171:1, 2.
Chisel					
	23		23-F/G-5 House 37	S1085/F48	Iron; end flattened; tang folded over; very corroded. P.
Spear					
	24		23-F/G-5 House 37	S1086/F49	Iron; in four pieces. P.
Tripod cup					
	25	12	23-D-1	TS	Buff ware; tan core; many small and large white grits.
Mortar					
	26		23-F/G-7/8 House 33	S1106/St76	Black basalt; smooth on inside. P. Fig. 170:3.
Tripod mortar					
	27		Street E of House 33	S1134/St78	Basalt fragment of tripod. P.

FIGURE 8

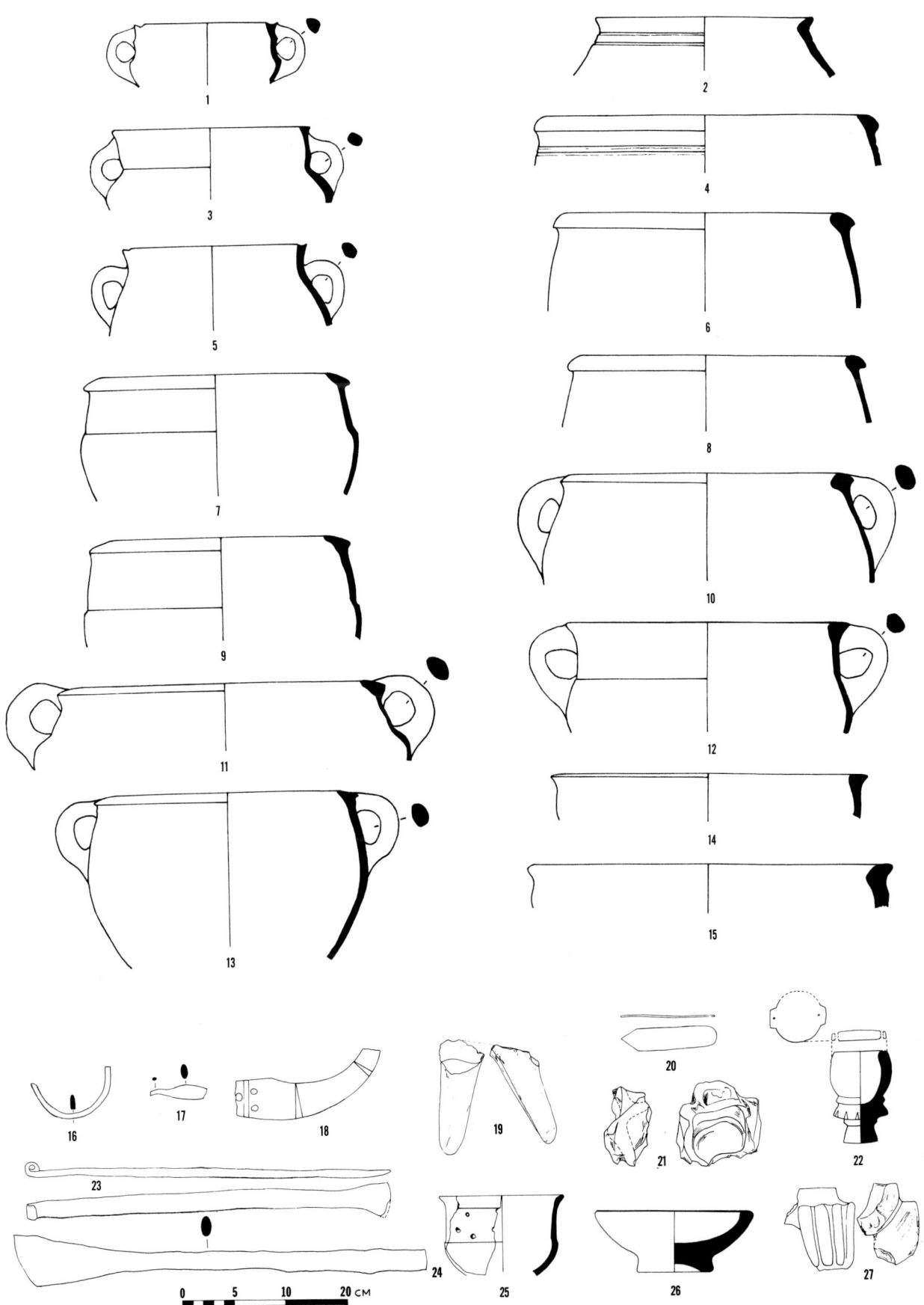

Pottery and other objects from Stratum VI.

Figure 9 (Stratum VI)

No.	Type	Provenience	Field No.	Description
Storage jar				
1		23-F-5	TS	Red-brown ware; tan core; many small black and white grits.
2		23-F-5	TS	Tan ware; tan core; some mixed black and white grits.
3		23-F-4	TS	Tan ware; tan core; many small black and some white grits.
4		23-D-1	TS	Tan ware; tan core; many small and medium black and white grits.
5		23-F/G-5 House 37	TS	Tan ware; tan core; many small black and white grits.
6		23-F/G-5 House 37	TS	Red-brown ware; tan core; many small and few medium black and white grits.
7	44	23-F/G-5 House 37	TS	Red-brown ware; gray core; many mixed black and white grits.
8		23-G-3	TS	Tan ware; burnished red on outside; tan core; small and medium black and white grits.
9		23-F-4	TS	Red-brown ware; gray core; many mixed white and crystalline grits.
Jug				
10		23-F-4	TS	Tan ware; tan core; mixed black and white grits.
Storage jar				
11	44	23-F-5	TS	Gray ware; gray core; many mixed white grits.
12	44	23-F-5 House 37	S1101/P642	Tan ware; tan core; some mixed white grits; buff slip. A. Fig. 167:1.
13	19	23-F/G-7/8 House 33	S1102/P643	Red-brown ware; gray core; many mixed black and white grits; tan slip. Fig. 167:4.
14		23-F-4/5	TS	Red-brown ware; gray inside; gray core; many mixed black and white grits.
Bowl				
15		23-G-2	TS	Tan ware; tan core; many mixed black and white grits; burnished inside and on rim.
Storage jar				
16		Street	TS	Buff ware; tan core; very many mixed white grits.
17		Street	TS	Red-brown ware; gray core; many mixed black and white grits.
18		Street	TS	Buff ware; buff core; very many mixed black and white grits.

FIGURE 9

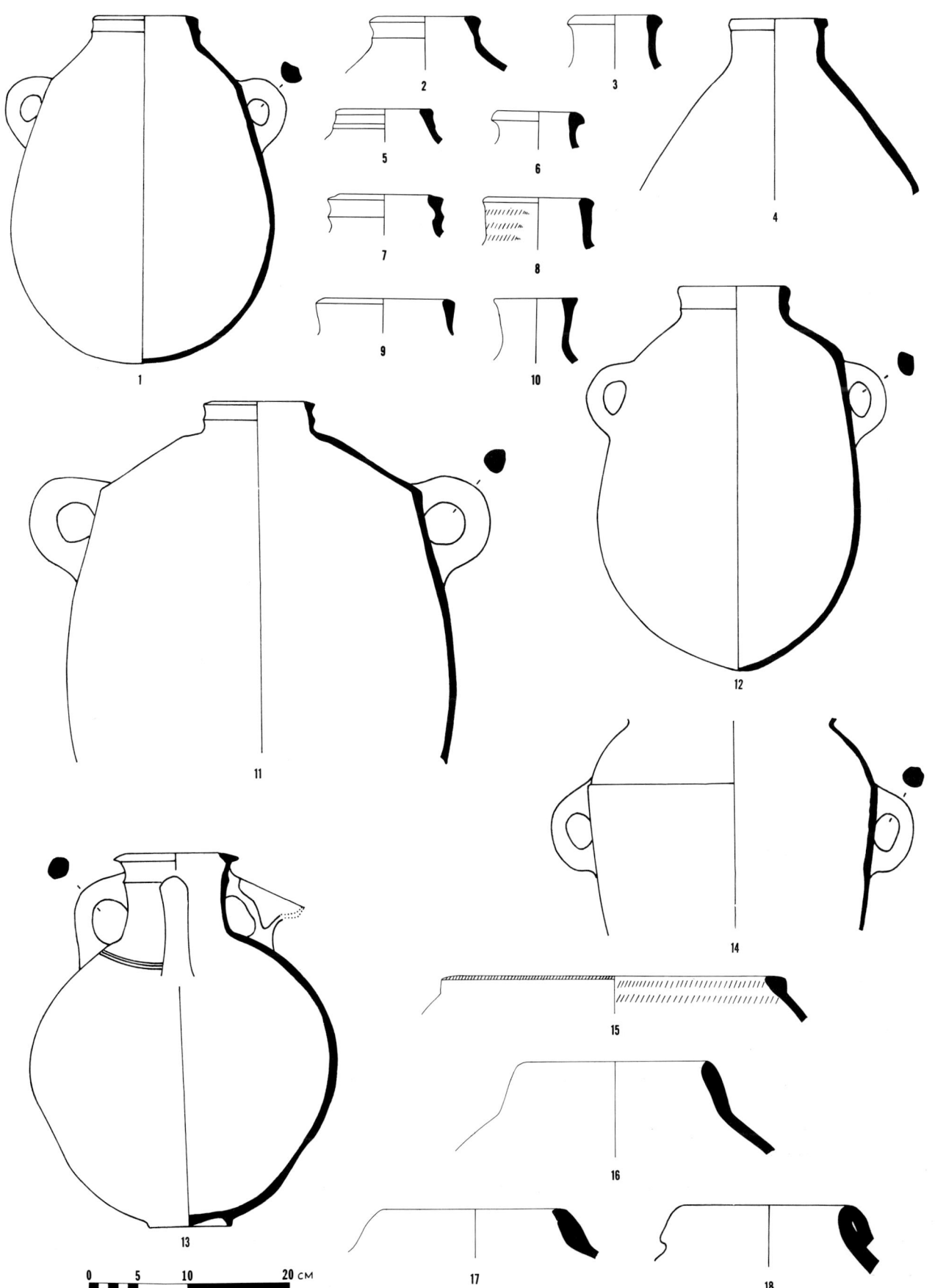

Pottery from Stratum VI.

Figure 10 (Stratum V)

	No.	Type	Provenience	Field No.	Description
Bowl					
	1	15	23-E-2	TS	Tan ware; tan core; some large and medium black grits.
	2	15	32-C-10	S817/P458	Red-brown ware; gray core; few medium and small white grits; metallic hard. P.
	3	21	23-F/G-1/2, 32-F/G-1 House 13	S1020/P611	Brown ware; brown core; mixed black and white grits; traces of two lines of burnishing on outside below rim. P. Fig. 164:2.
	4		23-F-4	TS	Tan ware; brown core; a few medium black grits; red-brown slip on inside and rim, dribbling over on outside.
	5		23-D/E-5 House 6	S217/P85	Buff ware; a few brown grits; red-brown slip; burnished inside and outside. P.
	6		23-F-5 House 7	S523/P281	Tan ware; tan core; many large white and few small black grits; painted red-brown inside and outside rim, spilled over outer surface. P.
	7	22	23-C-4	TS	Tan ware; red-brown slip on inside and spilled over outside; burnished on inside and on rim.
	8		23-C-2	TS	Tan ware; tan core; some medium black and white grits; burnished on outside and on rim.
	9	42	23-D-4 House 8	S103/P26	Tan ware; small black grits; red-brown slip; wheel burnished inside and outside.
	10		23-D-4 House 8	S105/P28	Red ware; gray core; few small white grits; burnished inside and on rim. P.
	11	42	23-E-5 House 6	S111/P34	Red ware; tan core; few large and many small black grits; red-brown slip on inside and rim; wheel burnished inside and on rim. P.
	12		23-F-4	TS	Buff ware; buff core; well-levigated clay; red-brown slip; wheel burnished on rim and interior; trace of burnishing below rim on exterior.
	13		23-E-6 House 6	S127/P46	Red-brown ware; tan core; some large and many small black, brown, and white grits; burnished inside and on rim; traces of burnishing outside; knobs on outside below rim. P.
	14		23-F-2	TS	Red-brown ware; brown core; many large and medium black grits; wheel burnished on inside and rim.
	15		23-G-4	TS	Brown ware; brown core; many mixed black and white grits; wheel burnished on inside and rim.
	16	25	23-E-3 House 10	S538/P296	Brown ware; brown core; some large and many small black grits; red-brown slip on inside and rim. P.
	17		23-E-4 House 8	S230/P98	Red-brown ware; tan core; small white grits; wheel burnished on rim and inside; traces of burnish outside. P.
	18		32-C-10	S820/P461	Red-brown ware; tan core; many mixed black and white grits; burnished on inside and rim. P.
	19		23-D-4 House 8	S107/P30	Tan ware; tan core; many small black grits. P.
	20		23-D-4 House 8	S106/P29	Red ware; tan core; slip on rim and inside; few medium black grits. P.
	21		32-C-10	S818/P459	Red-brown ware; red-brown core; many mixed black grits; burnished on inside and rim. A.
	22	23	32-C-9		Tan ware; tan core; many mixed white grits.
	23	24	32-C-9		Tan ware; tan core; many mixed white grits; traces of red-brown slip.
	24		23-F-4	TS	Buff ware; buff and brown core; many mixed black and white grits.
	25		23-C-2	TS	Gray ware; gray core; some mixed black grits; burnished on inside and rim.
	26		23-C-2	TS	Tan ware; tan core; many mixed black and white grits.
	27	26	23-F-2	TS	Red-brown ware; tan core; few medium black and many small white grits; burnished on inside and rim.
Tripod cup					
	28	33	23-G-4	TS	Tan ware; tan core; few large white and many small black and white grits.
	29	33	23-G-3 House 9 or 11	S744/P419	Tan ware; tan core; some mixed white grits. P. Fig. 168:10.
Animal figurine					
	30		23-D/E-5 House 6	S700/Pfig10	Red-brown ware; red-brown core; few small black grits; hole in center. Shown double scale. P. Fig. 169:1.
Human figurine					
	31		32-D/E-8 House 16	S979/Pfig18	Red-brown ware; tan core; some medium black grits. Shown double scale. A.
Tripod bowl					
	32		23-C-5/6 House 29(?)	S496/P256	Tan ware; many mixed black and white grits. P.
Base					
	33		23-E-4 House 8	S343/P181	Tan ware; coarse clay; brown core; many medium and small black and white grits. P.
Mortar					
	34		23-E-5 House 6	S69/St4	Dark gray basalt; part of bowl, one leg and attached strut; rough surface.
Sherd					
	35		23-D-5 House 6	S339/P176	Red-brown, highly burnished ware; "rivets" of clay pellets. P.

FIGURE 10

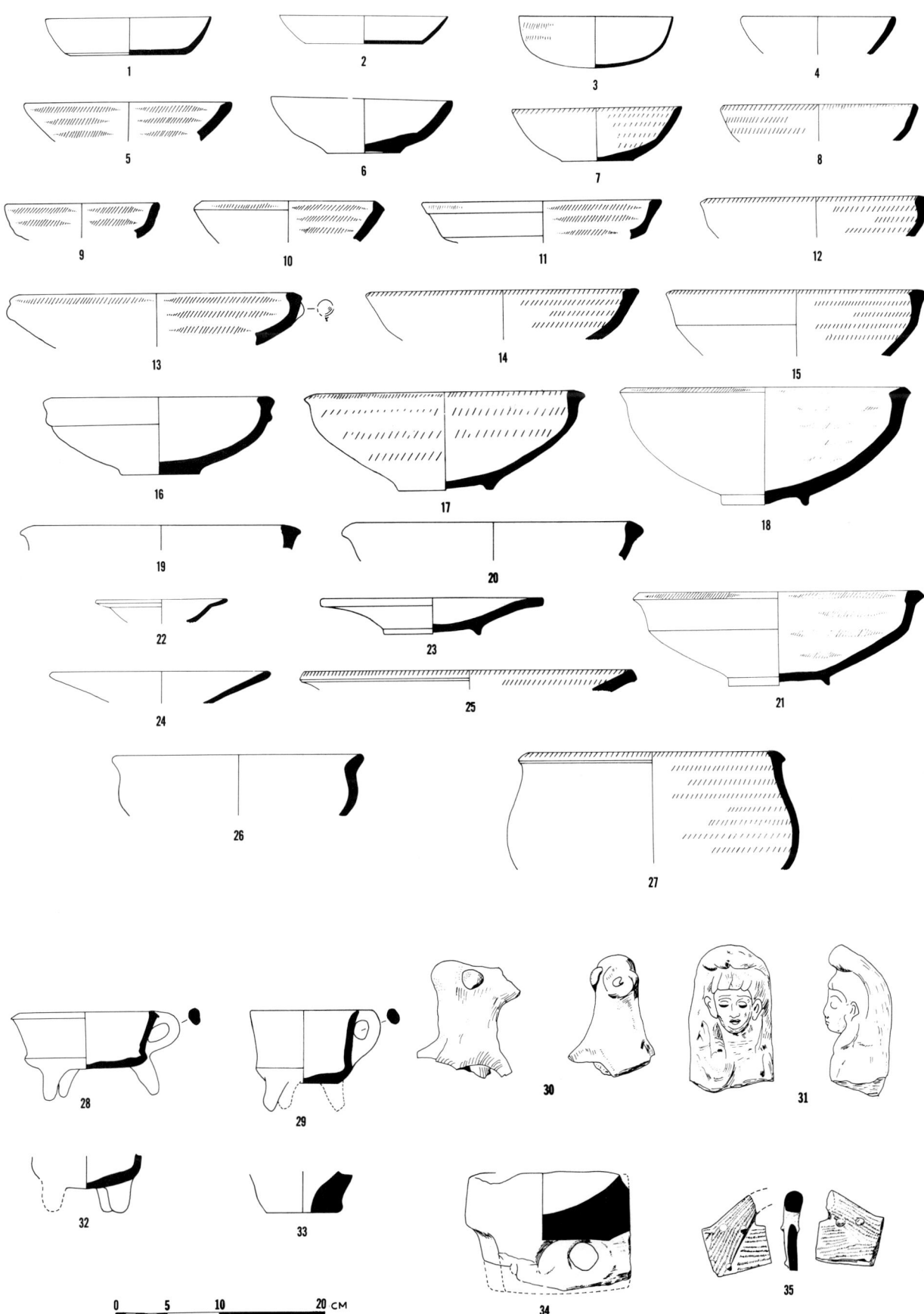

Pottery and other objects from Stratum V.

Figure 11 (Stratum V)

	No.	Type	Provenience	Field No.	Description
Juglet					
	1	16	23-F-4	TS	Red ware; tan core; few large white and some small black and white grits; vertical burnishing on body.
	2		23-D/E-4/5 House 8	S1003/P602	Tan ware; many large and small white grits. P. Fig. 164:11.
	3		23-E-2	TS	Buff ware; gray core; few large black and medium white grits.
	4		23-C-2 House 25	S842/P480	Buff ware; buff core; large and small black grits; very heavy ware. P.
	5	16	23-D-6 House 4	S334/P171	Gray ware; fine white grits; vertical burnishing on body. P.
	6		23-D-4 House 8	S1310/P700	Tan ware; many mixed black and white grits; vertically burnished. P.
	7		23-F-4	TS	Buff ware; few large black and small black and white grits; red slip?
	8	16	23-D-4 House 8	S312/P165	Tan ware; few large black and white and many small white grits; traces of burnishing outside. P.
	9	17	23-E-1	S757/P427	Black ware; gray core; traces of burnishing. P.
	10	17	32-D/E-8 House 16	S981/P566	Black ware; gray core; burnished vertically. P. Fig. 164:10.
Decanter					
	11	18	32-C-9 House 19	S892/P510	Gray ware; many mixed white grits. P.
	12	18	23-D-6 House 6 (or 4)	S265/P132	Gray ware; mixed black and white grits. P.
	13	18	32-E-9/10 House 14	S1006/P605	Gray ware; buff surface (?); mixed black and white grits. P. Fig. 166:7.
	14	18	32-E-2	TS	Gray ware; many mixed black and white grits.
	15		32-D-9 House 14	S893/P511	Red-brown ware; gray core; many large and small white grits. P.
Jug (?)					
	16		23-D-4 House 8	S104/P27	Tan ware; some medium and small black and white grits; red slip. P.
Pilgrim flask					
	17	31	23-D-6 House 6	S157/P67	Buff ware; some grits. Fig. 166:9.
	18	30	23-D-6	S421/P232	Tan ware; red lines painted on both sides of body. P.
Jug					
	19		23-C-2	TS	Tan ware; some mixed black and white grits.
	20		23-E-5 House 6	S182/P78	Red-brown ware; many mixed black and white grits. P.
	21		23-E-5 House 6	S118/P40	Brown ware; dark core; many mixed black and white grits. P.
	22	29	House 9	S1004/P603	Red, heavy ware; many mixed black and white grits. P. Fig. 165:1.
Jug with strainer spout					
	23	28	23-D-5 House 6	S222/P90	Buff ware; buff core; some medium and small black grits; red-brown slip on outside. Fig. 165:8.
Jug					
	24		23-F-5 House 7	S497/P257	Red ware; tan core; a few small white grits. P.
Decanter					
	25		23-D-4 House 8	S342/P179	Tan ware; tan core; few medium and large black and white grits; horizontal, wheel-made grooves on body continue around flat base. P.

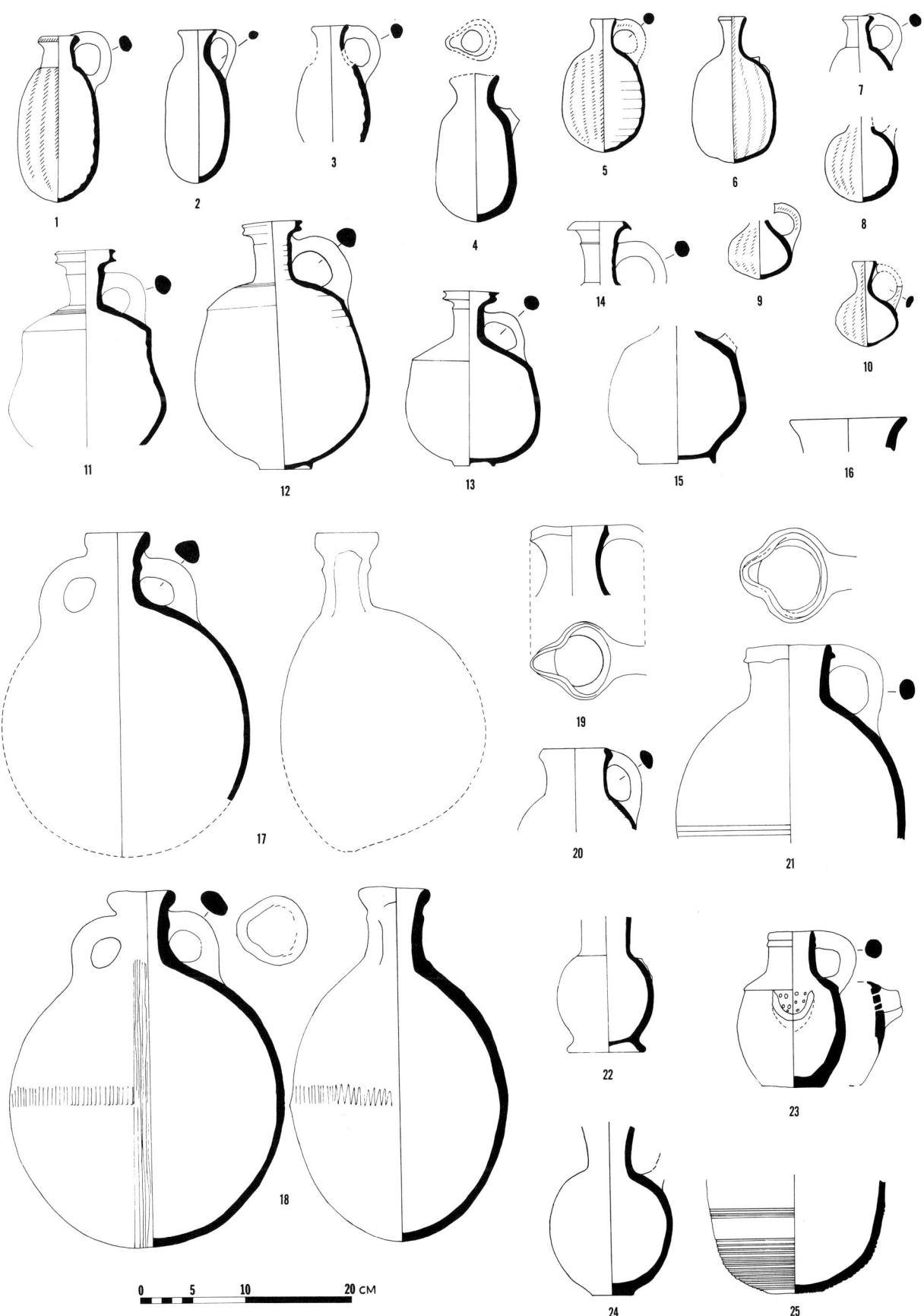

FIGURE 11

Pottery from Stratum V.

Figure 12 (Stratum V)

	No.	Type	Provenience	Field No.	Description
Krater					
	1		23-F-4	TS	Gray ware; many mixed black and white grits.
	2		23-D/E-5 House 6	S268/P135	Red-brown ware; brown core; large black and small black and white grits. P.
	3		23-F-2	TS	Red-brown core; many mixed black and white grits.
	4		23-D/E-5 House 6	S270/P137	Brown ware; some large and medium black grits. P.
	5		23-G-4	TS	Tan ware; tan core; few large and many small black and white grits.
	6		23-G-2	TS	Red ware; gray core; some large and many small black and white grits.
	7	27	23-G-4	TS	Buff ware; buff core; many mixed black and white grits.
	8		23-F-4	TS	Red-brown ware; brown core; some mixed black and white grits.
	9	27	23-D/E-5 House 6	S267/P134	Brown ware; dark gray core. P.
	10	20	23-F-4	TS	Red-brown ware; gray core; some large black and white and many small black grits.
	11		23-C-2	TS	Tan ware; brown core; some small black and white grits.
	12	20	23-G-2	TS	Red-brown ware; many mixed black and white grits.
	13		23-G-3	TS	Buff ware; tan core; many large and some small black and white grits.
	14	27	23-D/E-5	S333/P170	Buff to red-brown ware. A. Fig. 167:3.
	15		32-C-10	S846/P484	Buff ware; tan core; many mixed black and white grits.
	16		23-G-6 House 3	S845/P483	Red-brown ware; red-brown core; many mixed black and white grits.

FIGURE 12

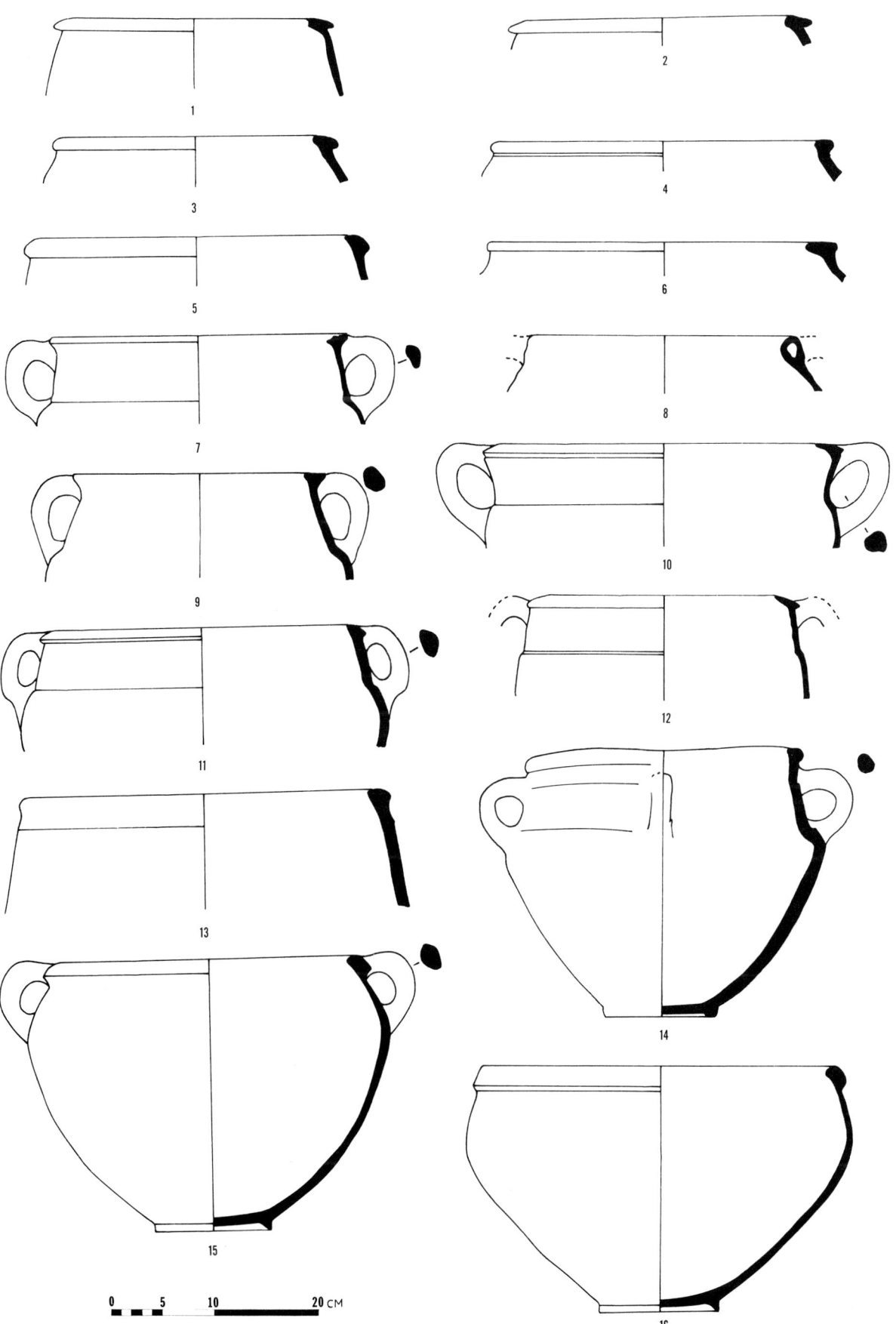

Pottery from Stratum V.

Figure 13 (Stratum V)

No.	Type	Provenience	Field No.	Description
Cooking pot				
1		23-C-2	TS	Dark brown ware; dark gray core; some large black and many small white and crystalline grits.
2		23-G-2	TS	Gray ware; gray core; many mixed black, white and crystalline grits.
3		23-D/E-5 House 6	S269/P136	Gray ware; gray core; some medium and many small white grits. P.
4	43	23-E-6 House 6	S124/P43	Red-brown ware; gray core; a few large and small black and many small white grits; possibly a bowl. P.
5		23-C-2	TS	Brown ware; dark gray core; many mixed black and white and crystalline grits; fired black in places.
6		23-G-2	TS	Dark brown ware; dark gray core; many mixed black, white and crystalline grits.
7		23-C-2	TS	Red-brown ware; dark gray core; many mixed black, white and crystalline grits.
8		23-C-4	S181/P77	Brown ware; gray core; many medium and small white grits. P.
9	43	23-D/E-5/6 House 6	S225/P93	Tan ware; brown and gray core; many mixed black and white grits. P.
10	43	23-E-5 House 6	S112/P35	Red-brown ware; brown core; a few large white and many small black, white and crystalline grits. P.
11	43	23-E-6 House 6	S125/P44	Red-brown ware; brown core; many small black, white and crystalline grits. P.
12	43	23-F-4	TS	Red-brown ware; dark gray core; many white and crystalline grits.
13	43	23-G-4	TS	Brown ware; brown core; many mixed black and white grits.
14	43	23-D/E-5 House 6	S266/P133	Dark brown ware; dark brown core; many small white grits. P.
15	43	23-F-5	TS	Brown ware; brown core; many mixed white and crystalline grits.
16		23-G-1 House 13	S751/P423	Brown ware; brown core; many mixed black and white grits. S.
17		23-G-5 House 7	S525/P283	Red-brown ware; grits in core. A.
18	43	23-G-2	TS	Red-brown ware; brown core; many mixed black and white grits.
19	43	23-F-3 House 9 or 11	S545/P303	Red-brown ware; brown core; fine white grits. P.
20	43	23-F-5 House 5 or 6	S530/P288	Brown ware; brown core; fine white grits. P.
21	43	23-G-2 House 11	S731/P406	Brown ware; brown core; many mixed black and white grits. A.

FIGURE 13

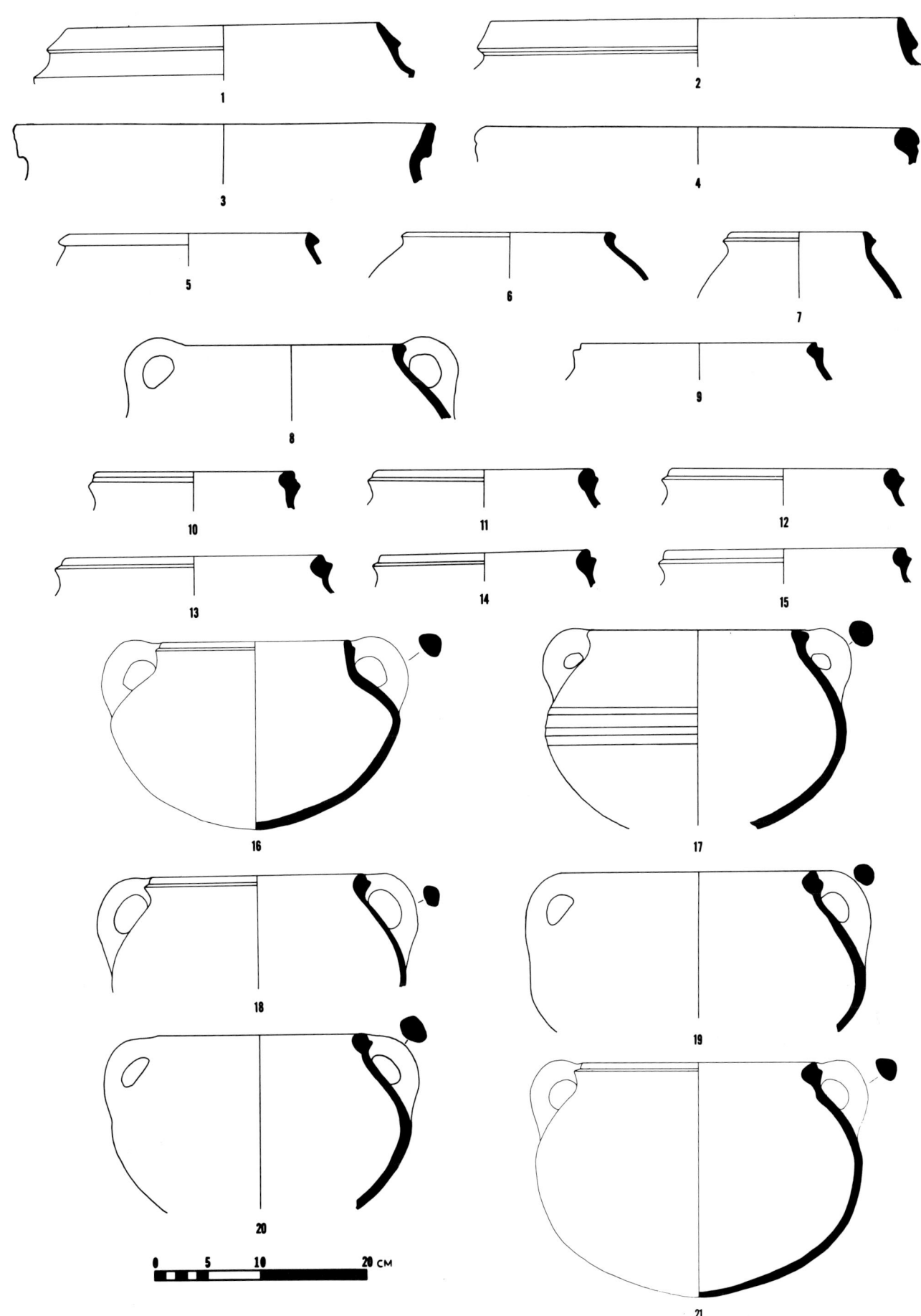

Pottery from Stratum V.

Figure 14 (Stratum V)

	No.	Type	Provenience	Field No.	Description
Storage jar					
	1	44	23-E-6 House 6	S126/P45	Red ware; gray core; many large and small white grits; some black grits. P.
	2	44	23-D-4 House 8	S108/P31	Buff ware; buff core; many mixed black and white grits. P.
	3	44	23-G-4	TS	Red-brown ware; dark gray core; many mixed black and white grits.
	4	44	23-G-4	TS	Tan ware; brown core; some black and white grits.
	5	44	23-G-4	TS	Brown ware; brown core; many mixed black and white grits.
	6		23-G-4	TS	Tan ware; gray core; many mixed large black and white grits.
	7		23-E-2	TS	Red ware; brown core; some mixed black and white grits.
	8		23-G-4	TS	Tan ware; gray core; many mixed black and white grits.
	9		23-G-4	TS	Buff ware; tan core; many mixed black and some mixed white grits.
	10		23-E-6 House 6	S122/P41	Buff ware; buff core; medium black grits; red slip on outside. P.
	11	32	23-D-5/6 House 6	S331/P168	Red-brown ware.
	12		23-C-2	TS	Red-brown ware; brown core; some medium and many small black and white grits.
	13	19	23-G-3	TS	Gray ware; dark gray core; many mixed black and white grits.
	14		23-E-2	TS	Tan ware; many small black and white grits.
	15		23-G-3	TS	Tan ware; brown core; many mixed black and white grits.
	16		23-E-5 House 6	S113/P36	Tan ware; tan core; some medium black and white grits; fired orange on inside. P.
Bowl					
	17	34	23-E-2	TS	Tan ware; gray core; many mixed black and white grits; burnished on inside and out; fired black inside.
	18	34	23-E-2	TS	Red-brown ware; gray core; many mixed black and white grits; fired black inside.
Lamp					
	19		23-G-3 House 9	S730/P405	Buff ware; carbon on nozzle. P.
Cosmetic palette					
	20		23-D/E-4 House 8 (or 10)	S311/St24	Stone. Fig. 169:2.
Cup with high base					
	21		23-F-5/6 House 5	S513/M149A	Faience (?); white; groove below rim. A. Fig. 171:3.
Game pieces					
	22		23-E-6 House 3 (or 4)	S70/M62	Seven round, flat pieces; red ware; burnished on one side. P. Fig. 171:4.
Spindle whorl					
	23		23-D-6 House 4	S1300/M300	Gray stone.
Clay disk					
	24		23-D-5 House 6	S365/P203	Buff ware; roughly made by hand; thicker at center. P.
	25		23-D-5 House 6	S366/P204	Buff ware; roughly made by hand; thicker at center. P.
Sickle					
	26		23-F/G-4/5 House 7	S1009/F40	Iron; in four pieces. P.
Arrowhead					
	27		23-E-4 House 8 (or 10)	S306/F3	Iron; corroded. P. Fig. 172:3.
	28		23-E-4	S307/F4	Iron; corroded. P. Fig. 172:2.
	29		23-G-6 House 5 (or 3)	S1007/Br50	Bronze; corroded. P.
Disk					
	30		23-F-4 House 9	S789/Br33	Bronze; 4 to 6 holes bored through; in five pieces.
Ring					
	31		23-F-4 House 7 (or 9)	S772/F21	Iron; corroded. P.
Fibula					
	32		23-G-6 House 5 (or 3)	S400/Br7	Bronze with iron needle. P. Shown double scale.
	33		23-E-4 House 10	S310/Br3	Bronze; triangular with buttonlike decoration; corroded. P. Shown double scale.
Nail					
	34		23-F-3 House 11	S786/F24	Iron; three pieces. P.
Spatula					
	35		23-G-3 House 11 (?)	S716/B20	Bone; brown; edges rounded. P.
Bead					
	36		23-D-6 House 4	S200/J2	Stone; white; two perforations lengthwise with a third broken away. P. Shown double scale.
Point					
	37		23-D/E-5 House 6	S368/B8	Horn; long and tapering; in two pieces. Fig. 171:9.

FIGURE 14

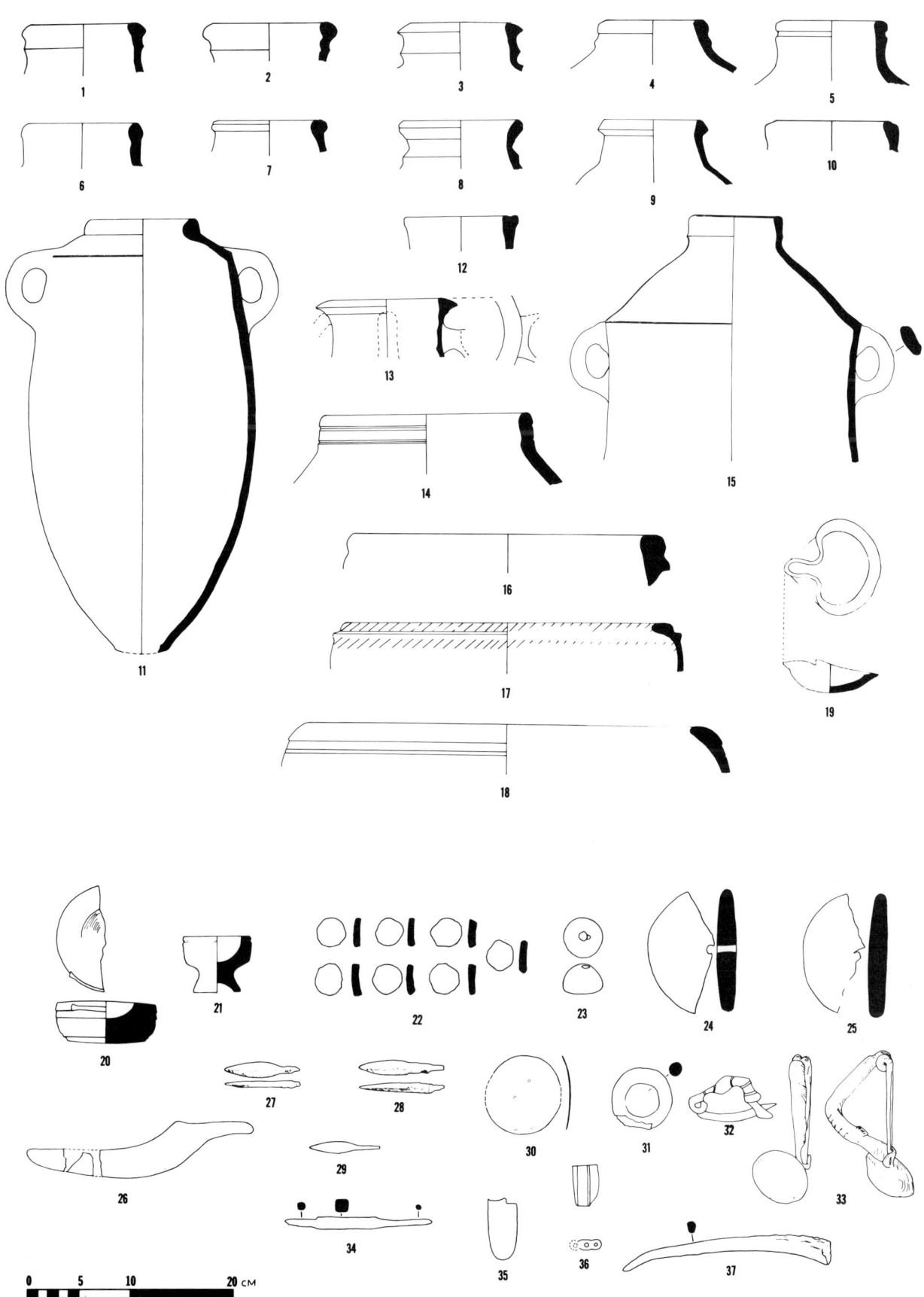

Pottery and other objects from Stratum V.

Figure 15 (Stratum IV)

	No.	Type	Provenience	Field No.	Description
Bowl					
	1		23-E-3	TS	Red ware; red and gray core; few small brown grits.
	2		23-E-3	TS	Red-brown ware; tan core; few small white grits; burnished inside and outside.
	3		23-E-3	TS	Gray ware; black core; many large and small white grits.
	4		23-E-3	TS	Tan ware; gray core; few small brown grits; wheel burnished outside and on rim inside.
	5	36	23-E-3	TS	Red-brown ware; black core; few large and small white grits; wheel burnished inside and outside.
	6		23-E-4	S2/P2	Red ware; black core; few small white grits.
	7	36	23-E-3	TS	Red ware; buff core; few black grits; wheel burnished on inside and on rim outside.
	8		23-E-3	TS	Black ware; black core; many small black grits; burnished inside and outside.
	9	38	23-E-3	TS	Tan ware; tan core; few medium black and white grits.
	10	36	23-E-3	TS	Tan ware; tan core; few medium and small white grits; burnished inside and on rim.
	11	36	23-E-3	TS	Brown ware; black core; some small white and black grits; black slip outside; burnished inside and out.
	12	35	23-D-4 Bins 11, 12	TS	Red ware; black core; few medium black grits; burnished outside.
	13	36	23-E-3	S141/P60	Red ware; red core; some large white grits; burnished inside and on rim.
	14	35	23-E-3	TS	Red ware; buff core; some small black grits; burnished inside and out.
Krater					
	15	39	23-D-4	S89/P13	Tan ware; black core; some medium white grits; burnished inside.
Bowl					
	16	37	23-E-3 Bin 3	TS	Buff ware; pink core shading into buff; many small black grits.
Krater					
	17	39	23-E-3	TS	Tan ware; gray core; few small white grits.
	18		23-E-4	S98/P22	Tan ware; black core; some mixed white grits.
	19	39	23-D-4	S90/P14	Red ware; gray core; few mixed white grits; burnished on rim.
	20		23-E-3	S139/P58	Tan ware; gray core; few small white grits.
	21	39	23-D-4 Bins 11, 12	TS	Red ware; black core; few large white grits; buff slip.
Bowl					
	22		23-E-3	TS	Red-brown ware; red-brown core; many small and medium white grits; burnished inside and on rim.
	23	40	23-E-6	S115/P38	Brown ware; black core; many large white grits.
Cooking pot					
	24		23-E-3	TS	Red-brown ware; gray core; many small and few large white and black grits.
	25	43	23-E-3	S137/P56	Brown ware; brown core; many mixed white grits.
	26	43	23-E-3	TS	Red-brown ware; gray core; some medium white grits.
	27	43	23-D-4	S92/P16	Red-brown ware; red-brown core; many medium black grits.
	28	43	23-E-3	S138/P57	Red-brown ware; black core; many mixed white grits.
	29		23-E-6	S114/P37	Brown ware; gray core; many small white grits.
	30		23-D-4	TS	Red-brown ware; red-brown core; many medium black and white grits.

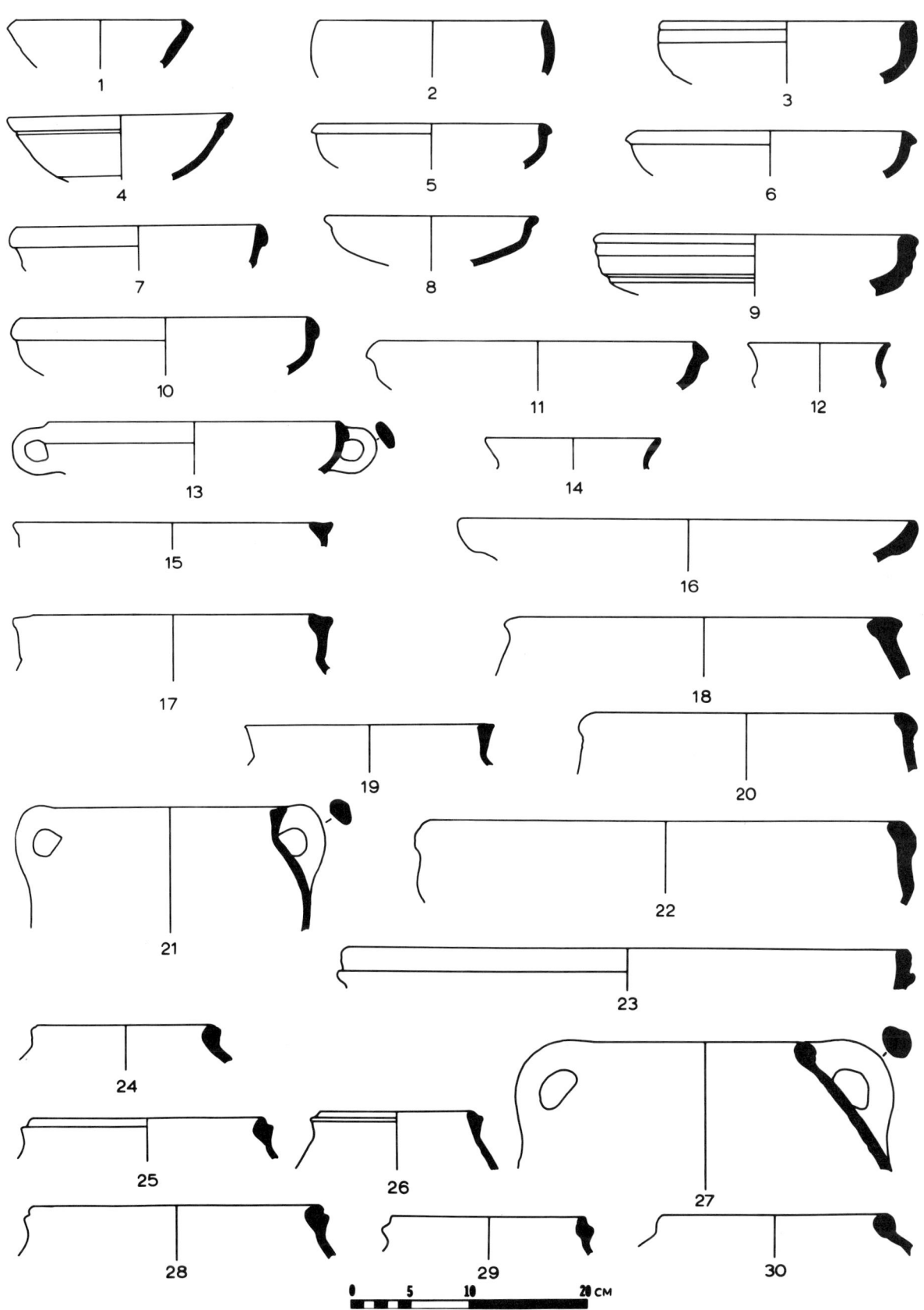

FIGURE 15

Pottery from Stratum IV.

Figure 16 (Stratum IV)

	No.	Type	Provenience	Field No.	Description
Jug					
	1		23-D-4	TS	Red ware; black core; some mixed white grits; tan slip.
	2		23-D-4	S85/P10	Red ware; gray core; some mixed white grits.
Storage jar					
	3	44	23-D-4	S88/P12	Brown ware; gray core; some mixed black grits.
Jug					
	4		23-E-6	S116/P39	Red ware; black core; some medium white grits.
	5		23-D-4	S91/P15	Red ware; black core; some mixed black and white grits.
Storage jar					
	6		23-D-4	TS	Tan ware; tan core; some small white grits.
	7	34	23-D-4	S87/P11	Red ware; gray core; many large white grits.
	8		23-D-4	S83/P8	Brown ware; brown core; many mixed black and white grits. Possibly cooking pot.
	9	34	23-E-3	TS	Buff ware; tan and red core; many large and small black and white grits.
	10	34	23-E-3	TS	Red ware; black core; many small white and few large black grits; buff slip; burnished outside.
Tripod bowl					
	11		23-E-3	S140/P59	Red ware; black core; many mixed black and white grits.
Human figurine					
	12		23-E-3	S142/Pfig2	Buff ware; light gray core. Shown double scale.
Storage jar					
	13		23-E-3	S338/P175	Red ware; gray core; very fine grits.
Bowl					
	14		23-E-4	S1/P1	Red ware; gray core; some small black grits; wedge-shaped incisions.
Sherd					
	15		23-D-4	S84/P9	Red-brown ware; red core; some mixed black grits; burnished inside and outside; incisions on outside; scratched after firing.
Jug					
	16		23-E-3	TS	Tan ware; red core; many small white grits and few large black grits.
Lamp					
	17		23-D-4	S66/P4	Tan ware; tan core; many mixed black and white grits. Fig. 168:6.
	18	41	23-E-3	S441/P245	Red ware; brown core; many small black and white grits.

FIGURE 16

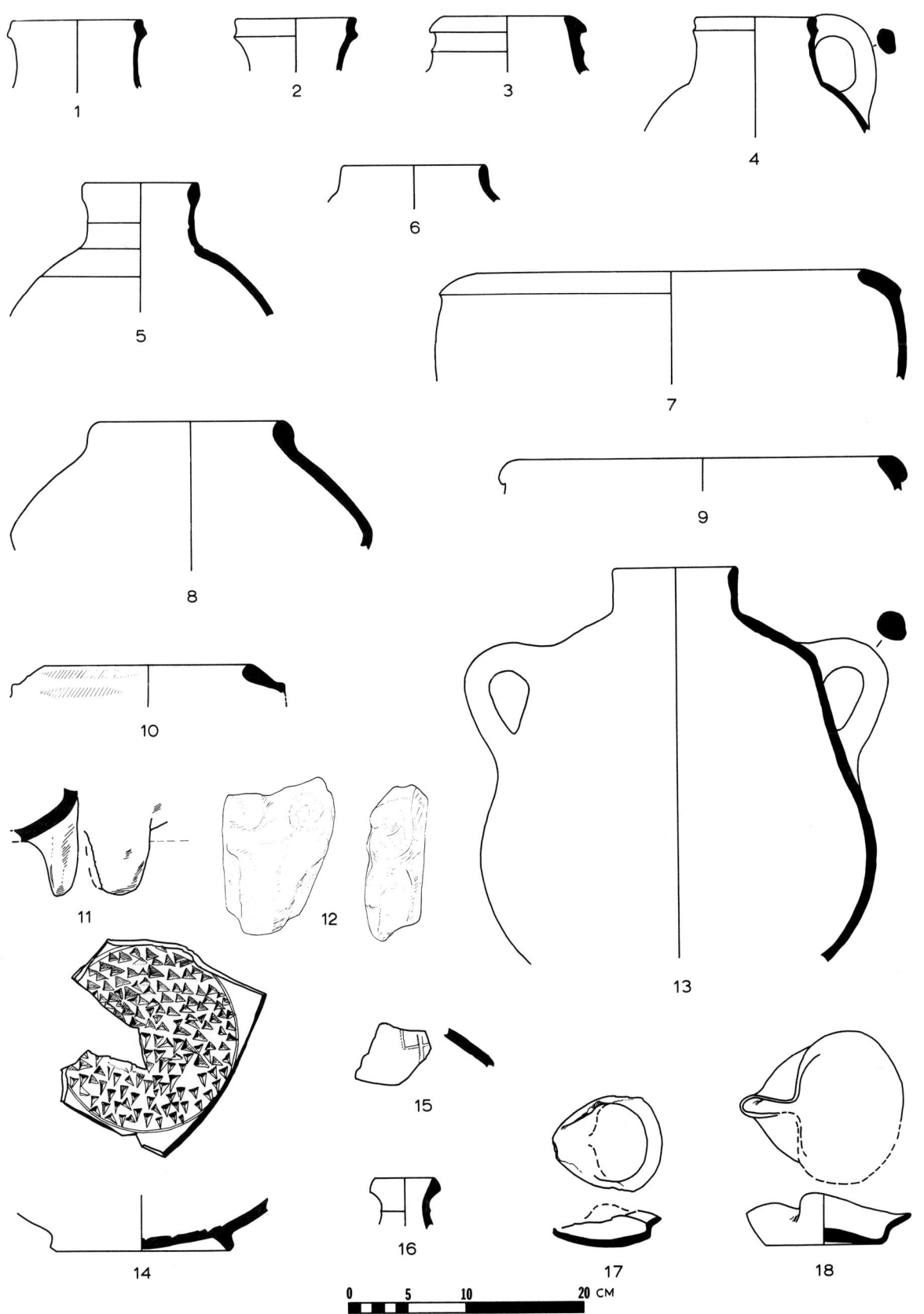

Pottery and other objects from Stratum IV.

Figure 17 (Stratum IV)

	No.	Type	Provenience	Field No.	Description
Bowl					
	1	37	23-E-2	TS	Buff ware; red-brown core; few large and medium black and white grits.
	2		23-G-3	TS	Tan ware; tan and brown core; many medium and small black and white grits; burnished on inside and rim.
	3		23-C-4	TS	Tan ware; tan core; some mixed black and white grits; burnished inside and on rim.
	4	36	23-F-2	TS	Tan ware; brown core; many large and small black and white grits; burnished on inside and on rim.
	5		23-C-2	TS	Red-brown ware; red-brown and gray core; some mixed black and white grits.
	6		23-C-1	TS	Red-brown ware; red-brown and gray core; some mixed black and white grits.
	7	36	23-F-2	TS	Red-brown ware; brown core; many medium and small black and white grits; burnished on inside and rim.
	8	35	23-F-4	TS	Brown ware; black core; few small black grits; metallic hard; burnished on outside rim.
	9		23-F-2	TS	Brown ware; brown and gray core; some small black and white grits.
	10		23-E-2	TS	Brown ware; brown core; few large and some small black grits.
Cooking pot					
	11		23-C-1	TS	Red-brown ware; brown core; some medium and many small black and white grits.
	12	43	23-D-2	TS	Brown ware; brown core; many mixed white grits.
	13		23-D-2	TS	Brown ware; brown core; some mixed black and white grits.
	14		23-G-3	TS	Gray ware; gray core; many medium and small white grits.
	15		23-G-3	TS	Brown ware; brown core; many small black and white grits.
Jug					
	16		23-C-2	TS	Brown ware; brown core; well levigated clay; metallic hard.
	17		23-C-2	TS	Buff ware; gray core; many mixed white grits.
Pilgrim flask					
	18		23-C-1	TS	Red-brown ware; red-brown and gray core; many mixed black and white grits.
Storage jar					
	19		23-D-7	TS	Gray ware; brown and gray core; many small black and white grits.
	20		23-G-3	TS	Tan ware; tan and gray core, many mixed black and white grits.
	21		23-C-1	TS	Tan ware; tan and gray core; some large black and many small white grits.
	22		23-G-4	TS	Brown ware; black core; many mixed black and white grits.
Cooking pot					
	23		23-G-3	TS	Red-brown ware; gray core; many mixed black and white grits.
	24		23-E-2	TS	Brown ware; gray core; many mixed black and white grits.
Krater					
	25		23-D-2	TS	Tan ware; brown core; many small black grits.
	26		23-E-2	TS	Red-brown ware; brown and gray core; many mixed black and white grits; burnished on inside and rim.
	27		23-C-2	TS	Buff ware; buff core; many mixed black grits.
Bowl					
	28		23-G-3	TS	Black ware; black core; many mixed black grits.
Storage jar					
	29		23-C-2	TS	Tan ware; tan core; many mixed black and white grits.
	30		23-G-3	TS	Tan ware; black core; many mixed black and white grits; burnished on rim.
	31	34	23-G-3	TS	Red-brown ware; brown core; many mixed black and white grits.
	32	34	23-G-3	TS	Red-brown ware; red-brown and gray core; many mixed black and white grits.
Tripod bowl					
	33			TS	Buff ware; gray core; many mixed white grits.

FIGURE 17

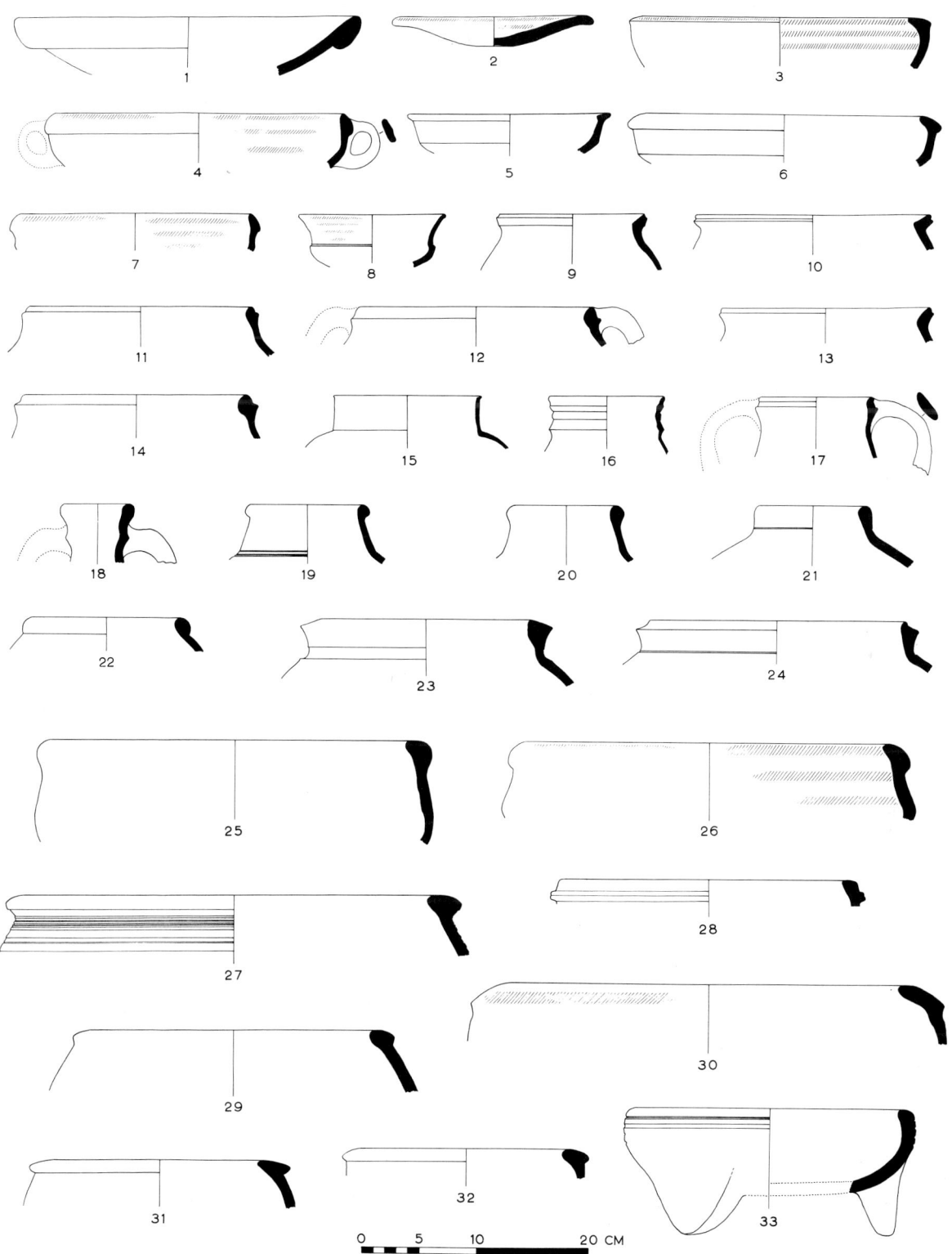

Pottery from Stratum IV.

Figure 18 (1–15 Stratum III; 16–31 Stratum II)

	No.	Provenience	Field No.	Description
Jar				
	1	31-F-8 Room 107W	S1218/P676	Tan ware; tan and gray core; many small black and white grits; red slip?; ring-burnished. P.
	2	31-E-5/6 Room 103	S1054/P616	Buff ware; many mixed white and some black grits. P.
Juglet				
	3	31-G-8 Room 107	S1190/P669	Tan ware; mixed white and some black grits.
Lamp				
	4	31-G-6/7 Room 101	S1186/P665	Tan ware; gray core; medium black and white grits. A.
Mortar				
	5	31-H-7 Room 109	S1105/St75	Basalt; black; very smooth inside. P.
Incense altar				
	6	31-E-6/7 Room 104	S1181/St82	Limestone; painted red on two opposite sides; inscribed designs identical on two opposite sides. A. Fig. 174:1–6. See pp. 00–00.
Kettle				
	7	31-G-9 Room 107	S1269/Br85	Bronze; iron handles passing through bronze loops, riveted with two rivets 4.7 cm. apart. P.
Anklet				
	8	31-E-5 Room 103	S1027/Br52	Bronze; slightly corroded. P.
Fibula				
	9	31-G-8 Room 107	S1160/Br72	Bronze; corroded. P.
Needle				
	10	31-E-8 Room 105	S1268/Br84	Bronze; corroded and bent. P.
Fibula				
	11	31-G-5/6 Room 102	S1075/Br57	Bronze; corroded slightly.
Ring				
	12	31-H-7 Room 109	S1217/J67	Silver. P.
Bead				
	13	31-G-8 Room 107	S1159/J65	Carnelian; dark amber color. P.
Spindle whorl				
	14	31-E-5 Room 103	S1017/M251	Gray stone; two incised lines near base. P.
Stopper				
	15	31-E-8 Room 105	S1201/M289	Buff ware; mixed black and white grits; two string impressions on top. P.
Bowl				
	16	31-E-5/6	S1005/P604	Tan ware; very small black grits; red paint inside and out; wide brown band around rim. P.
Spindle bottle				
	17	31-D-6	S936/P543	Gray ware, luminescent gray surface; burnished vertically. P.
Jug				
	18	31-B-6	S896/P514	Tan ware; few small black grits; grooves on body fragments. P.
Jar				
	19	31-B-6	S871/P497	Brown ware; gray core; many small and a few medium white grits. P.
Jug				
	20	31-C-8	S988/P568	Buff ware; brown core; small black grits and many small and large white grits. P. Fig. 166:1.
Lamp				
	21	31-F-9	S1135/P646	Tan ware; some medium black and white grits. (outside of building).
	22	31-E/F-6	S1022/P613	Tan ware; gray core; many mixed black and white grits; handmade. P. Fig. 168:8.
Stopper				
	23	31-E-5	S1046/M258	Tan ware; very porous; handmade. P.
Human figurine				
	24	31-E-6	S942/Pfig14	Tan ware; tan core; many mixed black grits. Shown double scale.
Point				
	25	31-D-5	S948/B21	Bone; three pieces. P.
Adze				
	26	31-C-5	S952/F31	Iron; almost complete. P.
Arrowhead				
	27	31-C-7	S888/F28	Iron; complete. P.
Spike				
	28	31-D-7	S873/F27	Iron. P.
	29	31-D-8	S872/F26	Iron. A.
Instrument				
	30	31-A-7	S950/F30	Iron; hollow half tube with three rivets punched through; trace of wood on inside with corrosion. P.
Fibula				
	31	31-A-7 (Stratum III)	S947/Br45	Bronze; two pieces. P.

FIGURE 18

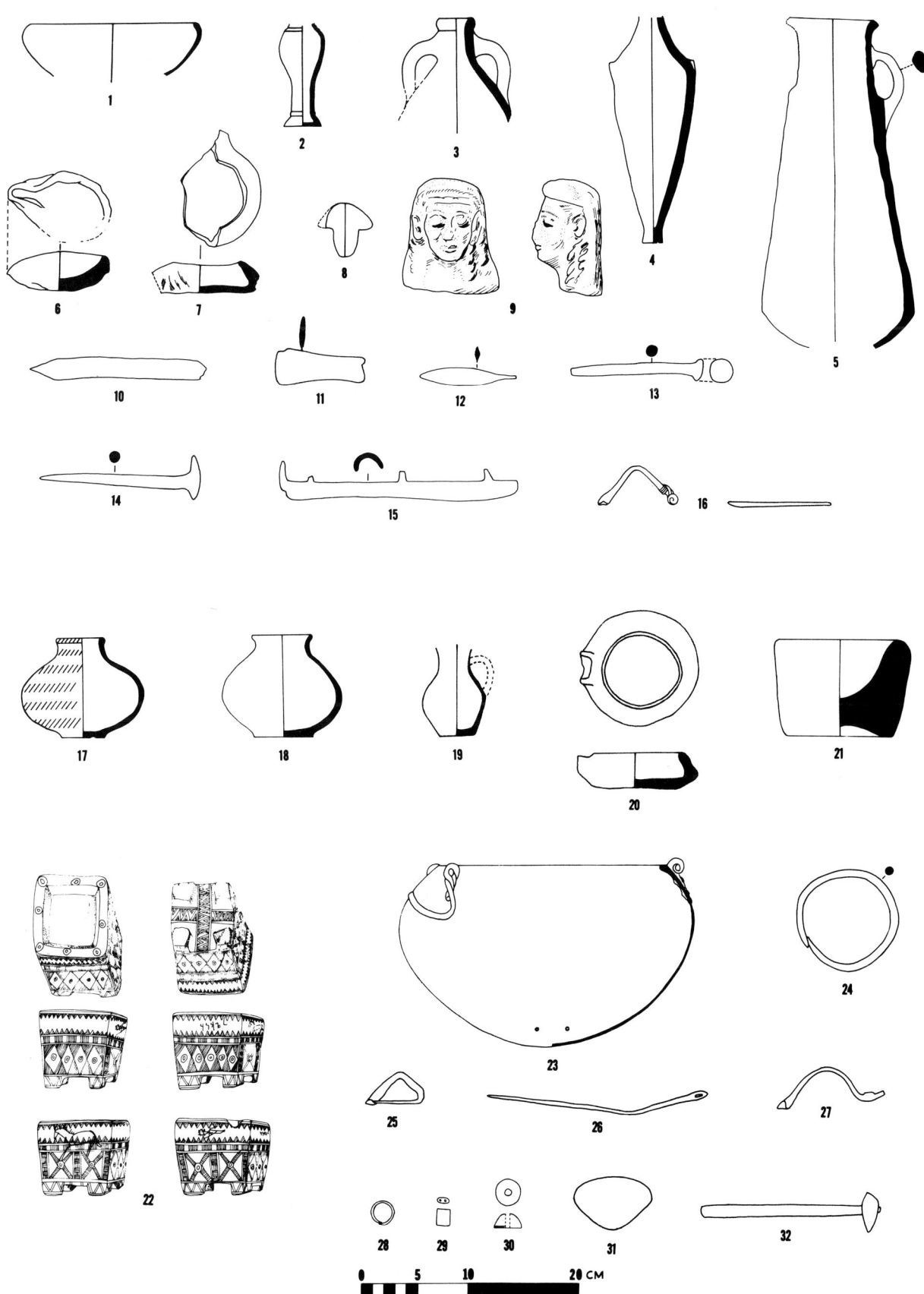

Pottery and other objects from Strata II (1–16) and III (17–32).

Figure 19 (Strata II (*) and I)

	No.	Provenience	Field No.	Description
Bowl				
	1		TS	Gray ware; gray core; many mixed white grits.
	2	31-B-6	TS	Tan ware; tan core; few small black grits; black slip.
	3	31-C-7	TS	Tan ware; gray core; some small black grits.
	4	31-C-7	TS	Tan ware; tan core; well levigated clay; silver-black surface.
	5		TS	Tan ware; tan core; some mixed white grits.
	6		TS	Tan ware; tan core; many mixed black and white grits.
	*7	31-C-6	S876/P499	Red ware; buff core; few small black and white grits; metallic hard. Fig. 164:3.
	8		TS	Tan ware; brown and gray core; few small black and white grits.
	9		TS	Pink ware; pink core; few small white grits.
	10		TS	Tan ware; tan core; some mixed white grits.
	11		TS	Buff ware; buff core; well levigated clay; red-brown slip.
	12		TS	Pink ware; pink and gray core; few small white grits; pink slip; metallic hard.
	*13	31-B-7	S832/P470	Brown ware; brown core; few small white grits; fired buff on outside.
	14		TS	Tan ware; tan core; some small black grits; brown to red-brown surface; metallic hard.
Sherd				
	15		TS	Tan ware; tan core; few small black grits; red-brown slip; metallic hard.
	16		TS	Tan ware; tan core; some mixed black grits; red-brown slip; metallic hard.
	17		TS	Pink ware; pink and gray core; few mixed black grits; black and white paint.
	18		TS	Tan ware; tan core; well levigated clay; red-brown slip; metallic hard.
Juglet				
	*19	31-B-5	S932/P539	Black ware; black core; some medium black grits; molded decoration.
Jar				
	*20	31-B-6	S890/P508	Gray ware; gray core; well levigated clay; molded decoration.
Lamp				
	*21	31-C-7	S815/P456	Tan ware; tan core; few medium and small black and white grits.
	*22	31-B-5	S937/P545	Black ware; black core; well levigated clay.
	*23	31-C-5	S938/P546	Black ware; hand burnished.
	24		TS	Gray ware; gray core; many small black grits.
	25		TS	Brown ware; brown core; well levigated clay; metallic hard.
Jar				
	*26	31-A-6	S894/P512	Red-brown ware; tan core; few small black grits.
	*27	31-D-7	S870/P496	Tan ware; tan core; many small black grits; buff slip.
	28		TS	Tan ware; tan core; many mixed white grits.
	*29	31-D-7	S933/P540	Red-brown ware; red-brown and gray core; few small black and white grits. Fig. 166:2.
Bottle				
	*30	31-C-5	S934/P541	Tan ware; gray core; many mixed white grits.
Jug				
	*31	31-C-6(?)	S895/P513	Light gray ware.
Bottle				
	32		TS	Tan ware; tan core; many mixed black grits.
	*33	31-D-5	S935/P542	Black ware; gray core; some small black grits; burnished vertically.
Jug				
	34		TS	Tan ware; tan core; many mixed black grits.
	35		TS	Buff ware; tan and gray core; few small black and white grits; metallic hard.
	36		TS	Tan ware; tan and gray core; many medium black grits.

FIGURE 19

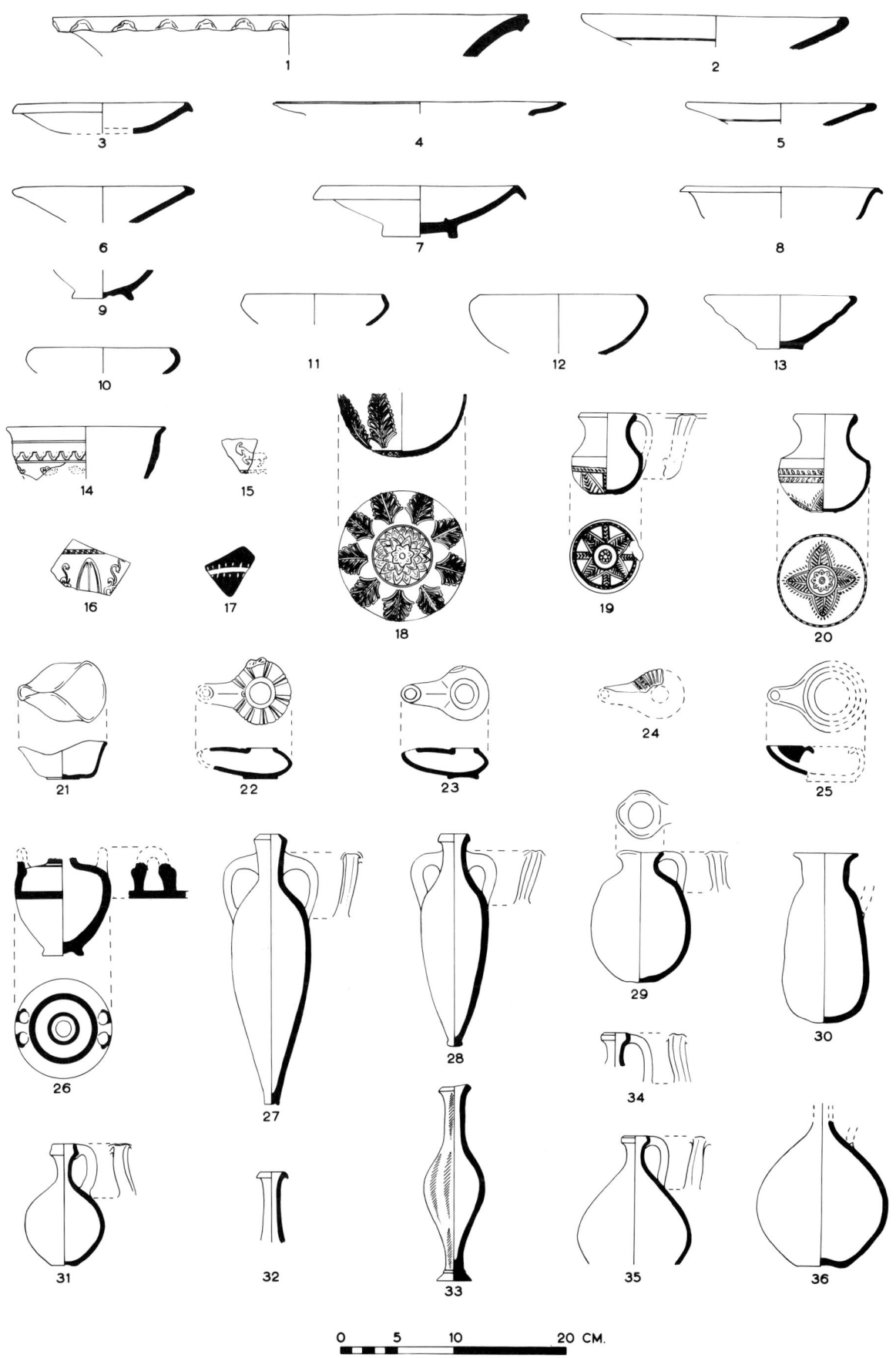

Pottery from Strata II (7, 13, 19–23, 26–27, 29–31, 33) and I.

Figure 20 (Strata II (*) and I)

	No.	Provenience	Field No.	Description
Krater				
	1		TS	Brown ware; brown core; many mixed white grits; buff slip.
Jar				
	2		TS	Tan ware; tan and buff core; many small black grits.
	3	31-B-6	TS	Brown ware; brown core; many mixed black and white grits.
	4		TS	Buff ware; brown and gray core; many mixed white grits.
Krater				
	5		TS	Brown ware; brown and gray core; many mixed white grits; buff slip.
Cooking pot				
	*6	31-C-7	S833/P471	Red-brown ware; red-brown core; many small black and few medium white grits.
	7		TS	Red-brown ware; red-brown core; many mixed black and white grits.
Storage jar				
	8	31-C-7	TS	Gray ware; gray core; many small black and few large white grits; buff slip.
	9		TS	Brown ware; brown and gray core; many mixed white grits.
	10	31-C-7	TS	Red-brown ware; brown core; many mixed white grits; buff slip.
Jug				
	11	31-B-6	TS	Brown ware; brown core; some small and large white grits; fired buff on outside.
Storage jar				
	12		TS	Buff ware; brown and gray core; many mixed black and white grits.
Jug				
	13	31-C/D-7	TS	Tan ware; tan and gray core; many mixed white grits; buff slip.
	14	31-D-7	TS	Red-brown ware; red-brown and gray core; many mixed white grits; brown and white paint.
Handle				
	15		TS	Brown ware; brown core; many mixed white grits; buff slip.
Jar				
	*16	31-B-7	S851/P487	Tan ware; tan clay; some medium and small black grits; red-brown slip; incised vine design.
Jug				
	*17	31-B-7	S816/P457	Brown ware; gray core; some medium and small white grits; fired buff on outside.
	*18	31-B-5	S939/P547	Tan ware; tan and gray core; few small black grits.

FIGURE 20

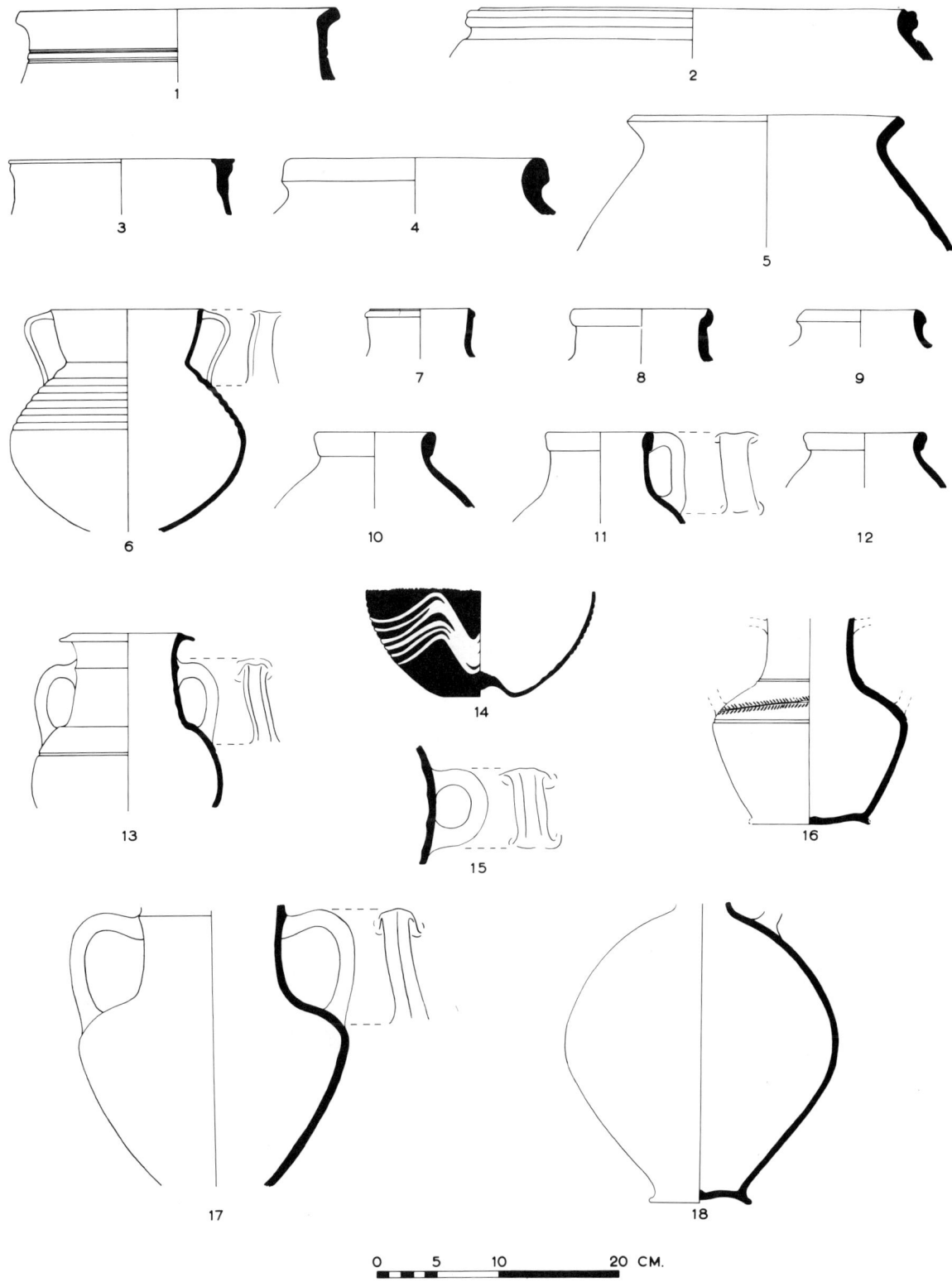

Pottery from Strata II (6, 16, 17–18) and I.

Figure 21. Tell es-Sa'idiyeh as seen from the east.

Figure 22. Tell es-Sa'idiyeh as seen from the north.

Figure 23. Tell es-Sa'idiyeh as seen from the west.

Figure 24. Tell es-Sa'idiyeh as seen from the south.

Figure 25. Paved area beside the city wall of Stratum VII, looking west.

Figure 26. Earlier and later phases of Stratum VII paving, with segment of the mud-brick city wall to the right, looking southwest.

Figure 27. Later phase of paving and the north wall of House 51, looking southeast.

Figure 28. Crushed pottery on a floor below that of Stratum VII.

Figure 29. Houses 51 (upper), 53 (center), and 55 (lower), looking northeast.

Figure 30. General view of Stratum VII, looking south.

Figure 31. Earlier phase of the main east-west street of Stratum VII, looking west.

Figure 32. Earlier phase of the main east-west street of Stratum VII, looking east.

Figure 33. Room 57, looking east.

Figure 34. North-south street in 23-F-2/5 of Stratum VII, looking south.

Figure 35. Room 62 in its earlier phase, looking west.

Figure 36. House 64 (lower) and House 66 (upper), looking south.

Figure 37. House 64, looking north.

Figure 38. Platform of House 64, looking northeast.

Figure 39. Tripod cup *in situ* on platform in House 64.

Figure 40. Shells and stone ring on floor of House 64.

Figure 41. House 66, looking north.

Figure 42. East-west street in 23-F/G-6, with House 35 at the right and House 37 at the left, looking west.

Figure 43. General view of the north-south street and Houses 41, 37–39, 35, 33, and 31, looking north.

Figure 44. Clay oven in House 35 constructed of broken cooking pots and jars.

Figure 45. Millstone and rider found in House 35.

Figure 46. Stone pavement in House 41, looking west.

Figure 47. House 37, looking west.

Figure 48. House 37–39 and kitchen area to the east beside main north-south street, looking southeast.

Figure 49. Crushed pottery vessels in House 39, looking southeast.

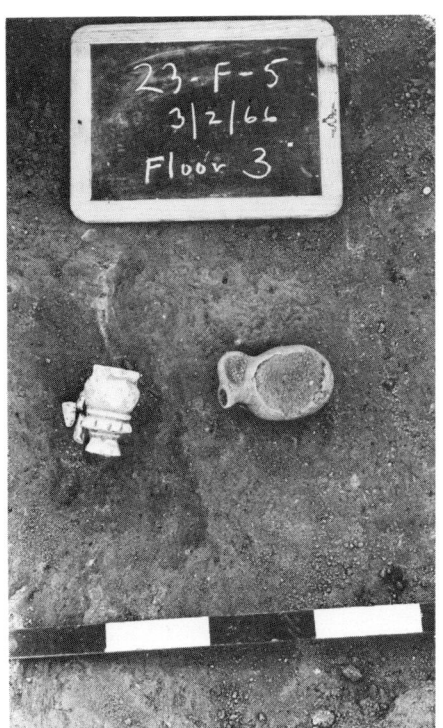

Figure 50. Faience cosmetic cup (S1084/M274) and juglet beside south wall of House 37.

Figure 51. Chalice (S1078/P625), jug (S1094/P635), and decanter (S1057/P619) found beside north wall of Room 37, looking west.

Figure 52. Loom weights and juglets along north wall of Room 39.

Figure 53. House 43, looking west.

Figure 54. Remains of pavement in House 1 (right center), looking east.

Figure 55. House 3, looking east.

Figure 56. House 3, looking west.

Figure 57. House 5, looking west.

Figure 58. House 5, looking east.

Figure 59. House 7, looking west.

Figure 60. Balk between 23-G-4 and 23-G-5, looking north.

Figure 61. House 7, looking east.

Figure 62. House 7, looking south.

Figure 63. House 9, looking east.

Figure 64. House 9, looking northwest.

Figure 65. Charred beam in House 9, looking north.

Figure 66. House 11, looking east.

Figure 67. Pavement of House 2, running beside foundation for city wall, looking west.

Figure 68. Original pavement in the northwest corner of House 4, looking north.

Figure 69. Second pavement imposed on original in the northwest corner of House 4, looking west.

Figure 70. Pit in the unpaved room of House 6 north of columns, looking west.

Figure 71. Plastered bin with hole, in House 6, looking south.

Figure 72. Skeleton of infant buried in the floor of House 6.

Figure 73. Lower layer of loom weights found in House 6, looking west.

Figure 74. Upper layer of loom weights found in House 6, looking west.

Figure 75. House 6, with its four columns, looking northwest.

Figure 76. House 6, looking southeast.

Figure 77. Bin between two columns of House 6, looking northwest.

Figure 78. House 8, looking east.

Figure 79. House 8, looking west.

Figure 80. House 25 (foreground, left), House 23 (foreground, right), and House 12 (upper), looking east.

Figure 81. Partition wall between front and back rooms of House 12, looking east.

Figure 82. Portion of pavement of House 12, and brick foundation for column, looking north.

Figure 83. House 13, looking east, cut by Bin A of Stratum IV.

Figure 84. Pavement of House 14, looking west.

Figure 85. House 16, looking east.

Figure 86. House 16, east part with stairs and bin, looking east.

Figure 87. Back room of House 16, with bin, looking north.

Figure 88. Loom weights on floor of back room of House 16, looking west.

Figure 89. Loom weights found beside column wall of House 16, looking northwest.

Figure 90. Street running north-south in 32-F-8/9, looking south.

Figure 91. Paved section of the front room of House 14 and the north-south street, looking southeast.

Figure 92. Houses 19 (foreground) and 17 (upper), looking south.

Figure 93. Paving of House 25, looking north.

Figure 94. House 27 (right) and courtyard between Houses 27 and 29, looking east.

Figure 95. Beam and roof material on floor of House 27, looking northeast.

Figure 96. West north-south street of Stratum V, looking north.

Figure 98. Upper course of west north-south street in Stratum V, looking south.

Figure 97. West north-south street of Stratum V, looking south.

Figure 99. Pit 14 with posthole, in Stratum IV, looking southwest.

Figure 100. Rectangular Bin A of Stratum IV, looking northeast.

Figure 101. Rectangular Bin A, looking southwest.

Figure 102. Rectangular Bin B of Stratum IV, looking northwest.

Figure 103. Rectangular Bin B (foreground) and Bin A (upper), looking east.

Figure 104. Rectangular Bin B of Stratum IV, looking southwest.

Figure 105. General view of west end of the north side of the tell.

Figure 106. North side of the tell at the beginning of the excavation of the stairway.

Figure 107. Segment of stairs in 14-H/J-5/6, looking south.

Figure 108. Stairway in 14-H/J-8/9, looking south.

Figure 109. Stairway seen from upper steps, looking toward the springs and the Wādī Kufrinjeh (upper).

Figure 111. Steps of the east-west segment of the stairway and the landing, looking west.

Figure 110. Treads of six steps between the landing at the bottom of the main north-south section and the first broad platform; to the right is the wall separating the tunnel from the street outside; looking west.

Figure 112. Street to the north of the east-west wall of the tunnel, looking south.

Figure 113. Plaster on a stone from the west wall of the stairway.

Figure 114. Stairway, looking south.

Figure 115. Lower part of stairway, with the north wall in the foreground.

Figure 116. Sounding 3, at the head of the preserved portion of the stairway, looking east.

Figure 117. Pavements of Rooms 101 and 102 of Stratum III, looking south.

Figure 118. Covered drain of Room 101 of Stratum III, looking west.

Figure 119. Opening to drain of Room 101 of Stratum III, looking east.

Figure 120. General view of Room 101 of Stratum III, looking southeast.

Figure 121. General view of Rooms 101 and 102 of Stratum III, looking southeast.

Figure 122. Pavements of Rooms 102 and 101 of Stratum III, looking northeast.

Figure 123. West side of doorway between Rooms 101 and 102 of Stratum III, looking west.

Figure 124. Room 102 of Stratum III, looking east.

Figure 125. Room 103 of Stratum III, looking north.

Figure 126. Paved area to the north of Room 103, looking west.

Figure 127. Room 108, looking west.

Figure 128. Room 108, looking southwest.

Figure 129. General view of building of Stratum III, looking southwest.

Figure 133. General view of stone foundations of the building of Stratum II, looking west.

Figure 134. Rooms 202, 205 (right), 207 and 206 (left), foundations of building of Stratum II, looking west.

Figure 135. Foundations of Rooms 203, 204, 205 (right), and 202 (left) of Stratum II.

Figure 130. General view of building of Stratum III, looking west.

Figure 131. General view of building of Stratum III, looking southwest.

Figure 132. General view of building of Stratum III, looking northwest.

Figure 136. General view of foundations of building of Stratum II, looking northwest.

Figure 137. Rooms 203 (center), 204 (upper right), and 202 (upper left) of Stratum II, looking southwest.

Figure 138. Rooms 205 (lower), 204 (middle), and 203 and 201 (upper); foundations of building of Stratum II, looking east.

Figure 139. Rooms 205 (lower left) and 202 (right of center) of Stratum II, looking east.

Figure 140. Rooms 202 (right of center), 205, 204, 203, and 201 (left) of Stratum II, looking east.

Figure 141. Rooms 206 (lower), 205 (center), and 204 (right of center) foundations of building of Stratum II, looking north.

Figure 142. Room 207 (center) of building of Stratum II, looking northeast.

Figure 143. Room 206 (center) at southwest corner of building of Stratum II, looking northeast.

Figure 144. East wall of building of Stratum II, looking south.

Figure 145. Rooms 203 (lower), 202, 208 (center), and 207 (upper right) of building of Stratum II, looking south.

Figure 146. Rooms 204 (lower), 202, 207 (center), and 206 (upper right) of building of Stratum II, looking south.

Figure 147. Room 205 (center) foundations of building of Stratum II, looking south.

Figure 148. Rooms 203 and 202 (center) and 208 (upper) of building of Stratum II, looking southeast.

Figure 149. Top of foundation with reed impressions on south wall of Room 202, opposite Room 207, looking west.

Figure 150. Reeds from the roof found on floor in 31-B-6.

Figure 151. Charred roof beam in Room 203 of building of Stratum II, looking west.

Figure 152. Two clay ovens outside of the building of Stratum II, looking west.

Figure 153. Foundations of Stratum I building in 31-C-8, built over the wall of the rectangular building of Stratum II, looking south.

Figure 154. Foundations of Stratum I building in 31-B-6, looking east, seen through the doorway between Rooms 205 and 202 of the building of Stratum II.

Figure 155. Foundation trench for wall of the building of Stratum I in 31-B-7, looking east.

Figure 156. Steps in the north reservoir in 31-E/F-7/8 of Stratum I, looking northwest.

Figure 157. South reservoir in 31-F-7, looking northwest.

Figure 158. South reservoir in 31-F-7, looking north.

Figure 159. City wall on surface of Areas 23 and 13, looking east.

Figure 160. City wall on surface of Area 23, looking west.

Figure 161. Surface walls in 32-E/F/G-10, looking west.

Figure 162. Bin lined with stones on surface of 32-F-9.

Figure 163. Shifted strata in 17-H-7/9.

FIGURE 164

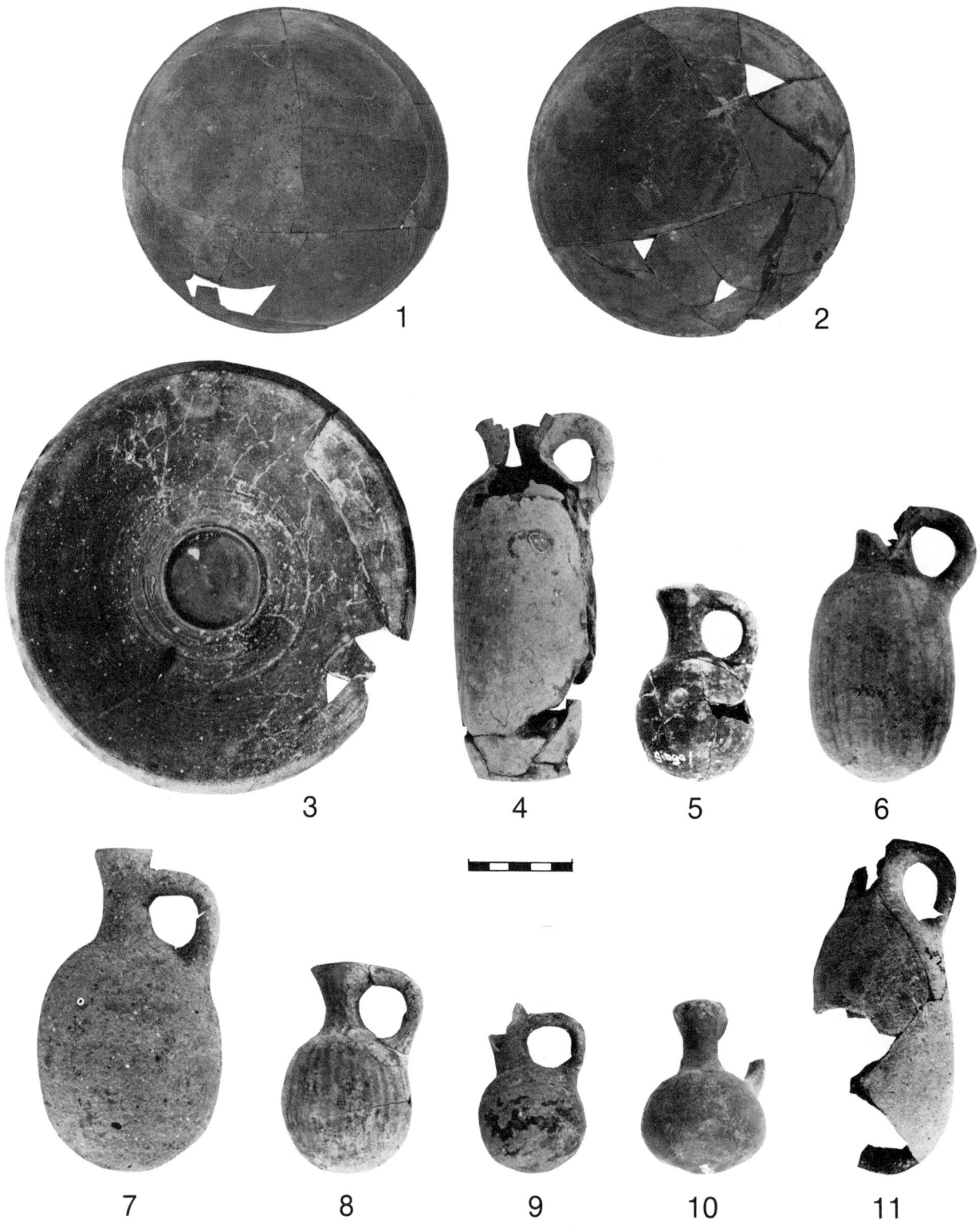

1: Bowl from Stratum VI (fig. 6:2). 2: Bowl from Stratum V (fig. 10:3). 3: Bowl from Stratum I (fig. 19:7). 4: Juglet from Stratum VII (fig. 5:7). 5: Juglet from Stratum VI (fig. 7:3). 6: Juglet from Stratum VI (fig. 7:8). 7: Juglet from Stratum VI (fig. 7:12). 8: Juglet from Stratum VI (fig. 7:4). 9: Juglet from Stratum VI (fig. 7:1). 10: Juglet from Stratum V (fig. 11:10). 11: Juglet from Stratum V (fig. 11:2).

FIGURE 165

1: Juglet from Stratum V (fig. 11:22). 2: Juglet S1103/P644, from 31-J-6, surface; red-brown ware; tan core; some small and medium black grits. 3: Jug from Stratum VI (fig. 7:25). 4: Jug from Stratum VI (fig. 7:21). 5: Jug from Stratum VI (fig. 7:24). 6: Trefoil-mouth jug S982/P567, from 32-F-8, Stratum V; tan ware; tan core; many mixed black and white grits; A. 7: Jug S615/P331, provenience undetermined; base-ring ware; buff to pink. 8: Jug from Stratum V (fig. 11:23). 9: Jar S715/P407, from 23-G-3, Stratum V; tan ware; brown core; many mixed black and white grits; handmade; reddish brown vertical and horizontal lines of paint on body; A.

FIGURE 166

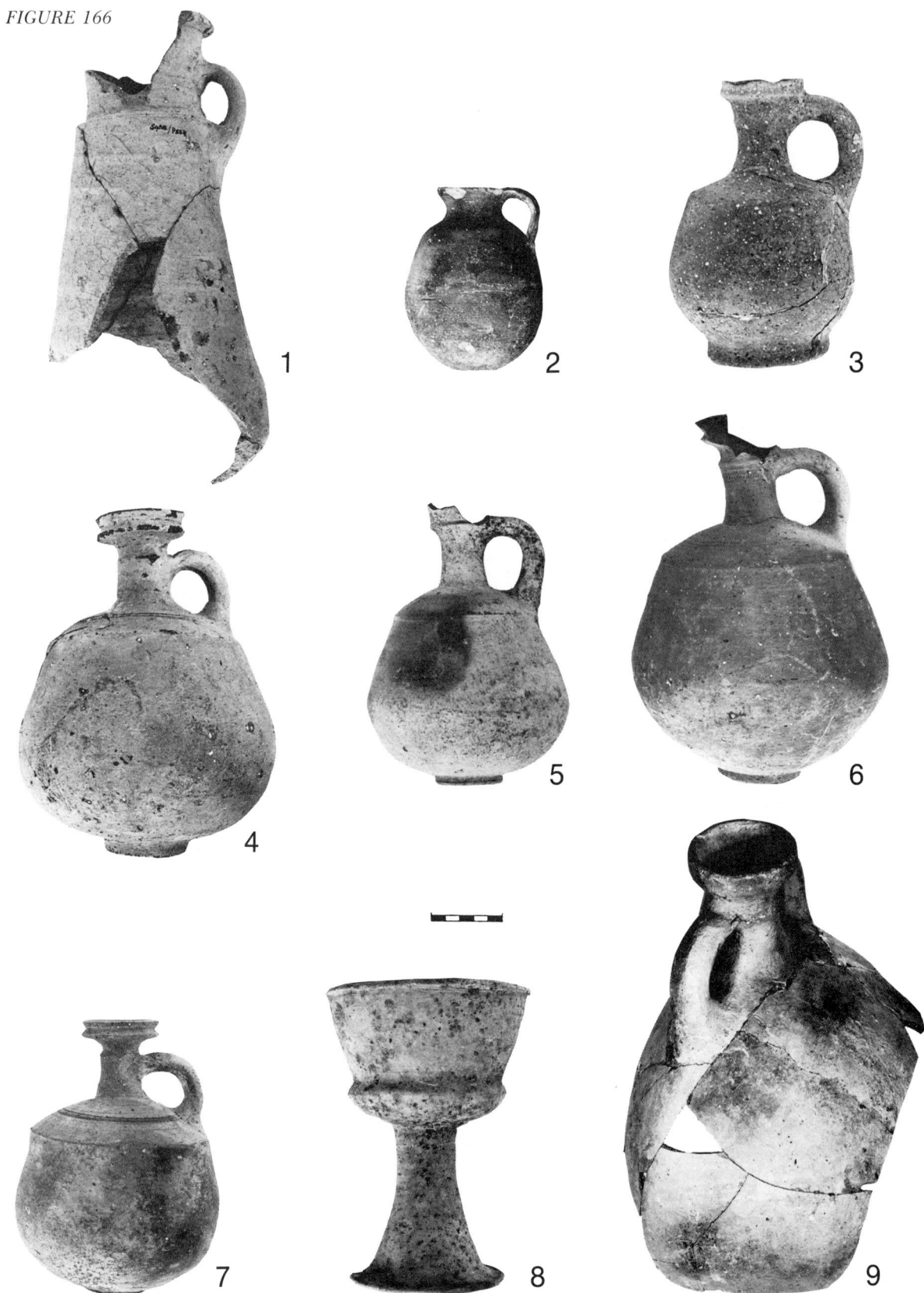

1: Jug from Stratum II (fig. 18:20). 2: Jug from Stratum I (fig. 19:29). 3: Decanter from Stratum VI (fig. 7:26). 4: Decanter from Stratum VI (fig. 7:27). 5: Decanter from Stratum VI (fig. 7:28). 6: Decanter from Stratum VI (fig. 7:29). 7: Decanter from Stratum V (fig. 11:13). 8: Chalice from Stratum VI (fig. 7:30). 9: Pilgrim flask from Stratum V (fig. 11:17).

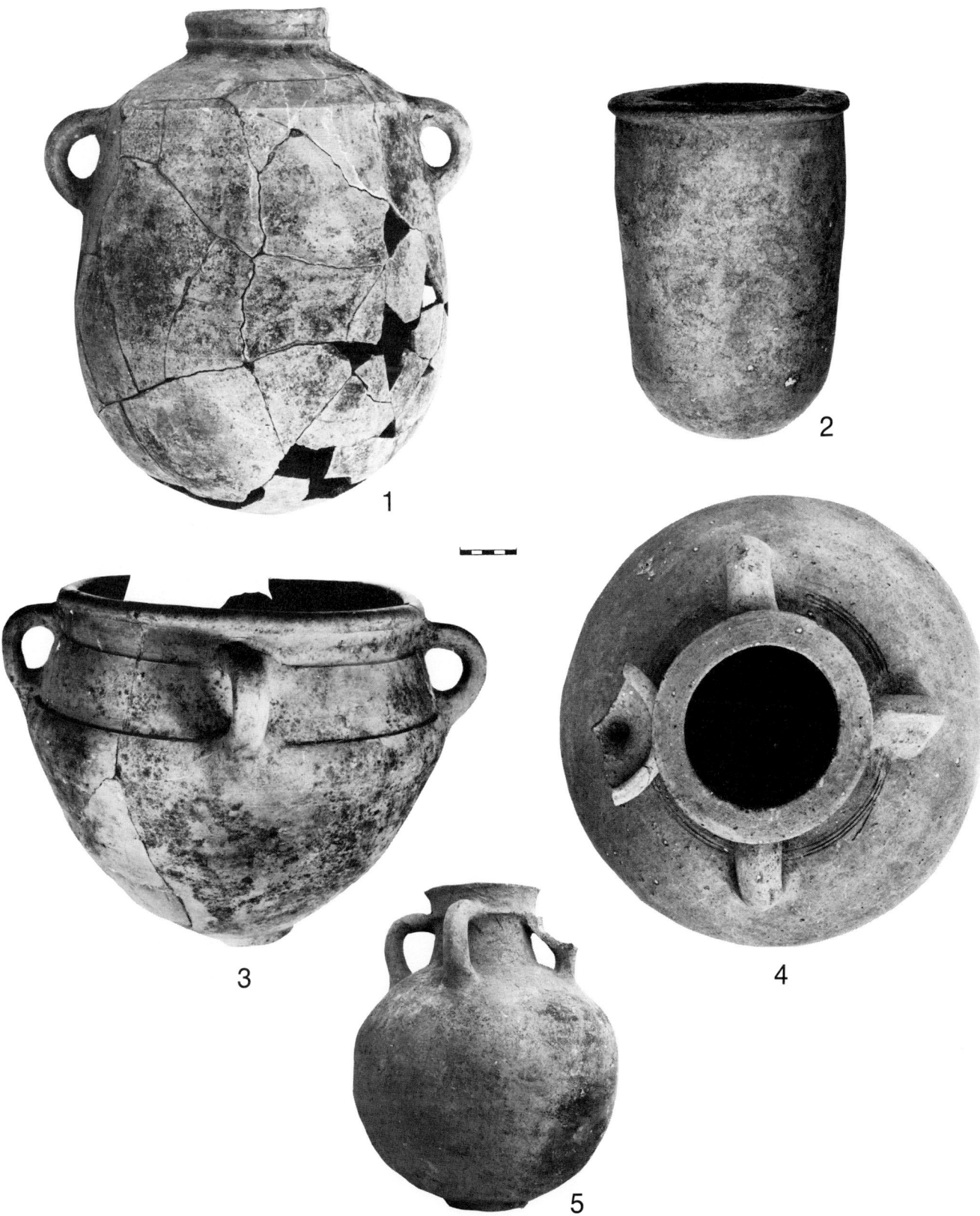

FIGURE 167

1: Storage jar from Stratum VI (fig. 9:12). 2: Storage jar S393/P221, from 23-D-6, Stratum IV; ware unrecorded. 3: Krater from Stratum V (fig. 12:14). 4: Jar from Stratum VI (fig. 9:13). 5: Three-handle jar S558/P308, from 23-F-7; buff to gray ware with dark gray core.

FIGURE 168

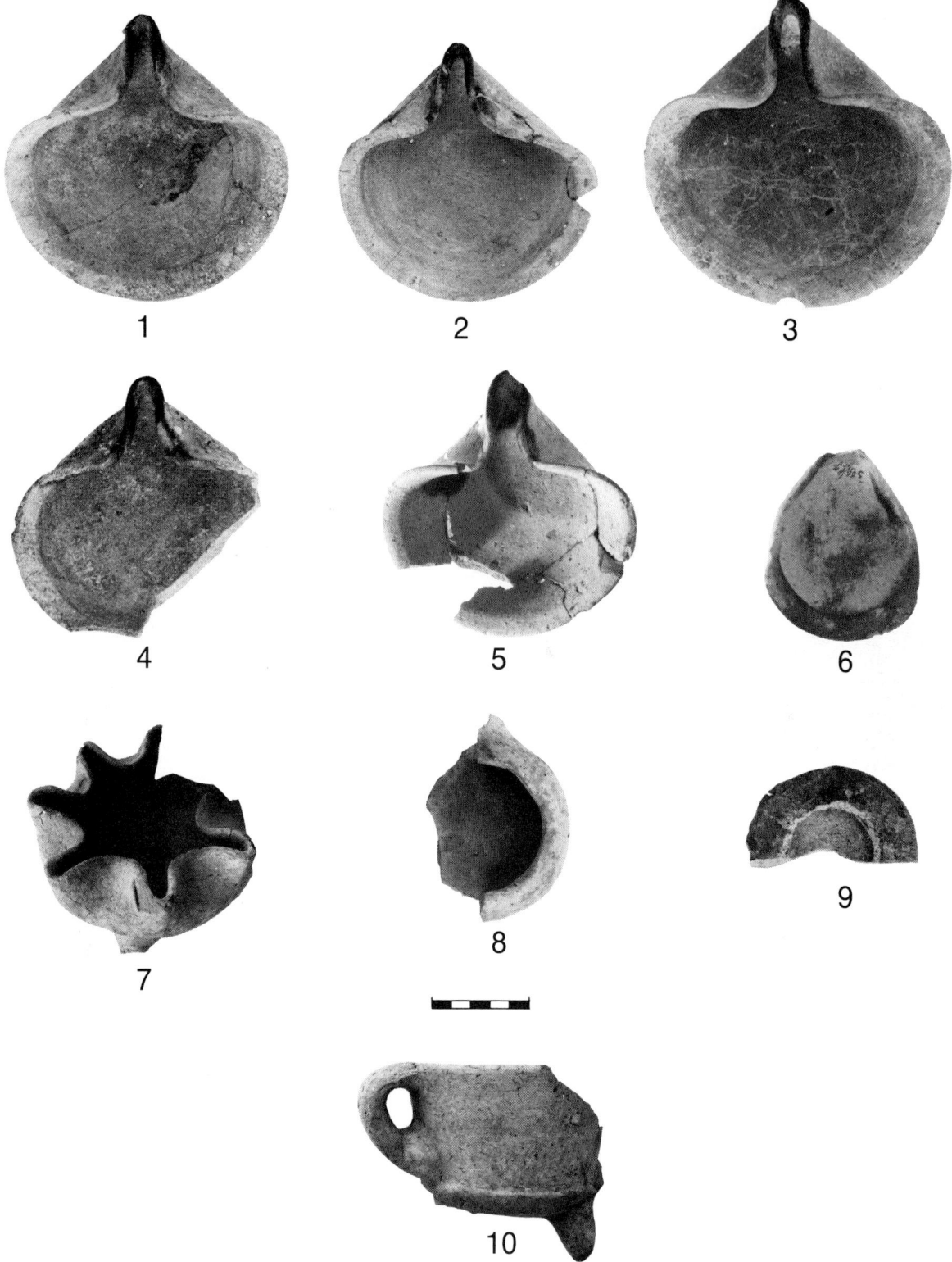

1: Lamp from Stratum VI (fig. 7:31). 2: Lamp from Stratum VI (fig. 7:32). 3: Lamp from Stratum VI (fig. 7:33). 4: Lamp from Stratum VI (fig. 7:34). 5: Lamp S362/P200, from 23-C-3, Stratum V; buff ware with gray core. 6: Lamp from Stratum IV (fig. 16:17). 7: Lamp S790/P443, from 23-F-1, below Stratum IV; tan ware; tan core; some mixed white grits. 8: Lamp from Stratum II (fig. 18:22). 9: Cosmetic palette 1024/St70, from 31-E-5, Room 103, Stratum III; white stone; two incised lines below rim on outside. 10: Tripod cup from Stratum V (fig. 10:29).

FIGURE 169

1: Zoomorphic figurine from Stratum V (fig. 10:30). 2: Zoomorphic figurine from Stratum V (fig. 14:20). 3: Human figurine S944/Pfig16, from 32-D-8, Bin 75, Stratum IV; tan ware with tan core; some mixed black and white grits; A. 4: Zoomorphic figurine S277/Pfig4, provenience undetermined; hollow body. 5: Human figurine S773/Pfig12, from 31-D-7(?), surface; red-brown ware; many small white grits. 6–7: Human figurine of seated pregnant woman S1140/Pfig21, from 31-C/D-5, Stratum III(?); tan ware with tan core; some small black grits; buff to tan slip; traces of red-brown paint on front and on headdress; A.

FIGURE 170

1: Group of clay loom weights. 2: Impression of woven cloth on clay, from 32-E-8, House 16, Stratum V. 3: Stone vessel from Stratum VI (fig. 8:26). 4: Stone mortar S599/St43, from 23-F-3. 5: Tripod mortar of basalt S80/St5, provenience unknown.

FIGURE 171

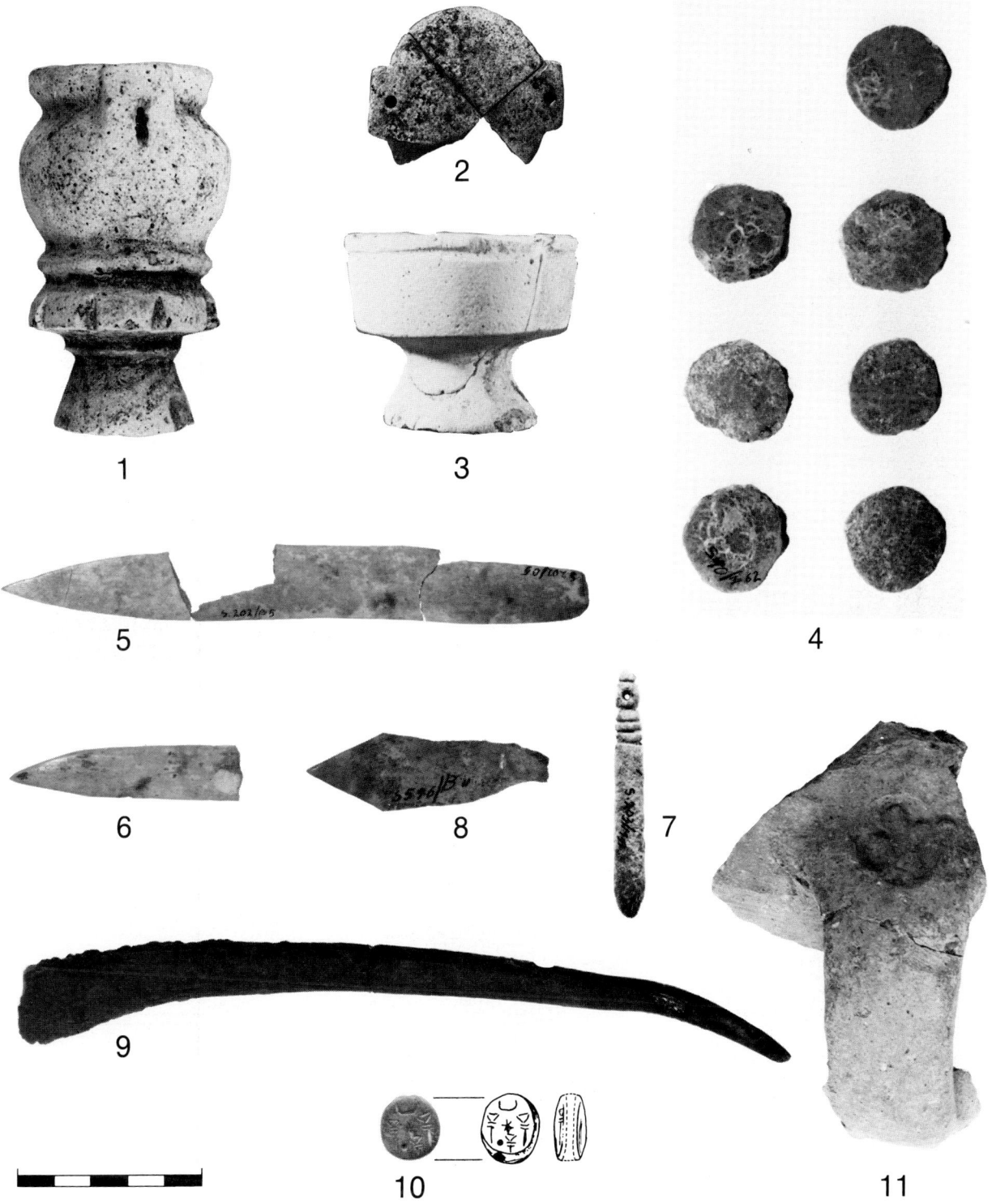

1–2: Faience cup with lid from Stratum VI (fig. 8:22). 3: Faience cup from Stratum V (fig. 14:21). 4: Game pieces from Stratum V (fig. 14:22). 5: Bone tool S202/B5, from Sounding 3, Layer I; light cream color. 6: Bone point S204/B6, from Sounding 3, Layer 1; cream color. 7: Pendant S203/M94, from Sounding 3, Layer 1; bone (?); orange-yellow. 8: Bone tool S596/B11, from 23-D/E-5, Stratum V; pointed blade; yellow; polished; A. 9: Bone point from Stratum V (fig. 14:37). 10: Bead S1039/St72, provenience unknown; pink stone; polished and pierced for stringing. 11: Stamped jar handle S1139/S12, from 31-C/D-5; brown ware; gray core; some mixed white grits.

FIGURE 172

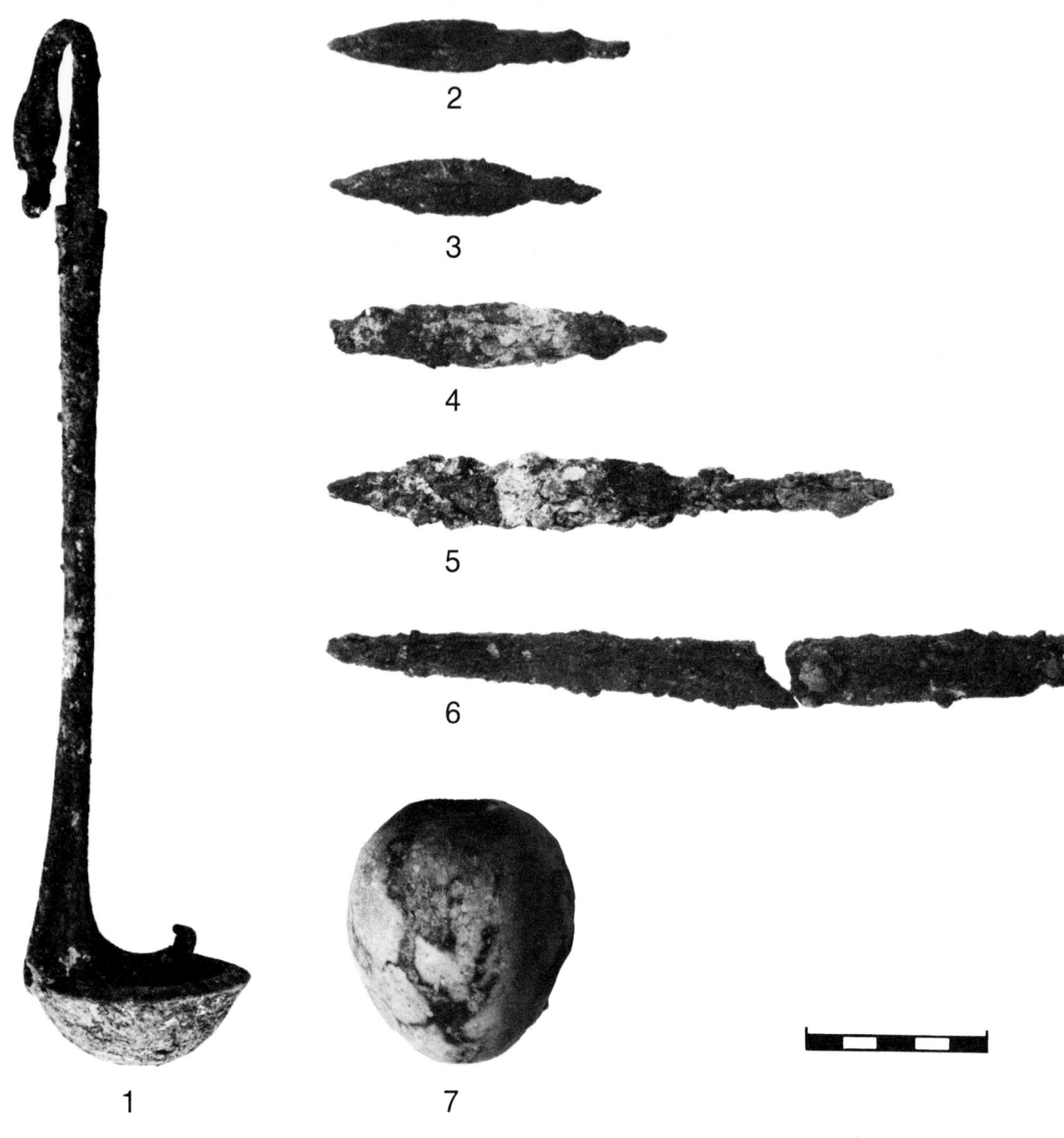

1: Bronze ladle S1147/Br71, from 31-A/B-7, Stratum II. 2: Iron arrowhead from Stratum V (fig. 14:28). 3: Iron arrowhead from Stratum V (fig. 14:27). 4: Iron arrowhead S554/F11, from 23-D-8; corroded. 5: Iron point S552/F9, from 23-F-4, Stratum IV; corroded. 6: Iron blade S553/F10, from 23-F-8; one rivet hole preserved. 7: Mace head S854/St61, from 17-K-10; stone; mottled white.

FIGURE 173

1: Cylinder seal S978/S5, from 32-E-8, Stratum V; brown stone; A. Drawing by Edith Porada. 2: Cylinder seal S977/S4, from 31-A-8; tan stone with red mottling. Drawing by Edith Porada.

FIGURE 174

1–6: Incense burner from Stratum III (fig. 18:6).

FIGURE 175

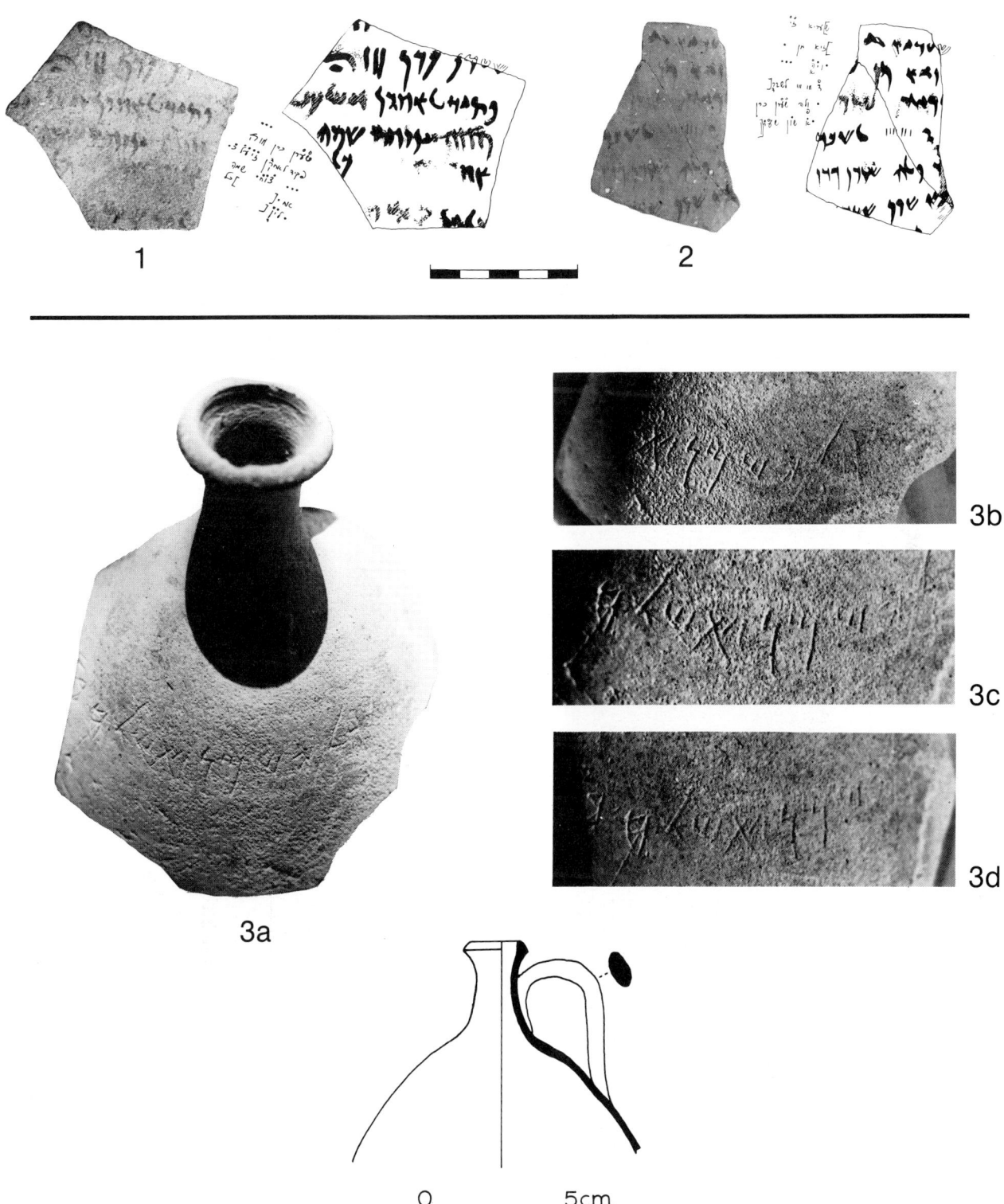

1: Ostracon S889/S3, from 32-G-8, Stratum IV; one side inscribed with six lines of Aramaic script in black ink; tan ware; tan and gray core; many mixed white grits; A. 2: Ostracon S1143/S13, from 31-C/D-5 and 31-A/B-6; six lines of Aramaic letters in black ink; on two pieces of the same ostracon each found in different plots; red-brown ware with gray core; some mixed white grits. 3a–d: Jug with inscription S1000/S10, from 32-E/F-8, Pit 80, Stratum IV; tan ware with tan core; few small white grits; buff slip.

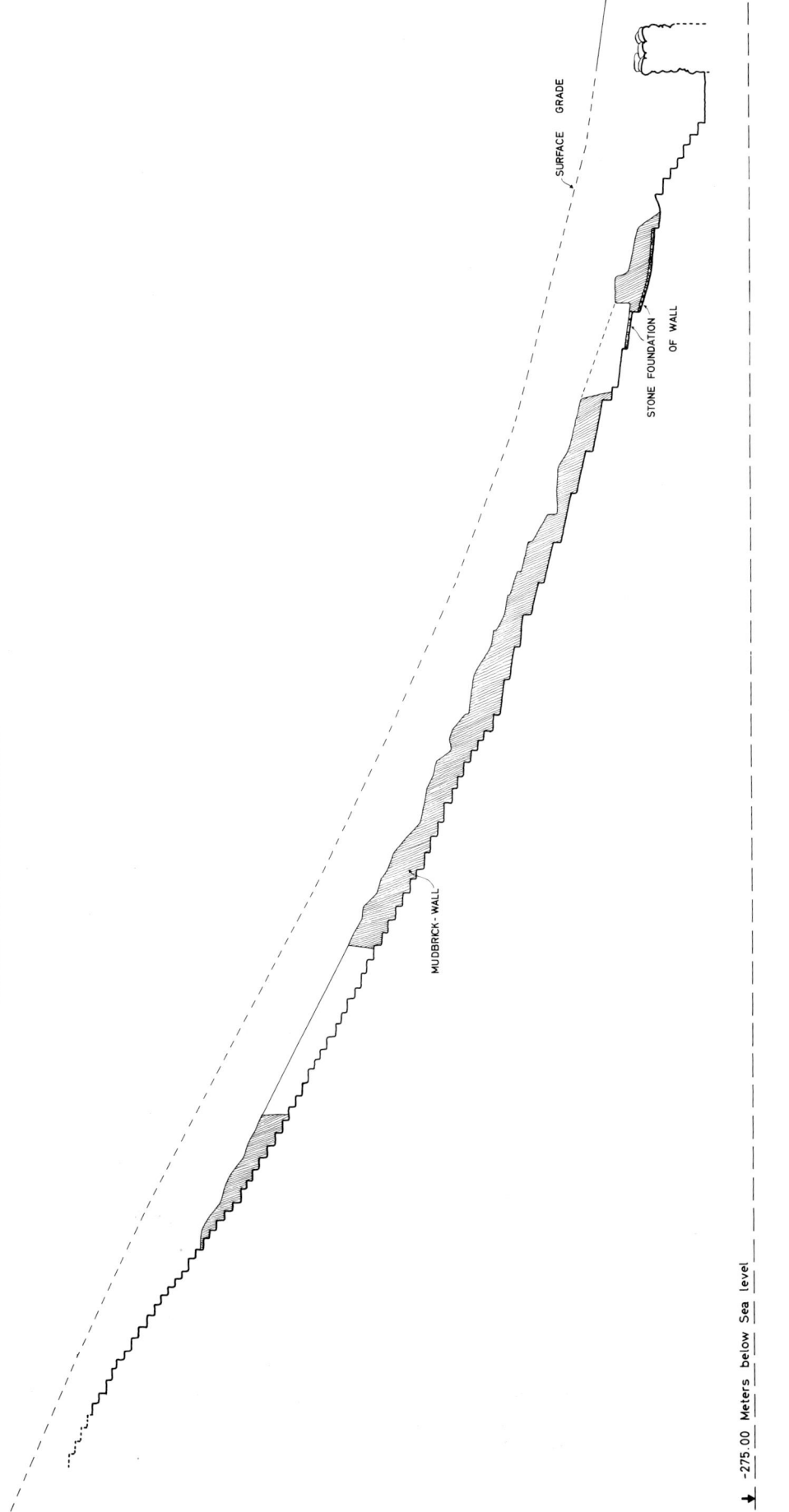

Section of central wall of stairway.

FIGURE 184

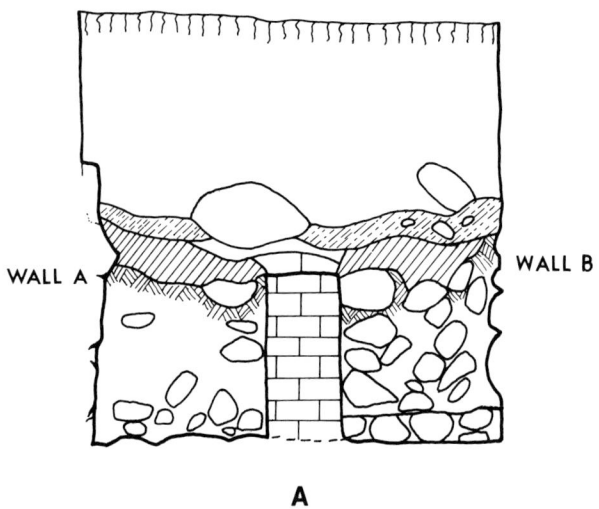
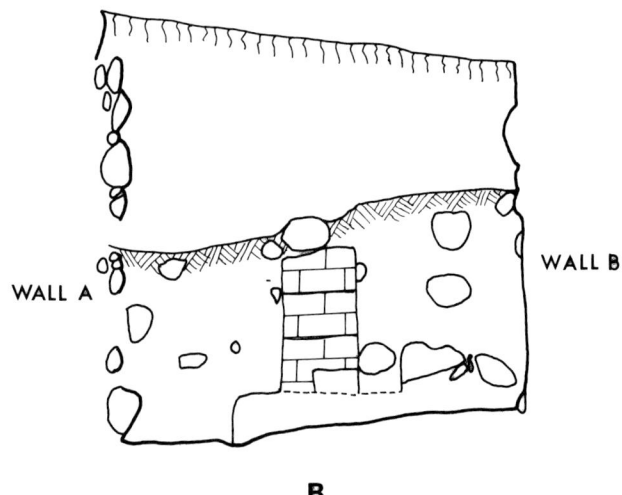
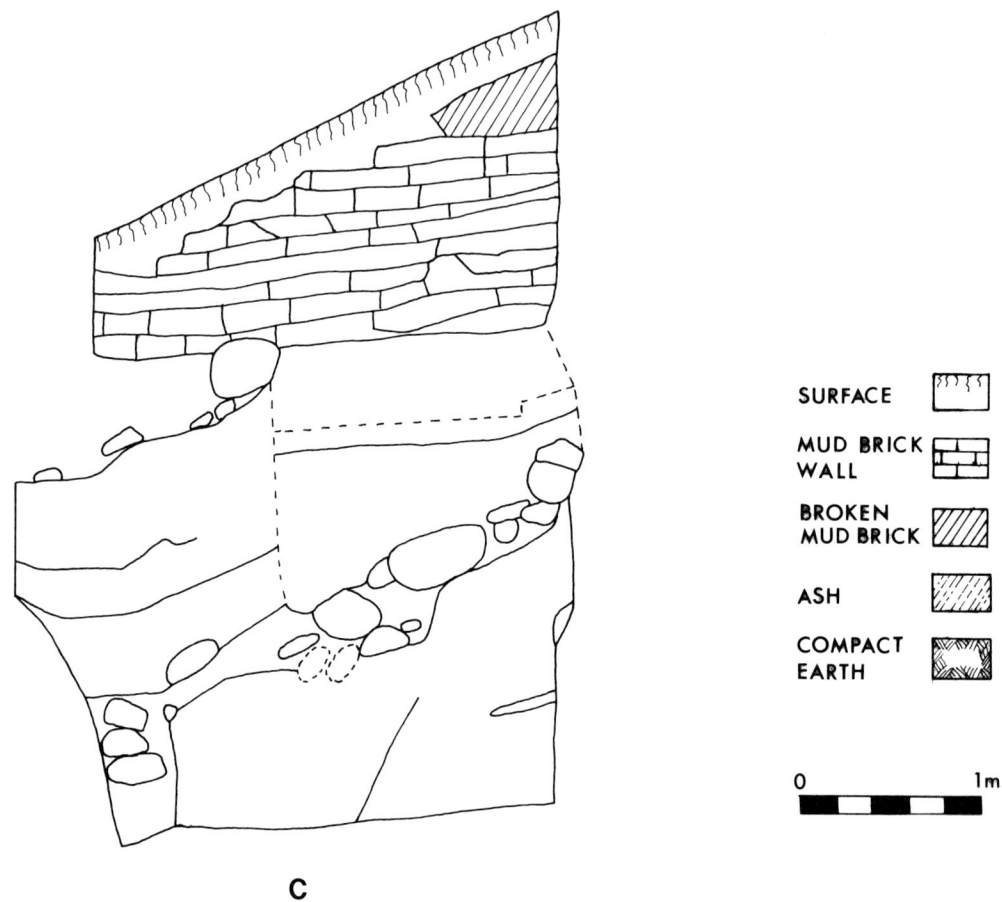

a. Section of Sounding 4 (14-H/J-9) looking south.
b. Section of Sounding 1 (14-J-5) looking south.
c. Section of Sounding 3 (14-J-2/3) looking east.

FIGURE 185

Plan of Stratum III.

FIGURE 186

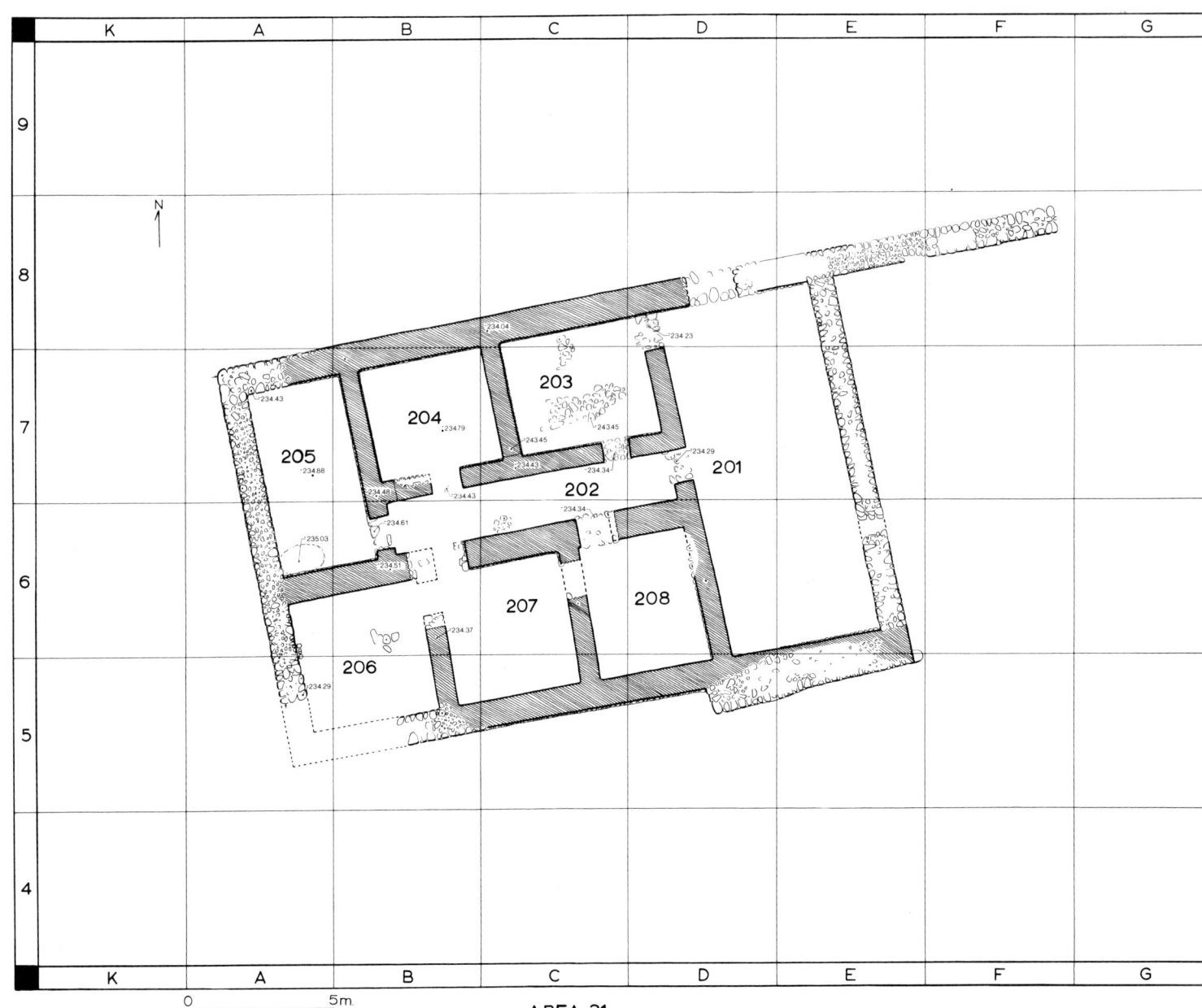

Plan of Stratum II.

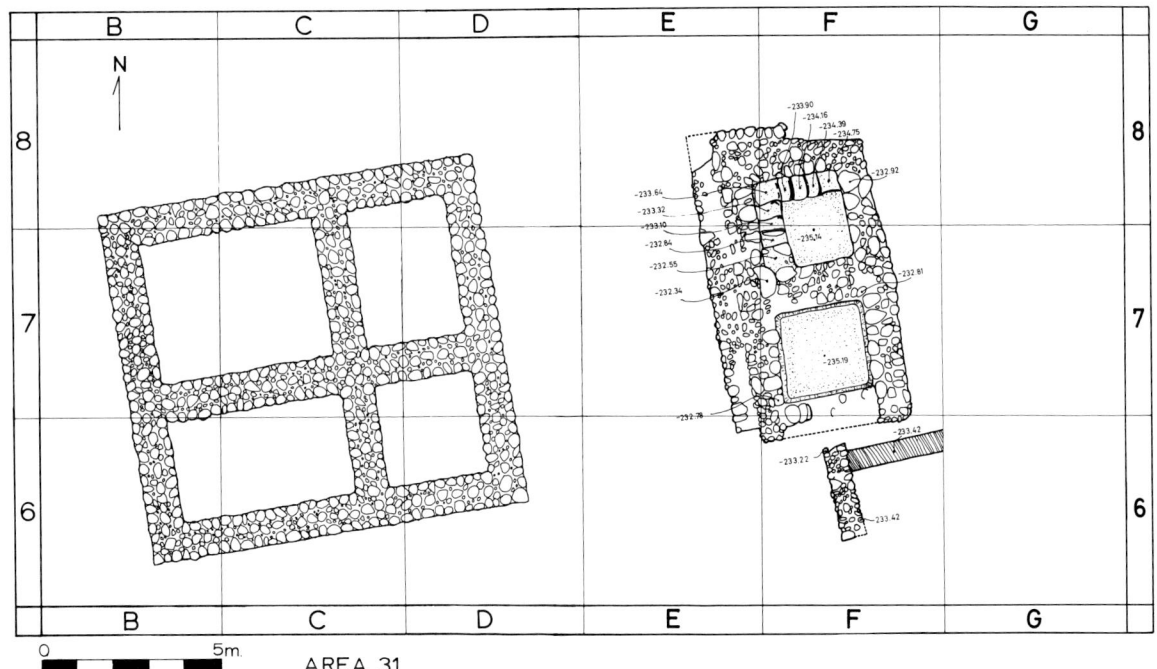

Plan of Stratum I.

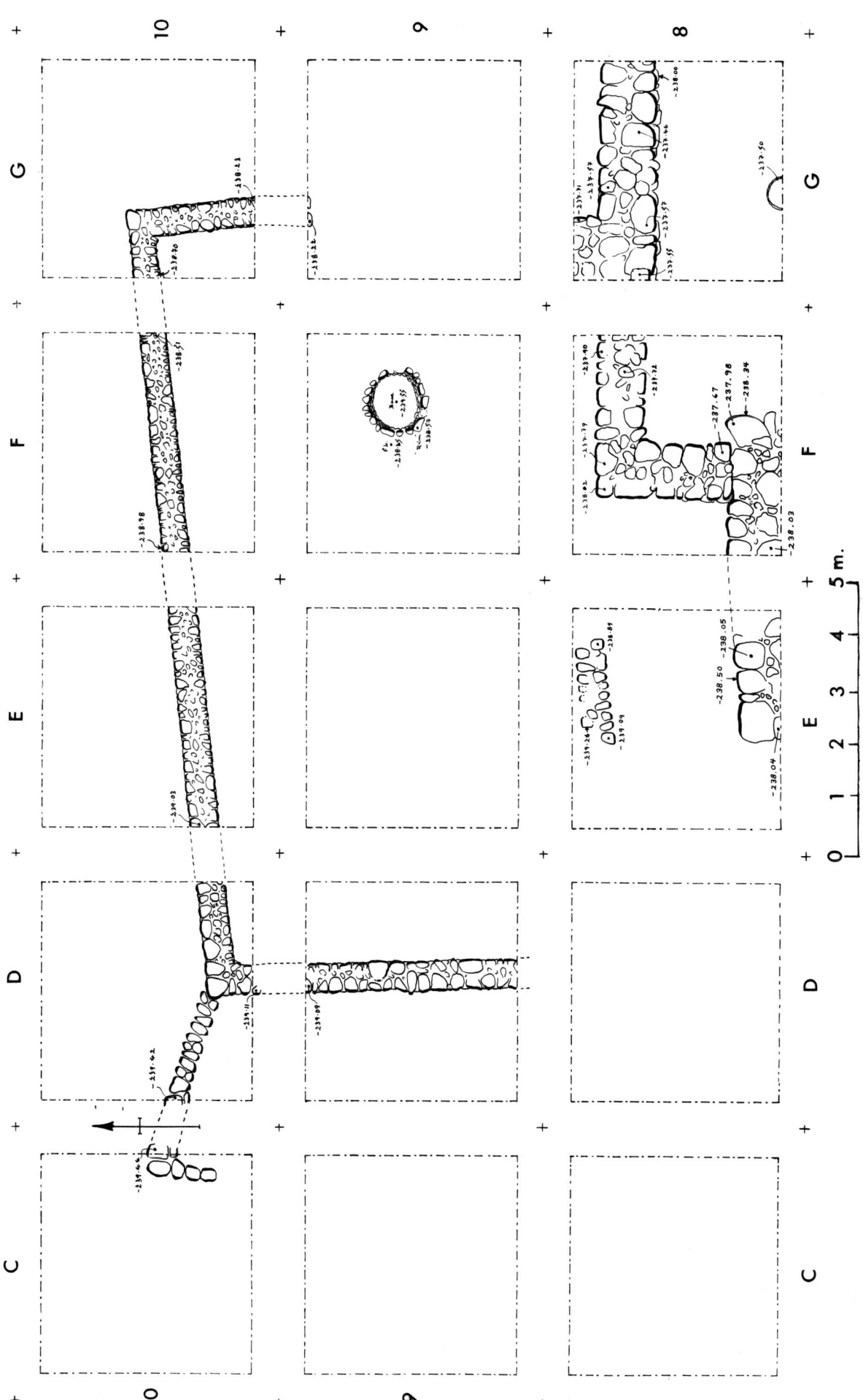

FIGURE 189

Plan of surface structures in Area 32.